Read On . . . Graphic Novels

Recent Titles in
Libraries Unlimited Read On Series
Barry Trott, Series Editor

Read On . . . Graphic Novels

Reading Lists for Every Taste

Abby Alpert

Read On Series
Barry Trott, Series Editor

AN IMPRINT OF ABC-CLIO, LLC
Santa Barbara, California • Denver, Colorado • Oxford, England

Copyright 2012 by ABC-CLIO, LLC

Library of Congress Cataloging-in-Publication Data

Alpert, Abby, 1961–
   Read on— graphic novels : reading lists for every taste / Abby Alpert.
      p. cm. — (Read on series)
   Includes index.
   ISBN 978-1-59158-825-2 (acid-free paper) — ISBN 978-1-61069-155-0 (ebook)   1. Graphic novels—Bibliography.   2. Libraries—Special collections—Graphic novels.   3. Public libraries—United States—Book lists.   4. Readers' advisory services—United States.   I. Title.
   Z5956.C6A43   2012
   [PN6710]
   016.7415—dc23   2011039792

ISBN: 978-1-59158-825-2
EISBN: 978-1-61069-155-0

16   15   14   13   12   1   2   3   4   5

This book is also available on the World Wide Web as an eBook.
Visit www.abc-clio.com for details.

Libraries Unlimited
An Imprint of ABC-CLIO, LLC

ABC-CLIO, LLC
130 Cremona Drive, P.O. Box 1911
Santa Barbara, California 93116-1911

This book is printed on acid-free paper ∞

Manufactured in the United States of America

*This book is dedicated to my son, Noah Alpert Taborda,
who makes it all worthwhile, and to the memory of
my grandmother, Sally Schramm, who
encouraged my love of books.*

Contents

Series Foreword

Welcome to Libraries Unlimited's Read On series of fiction and nonfiction genre guides for readers' advisors and for readers. The Read On series introduces readers and those who work with them to new ways of looking at books, genres, and reading interests.

Over the past decade, readers' advisory services have become vital in public libraries. A quick glance at the schedule of any library conference at the state or national level will reveal a wealth of programs on various aspects of connecting readers to books they will enjoy. Working with unfamiliar genres or types of reading can be a challenge, particularly for those new to the field. Equally, readers may find it a bit overwhelming to look for books outside their favorite authors and preferred reading interests. The titles in the Read On series offer you a new way to approach reading:

- they introduce you a broad sampling of materials available in a given genre;
- they offer you new directions to explore in a genre—through appeal features and unconventional topics;
- they help readers' advisors better understand and navigate genres with which they are less familiar;
- and they provide reading lists that you can use to create quick displays, include on your library web sites and in the library newsletter, or to hand out to readers.

The lists in the Read On series are arranged in sections based on appeal characteristics—story, character, setting, and language (as described in Joyce Saricks' and Reader's Advisory Services in the Public Library, 3d ed., ALA Editions, 2005), with a fifth section on mood. These are hidden elements of a book that attract readers. Remember that a book can have multiple appeal factors; and sometimes readers are drawn to a particular book for several factors, while other times for only one. In the Read On lists, titles are placed according to their primary appeal characteristics, and then put into a list that reflects common reading interests. So if you are working with a reader who loves fantasy that features quests for magical objects or a reader who is interested in memoirs with a strong sense of place you will be able to find a list of titles whose main appeal centers around this search. Each list indicates a title that is an especially good starting place for readers, an exemplar of that appeal characteristic.

Story is perhaps the most basic appeal characteristic. It relates to the plot of the book—what are the elements of the tale? Is the emphasis more on the people or the situations? Is the story action focused or more interior? Is it funny? Scary?

Many readers are drawn to the books they love by the characters. The Character appeal reflects such aspects as whether there are lots of characters or only a single main character; are the characters easily recognizable types? Do the characters grow and change over the course of the story? What are the characters' occupations?

Setting covers a range of elements that might appeal to readers. What is the time period or geographic locale of the tale? How much does the author describe the surroundings of the story? Does the reader feel as though he or she is "there", when reading the book? Are there special features such as the monastic location of Ellis Peters' Brother Cadfael mysteries or the small town setting of Jan Karon's Mitford series?

Although not traditionally considered appeal characteristic, mood is important to readers as well. It relates to how the author uses the tools of narrative—language, pacing, story, and character—to create a feeling for the work. Mood can be difficult to quantify because the reader brings his or her own feelings to the story as well. Mood really asks how does the book make the reader feel? Creepy? Refreshed? Joyful? Sad?

Finally, the Language appeal brings together titles where the author's writing style draws the reader. This can be anything from a lyrical prose style with lots of flourishes to a spare use of language ala Hemingway. Humor, snappy dialog, word-play, recipes and other language elements all have the potential to attract readers.

Dig into these lists. Use them to find new titles and authors in a genre that you love, or as a guide to expand your knowledge of a new type of writing. Above all, read, enjoy, and remember—never apologize for your reading tastes!

Barry Trott
Series Editor

Acknowledgments

I would like to thank my editors, Barbara Ittner and Barry Trott, for their patience and helpful feedback throughout the process of writing this book. Also, thanks to the staff of the Evanston Public Library Circulation Department who good-naturedly processed mountains of books multiple times a week over the past year. With gratitude to my brother Danny Alpert, who gave generously of his time to edit as I wrote and who provided encouragement when I needed it most. To my parents, Bernie and Fran Alpert, who make it all possible. To Chava, Andrea, Iris, and Judy, whose love and support keep me going. To Noah, who tolerated my distraction during this project and maintained his faith in me. With gratitude for all the good people in my life who have helped and enriched my life in countless ways, I couldn't do it without you! And, last but not least, appreciation to the cartoonists, writers, and artists who create graphic novels; the fruits of their labors have given me (and I hope they will give you) much to chew on and countless hours of enjoyment.

Introduction

Graphic Novels Defined

It almost takes a superhero to slide down the slippery slope of defining graphic novels. Are they a literary genre? Are they simply comic books? Part of the difficulty in describing graphic novels is that the term itself is a misnomer that has created divergent opinions. Most graphic novels aren't graphic (sex and/or violence), and many aren't novels (fictional prose narratives). In addition, comics imply humor, though many are not remotely funny. Graphic novels are most suitably defined as a format that uses the medium of comics, marrying text and image, to produce sequential art narratives that have shared conventions and vocabulary, including panels, captions, speech, and thought balloons. The fact that graphic novels are bound books, either paperback or hardcover, is what ultimately distinguishes them from comic books.

The term "graphic novel" is generally attributed to Will Eisner, who coined the phrase to facilitate the marketing of *A Contract with God* (1978) to mainstream book publishers. This term displayed the medium's ability to present high-quality content: mature and realistic with complex themes. Other terms that have been used are graphic books, sequential art, the ninth art, and auteur art. While "graphic novel" may have been an artificial name devised to frame comics in a more palatable light, it is the most widely recognized and used term for books that consist of sustained narrative arcs told in the comics medium.

Graphic novels are a unique blend of word and image. The medium has its own distinctive language that inherently communicates through space and time, from one panel to the next. They have plasticity capable of constructing all types of tales and expressing all ranges of emotion, from humor to despair. There are as many ways of representing humanity among graphic-novel authors as there are among movie directors and prose authors. Fundamentally, graphic novels, as a whole, offer a sweeping literary world of pictorial storytelling.

A Brief History of Graphic Novels

In the Victorian era, cartoons were geared toward adults, but by the early 1900s the majority of comics were intended to entertain a juvenile readership.

During the 1930s, because of the Great Depression and, later, the rise of fascism in Europe, comic books became very popular, particularly entertaining "funny animal" comics and comics featuring superheroes, whose supernatural powers could be used to defend the weak and to fight injustice. In the late 1940s, EC began producing crime and horror comics that were thematically more mature. Comic books were distributed through news agents and were sold at newsstands and revolving racks in drugstores. The popular attitude toward comics was that they were frivolous and that they were a danger to literacy. In 1955, psychiatrist Fredric Wertham wrote *The Seduction of the Innocent,* which sparked a public outcry based on a fear that comics could lead to juvenile delinquency. The comics industry reacted by creating the Comics Code Authority (CCA), a self-censoring seal of approval whose logo appeared on the cover of comics approved for lack of violence, sex, and antiestablishment messages.

In response to this self-censorship, a group of cartoonists in 1960s and early 1970s initiated an underground comic's movement, a vital break with the past. Comix, so called to distinguish them from code-controlled comic books and to suggest their X-rated content, grew out of the period's countercultural hippie community and dealt with adult themes such as sex, drugs, and radical politics. Underground comics redefined what topics the medium of comics could cover and claimed an entirely different readership from that of Marvel and DC. This underground movement created a niche market defined by younger adults with sympathetic sociopolitical viewpoints. It did not cross over commercially, in part because the comics were published by small-press publishers and sold through head shops, which kept them contained within the hippie culture from whence they had come and prevented the development of a broad retail network. In addition, Comix did not alter the popular attitude toward comics as juvenile, lowbrow, and subversive, and the movement died out as the counterculture declined.

The 1970s and 1980s gave rise to a new type of avant-garde adult comics that were more oriented toward high artistic quality and that explored subject matter that had previously been the realm of movies and books. Breaking with earlier comic-book conventions, these comics were referred to as commix, independents, or alternative comics. An academic community that was interested in comics developed, leading to the publication of *The Comics Journal,* a quarterly magazine focusing on evaluative criticism. This journal eventually started publishing comics and graphic novels under the Fantagraphics imprint, starting a small explosion of independent comics publishers that issued the new-style comics. Throughout the 1980s, this growth in comics' popularity resulted in a rise in specialty comic-book shops. The big publishers such as DC and Marvel were their bread and butter, but comic shops also stocked comics produced by independent publishers. The general public still perceived comics as "lowbrow," so the store customers tended to be fans of comic books, and the stores did not pull in a new readership.

In 1986, three pivotal graphic novels were published that initiated a new movement in the world of American comics: *Maus*, by Art Spiegelman, *Watchman*, by Alan Moore, and *The Dark Knight Returns*, by Frank Miller. These three graphic novels were revolutionary; they broke the barrier and rose above the critical radar, creating a new era in the comics medium, both in content and economically. The mainstream coverage and the praise showered on these titles precipitated a number of changes in the world of comics, including a broadening of the audience and a widening of distribution, increasing the presence of comics in libraries, bookstores, and school curriculums. Their success also contributed to a fresh climate of openness among cartoonists, who explored new types of subject matter and used the medium to grapple with serious, adult issues.

The Dark Knight Returns and *Watchmen* brought the superhero convention to adult audiences with dark satire and the introduction of the antihero. These stories upped the ante for superhero comics, taking the stories beyond clichéd adolescent fantasy and into complex, thought-provoking narratives with moral and ethical overtones. These two titles encouraged DC and Marvel to bind comic-book series for adult reading and to expand distribution.

Spiegelman's *Maus* recounts his parents' experience in Auschwitz and the impact it had on him. It was a radical piece of work, telling an extremely personal story and delving deeply into emotional realms. Addressing a particularly grave topic in cartoon format, particularly in the traditionally "funny animal" medium, was an exceptional leap in comics history. Initially published as a serialized, mini-comic in *RAW* magazine, *Maus* was rejected by 14 publishers prior to receiving an admiring full-page review in the *New York Times Book Review*. Subsequently, Pantheon, a mainstream literary publisher, published *Maus* in trade paperback and distributed it to bookstores with a marketing budget. It sold like crazy. *Maus* was a treated as a beautiful, compelling, serious piece of literature in graphic-novel format. It not only was reviewed in most major daily newspapers and magazines but was also discussed in academic journals as a breakthrough example of Holocaust literature. *Maus* also had cross-generational appeal, from teenagers up, significantly widening comics' readership potential audience. *Maus* was not only a critical triumph; it was also a commercial success. Within six months of publication, it went into its fifth printing and was nominated for the National Book Critics Circle Award in Biography. *Maus II* followed, published in 1992. Again, the sales and critical response were enormous, and the book was on the *New York Times* best-seller list for many weeks. Spiegelman was awarded the Pulitzer Prize, an unprecedented honor for a work in the comic-book medium.

The 1990s saw a turning point for comics for adults. In reading reviews of graphic novels throughout much of the 1990s, one often finds an opening sentence something like this: "Pow! Crash! Bang! Comics are growing up!"

Graphic novels moved into mainstream consciousness. Publishers stepped in to capitalize on the "new comics" with a flurry of publications of original material and series repackaged in graphic-novel format. Authors produced compelling nonfiction on issues such as Hiroshima (*Barefoot Gen*, by Keiji Nakazaw) and Sarajevo (*Fax from Sarajevo*, by Joe Kubert). Memoirs gained status, such as Howard Cruse's *Stuck Rubber Baby* (1995) and Harvey Pekars's *Our Cancer Year* (1994). Fictional works included two wildly popular and long-running series: *Sandman*, by Neil Gaiman, and *Love & Rockets*, by the Hernandez brothers. Public and critical opinion shifted to allow for the viewpoint that comics could be a sophisticated, serious form of inventive storytelling.

This shift resulted in increased availability of comic-book material in noncommercial locations such as libraries and schools in the 2000s. Some university and major research libraries collected comic books, usually in their Popular Culture collections. Public libraries rarely circulated comic books because of their poor reputation and the frailty of the format. *Maus* was one of the first to be catalogued and shelved in libraries with the Holocaust literature. Librarians and teachers began to promote graphic-novel collections and the comics medium as a valuable educational tool for helping reluctant readers, ESL students, and visual learners and for promoting literacy in general. Magazines that are used as basic collection-development review sources, such as *Publishers Weekly* and *Booklist*, began to review graphic novels. As Young Adult departments became increasingly common in libraries, YA associations started to champion graphic-novel collections as a way to draw teens into the library. In 2002, the American Library Association had a "Getting Graphic @ your Library" promotional conference, and Teen Read Week had a graphic-novel theme. The comics industry responded to this shift by catering to librarians. Diamond, a major U.S. comics distributor, has a website devoted to librarians that offers cataloging information and discounts for library purchases. There is no doubt that comics, primarily in graphic-novel format, are currently an active category in collection development in public libraries. In addition, with many titles achieving literary awards, including the Pulitzer, the National Book Award, and Guardian and Guggenheim fellowships, curriculums began to include graphic novels in courses from the elementary through the university level.

. The new millennium has also seen explosive growth in the graphic-novel trade book market. Mainstream publishers like Random House, W. W. Norton, Simon and Schuster, and Penguin began jumping on the graphic-novel bandwagon. Their generous marketing budgets exposed graphic novels to a wider audience. Houghton Mifflin added comics to its Best American Series, a series that has been defining literature since 1915, when it introduced the first Best American Comics 2006. Graphic novels were recognized by the *New York Times* with the introduction, in 2009, of weekly graphic-novel best-seller lists for hardcover, softcover, and manga. Graphic novels have become one of publishing's most popular mediums, with major best sellers such as Alison Bechdels's *Fun Home: A Family Tragicomic*, Chris Ware's *Jimmy Corrigan: The Smartest Kid on Earth*, and Craig Thompson's *Blankets*. A big boost to graphic novels was Hollywood's financial success with adaptations, beginning with Dan Clowes's *Ghost World* (2001), Marjane Satrapi's *Persepolis* (2007), and Alan Moore's *Watchmen* (2009).

Graphic novels are currently booming. The shift in distribution, publishing, and marketing encouraged cartoonists to think big, not only in terms of page numbers but also in originality, leading them to produce a wide array of visions both in form and in content. Free of their past stigma, graphic novels are now legitimized as appropriate adult reading material. The format has passed through its infancy, childhood, and teenage stages into a maturing category of literature that envelops all genres, fiction and nonfiction. Today, authors of diverse races, as well as women, gays, and lesbians, are creating material that has resulted in a significant expansion in adult readership, expanding from a narrow readership of young Caucasian males. We have entered a second golden era of comics in the form of graphic novels, with thousands of high-quality new titles every year.

The Appeal of Graphic Novels

Fundamentally, graphic novels are a way of telling a story using both text and pictures. As they cover all genres, all of the appeal factors present in prose novels can apply to a graphic novel. The storyline may be plot or theme based, told with varied pacing, in a linear or nonlinear progression. The main appeal may be the focus on character development, either of one character or a group of characters that present differing viewpoints. Perhaps it is the playful, nostalgic, or dark mood that draws the reader in. The period setting or the setting of the personal world the artist has created may be what tempts the reader. Or the hook may be witty dialogue, the lack of words, or the language of the art.

The major defining and unique appeal element is the visual narrative. There is a huge variety of styles of cartooning, from simple, old-fashioned cartoon art to digitally enhanced illustration. The reader grows to identify with the characters through both words and images. The mood may be set by the color palette or through illustration details. Images in this medium lend themselves to devices that are difficult to achieve with text only, including movement through time (past, present, and future) and to the depiction of deep emotional states; authors can even be self-referential. In addition, the illustrations bring the reader into the midst of the story in a distinctive way. As when watching a film, readers don't have to use their imaginations in the same way they do when called on to picture the descriptions presented in text. Where the reader's imagination does have to work is in understanding what is happening between the panels and to grasp the cartoonist's unique iconographies; the reader must simultaneously "read" text and image together. Graphic novels might also appeal because they are generally a quick read. Compelling ideas, profound stories, and entertaining escape are all to be found with a minimum of time invested.

How to Use This Book

Despite the amazing rise in publication and quality, graphic novels remain terra incognita to many readers' advisers and to adult readers alike. Many excellent graphic-novel resources have been published that provide core lists, collection development information, and genre guides. *Read on ... Graphic Novels* is intended to aid readers and readers' advisers in finding graphic novels that meet readers' interests. Titles are categorized according to prominent appeal elements, including Story, Setting, Character, Mood, and Language. Each section has annotated lists, organized alphabetically by author, that highlight aspects of the medium that go beyond subject headings or genre guides. In each list, a good starting title is marked with the ▶ symbol. About 500 titles are annotated in this book to provide a broad spectrum of graphic novels that appeal to adults with a wide range of reading tastes. The annotations provide a plot summary and some indication of why it was chosen for inclusion in the list.

The lists in this book comprise titles that are frequently available in large public library collections. Included are stand-alone original graphic novels, short-story anthologies, weekly strip collections, and previously published comic-book series collected in a single bound volume. Items that are excluded, although they are often shelved with graphic novels, are daily comic-strip and single-panel cartoon collections. Select titles of international graphic novels, including manga, and superhero genre titles are included, but these categories are too substantial to be covered in any depth in a book of this length. While the lists contain a broad variety of graphic-novel titles, they are by no means comprehensive.

The intended audience for this book is adult readers and the readers' advisers who assist them. The young adult audience covers a broad age range, and, while some of the titles within are appropriate for tweens and younger teens, the [Y][A] notation indicates content appropriate for older teenagers ages 16 and up.

New graphic-novel readers will find an introduction to the comic's medium that allows them to find materials appropriate to their general reading and viewing preferences. Arrows next to a title designate a good starting place in that list. Readers familiar with graphic novels will find original, diverse access points for discovering additional titles. This book is also a navigational aid for librarians to use in helping users and also has suggestions for collection development and ideas for displays and book discussion groups.

So, go ahead, dive in, and indulge yourself with the host of brilliant, eye-catching, and entertaining graphic novels. The possibilities for every stripe of storytelling are endless in the graphic-novel format; there is something for every reader to enjoy. For those of you who are already fans, this is an opportunity to broaden your horizons. For you first-time graphic-novel readers, you're in for an unexpected treat. However you use this book, enjoy! You're reading book-length comics, and they're fun!

Symbols Used in Annotations

▶ Start Here

☯ Book Award Winner

Ⓨ Ⓐ YA Friendly

Chapter One

Story

Pictorial storytelling has existed since prehistoric times when cave paintings were used to tell stories. People respond to stories, whether they are listening, viewing, or reading them. Storytelling is one of the most fundamental forms of communication. Both the intimacy and the plasticity of the format allow for many variations on the basic story: a problem is presented, the conflict is addressed, and the end offers a resolution of some sort.

Graphic novel fans know that the lines between fiction and nonfiction are blurred in the graphic format: nonfiction in the form of memoir, narrative nonfiction, and educational material all stand alongside pure fictional stories. Storylines in graphic novels carry all the same diverse appeals as prose works. The storyline may be explicit, violent, or action oriented or thought provoking and issue oriented. Complex plots with plot twists or multiple plotlines are as frequent as a slice-of-life tales or a gentle romp with a simple beginning, middle and end. There are recurring themes and favored plots that the graphic novel reader can count on.

The stories in these lists tend to vary more than those in prose novels, as they are not bound by genre conventions. As you read, you discover how the visual dimension enriches the text, communicating the story through the characters' facial expressions and body language, through settings and action, and through color and line. Whether theme driven or plot driven, the graphic novels included in the following lists share well-conceived narrative arcs that, whatever their form, carry all the same appeal as those in prose works.

1

Graphic Love: Romance Stories

Romances, popularized in the late 1940s, reached their peak in the 1950s when they accounted for more than a quarter of the comic-book market. Romance in the graphic format is currently dominated by manga geared to a teenage audience. This is a medium that is a natural for expressing the language of love—the "marriage" of text and image produces emotionally nuanced romances that will be appreciated by mature readers.

Beland, Tom

▶ *True Story, Swear to God: Archives.* 2008. Image Comics, ISBN 1582408815, 512p. Nonfiction.

What are the chances of a Californian cartoonist meeting a Puerto Rican radio personality at Disney World and falling in love? It's all true, as you will discover in this charming collection of Beland's comics that present vignettes of a loving romantic relationship. The simple line cartooning is just right for these matter-of-fact tales of love. The magic of this true love story is that, despite the straightforward storytelling, on completion, the reader is left feeling as if she had just finished a fairy tale.

Johnston, Antony

Three Days in Europe. 2003. Oni Press, ISBN 1929998724, 152p.

Jack and Jill, successful young professionals, are trying to put the spark back in their romance. Traces of O'Henry in the set-up: each plans a surprise Valentine's Day getaway for the other: he to Paris for an art exhibit she's dying to see, she to London for his favorite band's concert. On the way to the airport, their tickets are exchanged, setting off a chain reaction that leads to screwball comedy shenanigans. While not on par with a Hepburn-Grant movie, the art has that period look, with a contemporary edge. Snappy dialogue and sufficient twists and turns leading up to the unavoidable clichéd ending will keep the romantic comedy lover engaged.

Moore, Terry

Strangers in Paradise. 2004. Abstract Studio, ISBN 1892597268, 360p. ☿ Ⓨ Ⓐ

The romantic triangle is explored with great emotional depth in Moore's complex, 15-year-old saga of three friends. Dynamic, aggressive Katchoo loves her high school best friend and roommate, Francine. Devoted friend David loves Katchoo. Francine, plump and pretty, is so unsure of herself she doesn't know whom to love. Sound like the makings for a soap opera? Moore's honest characterizations and sympathetic treatment of the dramatic highs and lows the characters have experienced keep this complicated threesome real. That's what keeps fans caring and coming back for more of this modern-day take on affairs of the heart.

Okasaki, Mari
Suppli. 2007. TokyoPop, ISBN 1427803145, 224p.

Manimi, a 27-year-old workaholic, is heartbroken when her boyfriend of seven years breaks up with her. Reflecting on this and the professional rut she's been in, Manami promises herself to live more fully. This sweet workplace romance introduces Manimi's flirtations with two of her co-workers. The reader can identify with the fully realized characters and the maturing protagonist's efforts to juggle various aspects of her life. Many romantic moments keep romance readers engaged and wondering who Manimi will eventually fall in love with.

Rich, James S.
Twelve Reasons Why I Love Her. 2006. Oni Press, ISBN 1932664513, 144p.

This love story is unveiled through 12 nonlinear vignettes, each relaying an interaction in the ups and downs of Gwen and Evan's life together. The reader is drawn to care about the couple from the first chapter, which conveys a comfortable moment in an established romance. A rich make-up scene revealing their strong love is placed well before the trivial quarrel that prompted it, a reminder of the need to maintain perspective in the heat of a moment. The situations feel genuine, although at times the emotions come through more clearly in the excellent line drawing than in the dialogue. If you enjoy this, be sure to check out Rich's other nuanced romance graphic novels.

Watson, Andi
Love Fights. 2004. Oni Press, ISBN 1929998864, 160p. ☒

Jack is a newspaper cartoonist who draws the real life adventures of The Flamer, one of a cast of superheroes who inhabit his world. Love seems to elude Jack due to insecurities about his less-than-super human qualities until a chance meeting with Nora, a superhero gossip columnist investigating a scoop about The Flamer. Affection develops slowly and awkwardly, at an authentic pace, as the couple must overcome obstacles related to the cult of superhero celebrity. Romance readers, never fear; British cartoonist Watson keeps the superheroes off stage, his spare and concise art and text focused on this delightful, down-to-earth love story.

Graphic Witness: The Fallout from Fanaticism

This list contains historical events caused by tribal and religious fanaticism, imperialism, and fascism. The effects on the innocents who are victims of repression and genocide are explored in the following titles.

Giardino, Vittorio
Loss of Innocence, <u>Jew in Communist Prague</u>. 1994. NBM Comics Lit, ISBN 1561631809, 46p.

Jonas Finkel's life is dramatically altered after his physician father is arrested and disappears as a capitalist sympathizer in 1950s Communist Prague. Forced to leave school, he is isolated from his friends and finds work as a day laborer. His mother's life also grows smaller and more difficult every day, as she moves from being a French teacher to a factory job and is evicted from the family home, all the while writing to find out what happened to her husband. It's a dangerous world they are navigating, fraught with anti-Semitism and antibourgeois sentiments, where any small thing can be used against you by the totalitarian Communist rulers.

Kouno, Fumiyono
Town of Evening Calm; Country of Cherry Blossoms. 2003. Last Gasp, ISBN 9780867196658, 103p. ⅋ ⓎⒶ

The year is 1955, and adolescent Minami works and lives with her mother in postbomb slums in Hiroshima. Ten years after the bomb, she gets sick, and her death is foreshadowed, putting to end her guilt over surviving when her father and many of her siblings died. The next story starts in Tokyo in 1987, where young Nanami lives with her father, a *hibakushi* (survivor) and her brother, who suffers from asthma. Many years later, in 2004, she follows her father to see where he goes on his very long walks and ends up in Hiroshima, where he visits the family grave and relatives to talk about the dead. Numerous small details and dialogue enlighten readers, without preaching, about the physical, psychological, and social aftereffects of the atomic bomb.

Lockpez, Iverna, Dean Haspiel, and Jose Villarrubia
Cuba: My Revolution. 2010. Vertigo, ISBN 9781401222178, 144p. ⅋ ⓎⒶ

Seventeen-year-old Sonya is full of hope that justice and equality will come to her beloved Cuba following Fidel Castro's 1959 overthrow of the Batista regime. She sacrifices her dreams of becoming an artist to become a doctor for the revolution. As Sonya and her peers suffer through imprisonments and torture, she struggles with her shifting beliefs and loyalties. Based on Lockpez's personal experiences, the narrative and the expressive art track the painful process of the erosion of idealism in the face of destructive and sorrowing effects of dictatorship.

Nakazawa, Keiji
Barefoot Gen: A Cartoon Story of Hiroshima, <u>Barefoot Gen</u>. 2004. Last Gasp, ISBN 9780867196023, 284p. Nonfiction. ⅋ ⓎⒶ

The first volume in a series of 10 begins four months before the horrific day when the United States dropped the A-bomb on Hiroshima, a civilian city of 400,000. The protagonists are Gen and his proud family, who are bullied and ostracized for their antiwar views. Life is harsh under the military dictatorship, where the rich get richer while the poor starve as they watch their sons die in futile kamikaze missions. When the bomb is dropped, Gen and his mother survive, but how will they endure the horrendous things, from people's skin melting, to their loved ones being burned to death, that they have witnessed? The final tenth of this volume portrays what it was like a few hours after the bomb; read on to bear witness to the short- and long-term aftereffects for the people of Hiroshima.

Satrapi, Marjane

Persepolis: The Story of a Childhood. 2003. Pantheon Books, ISBN 0375422307, 153p. Nonfiction. ⚥ Ⓨ Ⓐ

Satrapi is the only child of loving, upper-class, Marxist parents and the granddaughter of one of Iran's last emperors. At the age of six, under the Shah's regime, she loves religion. By the time she is 10, the Islamic Revolution brings new fundamentalism, with changes ranging from involuntary head-covering to the execution of beloved family members. When the war with Iraq breaks out, friends are killed, and her neighborhood is bombed. Her parents send her to safety in Austria. Satrapi's keen perspective and charming, stark black-and-white art portray a child's attempts to understand shifting ideals in the face of various forms of totalitarianism in this stunning memoir.

Spiegelman, Art

▶ *Maus: A Survivors Tale.* 1986. Pantheon Books, ISBN 0394747232, 159p. Nonfiction. ⚥ ⚥

Spiegelman interviews his cantankerous father, Vladek, about his life in Poland from mid-1930 through the liberation of the concentration camps. Vladek narrates his story, his marriage, his experiences as a prisoner of war, the ghettoization of the Jews, and the death of his son at Auschwitz. The characters are depicted with the heads of different animals according to nationality: Jews are mice, Germans are cats, and Poles are pigs. This Pulitzer-Prize-winning graphic novel is striking in its use of the "funny animal" convention for subject matter as grave as genocide, the harrowing depiction of what it took to survive Auschwitz, and the portrayal of the guilt suffered by children of Holocaust survivors. Spiegelman's memoir is a benchmark in graphic-novel history, opening the doors for an adult readership on serious topics rendered in the comics medium.

Stassen, J. P.

Deogratias: A Tale of Rwanda. 2006. First Second, ISBN 9781596431034, 96p. ⚥ Ⓨ Ⓐ

Deogratias is a Hutu, and his close friends are Tutsi in the period when racial tensions were rising prior to the brutal 1994 genocide of 800,000 Tutsis. The story is told in flashbacks, showing Deogratias as a carefree adolescent, hanging out with his friends, and looking for his first sexual conquest. When the Hutus begin the massacre, Deogratias is driven mad when he is forced to choose between joining them or sharing the fate of his dead friends. He believes he is a dog, is unable to sleep, and is continuously drinking banana beer. Stassen's story and the moody art depict the consequences of racial oppression taken to the extreme.

Striking Crime: Bizarre Investigations

The crime genre, both fiction and nonfiction, has been as popular in comics as it has in all other forms of media. The entertainment value lies in shocking readers with nasty wrongdoings, from brutal murders, to robbery, to bloody fights. The following investigations all have a peculiar twist that pushes them over the edge.

Bertozzi, Nick
The Salon. 2007. St. Martin's Press, ISBN 0312354851, 192p. ℧
It's Paris, 1907, and someone is brutally murdering Modernist artists. Gertrude and Leo Stein team up with their salon regulars, including Matisse, Picasso, and Braque, to follow up on their suspicions that the villain is Gauguin's lover. This mystery is intertwined with salon meetings in the Steins' art-filled home, which elucidates this period in art history: the innovation of styles such as cubism, the theoretical debate, and the personalities of the artists. Award-winning cartoonist Bertozzi's bold art, saturated with a colorful palette, brings this wacky mystery alive.

Brubaker, Ed
Scene of the Crime: A Little Piece of Goodnight. 2000. DC Comics, ISBN 9781563896702, p105.
Jack Herriman has faced his own demons and works as a P.I. When his father's police partner gives him a missing-persons case, it leads to one murder after the next until he is submerged in a thorny family tale that has its roots in a tragedy that took place in a 1970s free-love commune. In the course of the investigation, Herriman's emotions about his father's death are stirred up, and he has to come to terms with his history all over again in award-winning cartoonist Brubaker's well-executed hard-boiled private-eye story.

Butcher, Jim, and Ardian Syaf
Welcome to the Jungle. 2008. Dabel Brothers Publishing, ISBN 9780345507464, 160p. ℧
The cops are stumped over the brutal murder of a night watchman at the Lincoln Park Zoo. The killer couldn't be human or animal, so they call their go-to guy for the supernatural, Harry Dresden, the only wizard in the Chicago phonebook. Harry, a white wizard, follows the forces of darkness, until he finds the culprit who has been killing off zoo staff and animals to use their blood in a ritual to achieve eternal power.

Gage, Christos N.

▶ ***Area 10.*** 2010. Vertigo Comics, ISBN 9781401210670, 180p.

NYPD Detective Adam Kamen is on a grisly case of "Henry the Eighth," a serial murderer who severs the heads of his victims and keeps them. When Kamen is accosted by a murderer who drills a hole in the middle of his forehead, he begins to see people's futures. He learns that this is a side effect of trepanation, a grisly practice of drilling holes in the "third eye" chakra to attain enlightenment. It soon becomes apparent that this bizarre ritual is tied into the serial murders, when a collection of the victim's heads is found, all with holes drilled into them. A compelling page-turner, this is weird crime fiction at its best.

Gallaher, David, and Steve Ellis

Box 13. 2010. Red 5 Comics, ISBN 9780980930269, 124p.

Dan Holiday, a well-known espionage author, is on a book tour for his new work of investigative journalism into the government-backed MKULTRA project, which alters brain function in humans to program them as super-soldiers. At a signing, he is left a box, labeled Box 1. When he opens it, his mind is altered, and he finds himself in a hospital, hooked up to multiple wires and computers. This is the first of 13 boxes that lead him on a wild chase to figure out who is sending the boxes and what they mean. The finale of this suspenseful search brings Holiday face to face with the odd truth of his existence.

Laymon, John, and Rob Guillory

Taster's Choice, Chew. 2009. Image Comics, ISBN 1607061597, 128p. YA

Tony Chu is a detective with a very peculiar gift: he is cibopathic; whatever he takes a bite of (except beets!) gives him psychic information about the history of that object. Chu works for the FDA, the most powerful governmental agency after an endemic avian flu results in all poultry being declared illegal. While Chu is at a restaurant, investigating the chicken black market, he eats a bowl of soup and has visions of the chef killing the people whose body parts are in the broth. Later, he eats the remaining finger of a murdered investigator to uncover his killer. Laymon's wacky premise allows for many gruesome, cannibalistic plot turns, and Guillory's art takes this strange crime series to the limits of good taste and humor.

Otsuka, Eiji, and Housui Yamazaki

The Kurosagi Corpse Delivery Service. 2006. Dark Horse Manga, ISBN 1593075669, 197p.

Kuro Karatsu, a student at a Buddhist university, comes across a strange flyer for volunteers while hopelessly looking for a job. He volunteers and finds himself among a group of fellow students, all with a talent related to the dead, including a dowser, who finds corpses rather than water; someone with embalming skills; and Kuro, who can communicate with the dead. When they find a winning lottery ticket on a corpse, they start a business to transport the corpses wherever they want to go! The intriguing account of their deliveries can be disturbing and is not for every reader.

Sala, Richard
  The Chuckling Whatsit. 1997. Fantagraphics, ISBN 1560972815, 200p. ☿
      A grisly murderer reappears years after gruesome serial killings and begins to kill astrologers. Reporter Broom, bold but dense, lurches through an increasing convoluted mystery, with creepy human-skinned dolls (the titular Whatsits), obsessed doll collectors, a cryptic masked assassin, and a murder-loving secret society called G.A.S.H. The cityscapes are full of tilting Gothic buildings built on twisting roads strewn with warped characters casting long shadows. Sala's distinctive dark gothic expressionism creates an unsettling emotional landscape that supports the mystery's bizarre plot twists, arcane occult tidbits, and droll humor.

Drawing Dis-ease: Triumph over Corporal Suffering

Graphic novels provide an intimacy and directness that allow creators to portray their experience of illness with depth and resonance. In each of the titles on this list, the protagonists go through transformations in response to grappling with the profound uncertainties and physical pain that come with disease.

Dahl, Ken
  Monsters. 2009, Secret Acres, ISBN 9780979960949, 200p. Ⓨ Ⓐ
      Dahl's confessional tale reads like a cross between 1960s underground comix and educational health materials. When Dahl's girlfriend finds out that she has herpes, their relationship crumbles. Dahl starts to feel isolated, sad, and frustrated. Grotesque drawings portray his experience of morphing into a contagious monster composed of shed viral cells. The educational section in the middle provides information for a disease that 70 percent of adults have but rarely speak of. With many graphic drawings of infected genitalia and sex, this one is not for the faint of heart.

Davison, Al
  The Spiral Cage. 2003. Active Images, ISBN 9780974056715, 140p.
      When British Davison, born with severe spina bifida, starts to walk, he astonished the doctors who had given him up as hopeless. His optimistic outlook and hard work allowed him to transcend the "spiral cage" of his DNA, becoming adept in martial arts, practicing Buddhism, and finding love and marriage. A dazzling array of cartooning styles successfully portray his dreams, his fantasies, and the facts of his life as Davison learns to accept himself in the face of misconceptions and discrimination against people with disabilities.

French, Rene
The Ticking. 2005. Top Shelf Productions, ISBN 9781891830709, 216p.

When Edison Steelhead's mother dies in childbirth, his father whisks him away to an isolated island lighthouse to hide the facial deformities that they share. Edison wears a mask to hide his face from the visitors, yet he is enchanted by the world around him, recording small insects and his father's scars in detailed drawings. Rejecting the surgery his father had to make him more "normal" looking and the isolation his father's discomfort has created, Edison accepts his appearance and opts to live in the real world. Award-winning cartoonist French's small, jewel-like pencil illustrations walk the line between being cute and monstrous in this touching and bizarre tale of a child coming to terms with himself, despite the deformities that make him different.

Marchetto, Marisa Acocella
Cancer Vixen. 2006. Alfred A. Knopf, ISBN (0307263576), p212.

Marchetto's memoir of facing breast cancer is both a funny and a serious take on lumpectomy, chemo, and radiation. Diagnosed at age 43, just weeks before her wedding, Marchetto struggles with finding her "higher self" within the high-fashion, superficial New York worlds in which she travels. With a spirited slap in the face to cancer, she continues to live a full life and even wears a different pair of designer high heels to her chemo sessions! In addition to her family and multitudes of friends, she consults two Kabbalistic rabbis, a priest, a therapist, even a call-in spiritualist. The admirable, honest story and the bold, bright comics result in an uplifting story about fighting cancer and coming away changed for the better.

Milner, Jude
Fat Free. 2006. Jeremy P. Tarcher/Penguin, ISBN 9781585425013, 64p. Nonfiction. ⚥

Young Jude grows progressively fatter when she begins to secretly gorge herself with sweets after a family disaster. Envious of the "litte Ginas," the petite girlie-girls, she runs away from home, only to get raped by a truck driver, which furthers her complex negative sense of self. She becomes a counselor and a telephone sex operator and finds a place with the fat-acceptance movement (PHAT). Her journey from self-hatred is a winding road, but she eventually finds confidence and commits to helping other overweight people.

Peeters, Fredrik
Blue Pills. 2008. Houghton Mifflin, ISBN 061882099, 190p.

Peeters connects strongly with Cati at a party in their hometown of Geneva. They enjoy each other's company, have little conflict, and feel a strong desire for each other. Before becoming intimate, Cati reveals that she and her three-year-old son are both HIV positive. Peeters's wonderful brushwork reveals both his inner conflicts and his deepening love. In this beautiful graphic novel, Peeters reveals how each of the characters comes to terms with living with fears, accepting the parameters it imposes on them and ultimately appreciating how living with illness facilitates the ability to relish each moment of their love.

Pekar, Harvey, Joyce Brabner, and Frank Stack
▶ *Our Cancer Year.* 1994. Four Walls Eight Windows, ISBN 1568580118, p 252. ⓨⒶ

Harvey Pekar chronicles his daily life as a file clerk at Cleveland's VA Hospital in his renowned comic-book series *American Splendor*. In the same year as Iraq's invasion of Kuwait and Operation Desert Storm, Pekar discovers he has lymphoma. The story of his chemotherapy and radiation treatments is interwoven with his wife's political work with a group of international students and their move from apartment living to home ownership. Pekar and Brabner struggle through the fears and pain together, as Harvey struggles with his neuroses, feelings of powerlessness, and inclination to overwork, even while fighting cancer.

Shivak, Nadia
Inside Out: Portrait of an Eating Disorder. 2007. Atheneum Books, ISBN 9780689852169, 64p. ⓧ

Shivak recounts her nearly lifelong struggle with bulimia, going deeply into the addictive quality and physical ramifications of this disease. Her narration and illustrations show her obsession with food and the shame and self-hatred that come from feeling powerless against the "Eating Disorder Monster." Hard emotional work and multiple hospitalizations have brought her to a place where she feels she is in control of the monster. Boxes containing alarming facts are spread throughout the book, with a list of resources for those who suffer from eating disorders.

Tobe, Keiko T.
With the Light: Raising an Autistic Child. 2001, 2007. Yen Press, ISBN 0759523568, 523p.

Sachiko is struggling to do her best as a young mother with a critical husband and mother-in-law blaming her for her son Hikaru's frequent tantrums and aversion to affection. When he is diagnosed with autism, Sachiko becomes his advocate for accommodations at school and responds to people's discomfort with his disorder. This manga follows Hikaru's experience from birth through elementary school. Despite a soap-opera quality, it contains a wealth of information about autism and the varied challenges a family faces as it learns to live with it.

Unmasked: Supersized Identity Crises

Fundamental to the superpowered ethos is a secret identity, usually composed of a nom de guerre and a costumed disguise. Undisguised, superheroes can lead ordinary lives without making themselves or their loved ones vulnerable. When masked, they have unlimited power and the freedom to abide by their own rules. The following stories explore this common superhero convention through the crisis that occurs when a secret identity has been exposed.

Bendis, Brian Michael, Alex Maleev, Manuel Gutierrez, and Terry Dodson
Out, **Daredevil**, **Vol. 5.** 2003. Marvel Entertainment, ISBN 9780785110743, 208p.

A gangster's thwarted attempt to usurp Kingpin leads him to the police seeking protective custody. In return, he gives the FBI Daredevil's secret identity. His cover leaked to a tabloid newspaper, lawyer Matt Murdock is in for a superhero's worst nightmare, including nonstop media attention, pressure to stop being a superhero, and repercussions for his masked friends. Murdock also grapples with the potential consequences of being a lawyer by day and a vigilante by night. Award-winning author Bendis's portrait of a flawed man, struggling to maintain his privacy and sanity while under extreme public scrutiny, is completed by excellent dark, moody art.

Brubaker, Ed, and Sean Phillips
Incognito. 2009. Marvel Comics, ISBN9780785139799, 176p.

After betraying his cartel of supervillains, Zack Overkill is given a new identity in a witness protection program. His powers suppressed by government prescribed meds and the daily grind of working as a lowly file clerk force him to conform to the rules of the common folk. Severe boredom and the discovery that illegal drugs override the effect of his meds drive Overkill back to his old superpowered ways, but with a new twist. This supervillain variation on the secret-identity theme is a dark and complex look at the powers and thrills of life above the rat race.

Busiek, Kurt, and Stuart Immonen
Superman: Secret Identity. 2004. DC Comics, ISBN 1401204511, 206p. ⛃

A thoughtful, teenage loner in Kansas has finally come to terms with getting teased because his name is Clark Kent when he discovers that, in addition to sharing his name with Superman, he also has his powers! He saves lots of people, falls in love, fathers two daughters, and grows old. All along, he worries about getting caught by immoral government agents and the danger he is putting his family in. Busiek's Superman represents the everyman, coming to terms with the challenges that each stage of life presents. Immonen's stunning artwork adds intricacy to this unusual superhero story, where a secret identity symbolizes the concealed parts of us that are common to human experience.

Meltzer, Brad, and Rags Morales
▶ *Identity Crisis.* 2005. DC Comics, ISBN 1401206883, 242p. ⛃

When Elongated Man's beloved wife is murdered, it pierces to the heart of the fears that lurk in every superhero—that his calling will endanger the ones he loves most. The whole DC superhero universe converges to mourn with him, unravel the mystery, and bring the villain to justice. Each character wrestles with events and the role he played in superhero history and with his own conflict about continuing to protect and defend. This incredible thematic and artistic study of the combination of the heroic and the human permits the reader to identify with the superpowered in a deep way while unmasking the mythology of their universe.

Pope, Paul, and Jose Villarrubia
Batman: Year 100. 2007. DC Comics, ISBN 9781401211929, 228p. ☙ Ⓨ Ⓐ
   The year is 2039, 100 years after Bob Kane's creation of Batman, in a world where a technological "Big Brother" has taken privacy away from humans and superheroes alike. Supervillains have been eradicated, leaving the treachery to those who supposedly protect civilians. An elderly but fierce Batman is the only superhero who is still masked. When he is framed for the murder of a federal agent who is transporting an electronic doomsday plague formula, his identity becomes of paramount importance to the powers that be. Instead, Batman unmasks government conspiracies and retreats back into privacy in this dystopian science fiction superhero story that questions the use of technology as a means of control.

Straczynski, J. Michael, and Ron Garney
Civil War: The Amazing Spider-Man. 2007. Marvel, ISBN 0785123370, 168p. ☙
   When the U.S. government introduces the Superhero Registration Act in order to protect civilians from the superpowered, Spider-Man is urged by Iron-Man, a supporter of the act, to register. After an emotional conversation with MJ and Aunt May, Spiderman reveals his real name as he removes his mask at a press conference. He rethinks his actions when he discovers how vulnerable he and his family are to attacks from antiregistration superheroes led by Captain America, criminals he has captured, and his friends and co-workers in his life as Peter Parker. An allegory of post–Patriot Act loss of privacy, the *Civil War* series explores the multifaceted realities of living with a secret identity.

Mad Scientists, Contraptions, and Victoriana, Oh My!: Steampunk Yarns

Steampunk is usually a mix of science fiction, speculative fiction, adventure, romance, and mystery set in an alternate Victorian era on the brink of the Industrial Revolution. Typical to steampunk fiction are sinister scientists, literary and historical characters, and futuristic vehicles and devices that are powered by a mix of mechanics, steam, and advanced technologies. Fans of the visions of 19th-century "retro science fiction" (H. G. Wells and Jules Verne), fin-de-siècle aesthetics, and rip-roaring, over-the-top adventure may find satisfaction with the following steampunk graphic novels.

Fraction, Matt
Five Fists of Science. 2006. Image Comics, ISBN 1582406057, 1v. (unpaged).
Mark Twain and Nikola Tesla team up with other prominent supporters of the Armistice Movement in an attempt to end war by supplying every country with Tesla's superweapon, a motion-guided giant robot soldier. Their blend of science and showmanship is upstaged by superfinanciers J. P. Morgan and Andrew Carnegie, who recruit Thomas Edison into a black-magic secret society that aims to control the world. Industrial and scientific growth in Victorian New York is accurately presented, and celebrities of the period are well represented in this fun and appealing steampunk graphic novel.

Moore, Alan, and Kevin O'Neill
▶ *League of Extraordinary Gentleman,* **Vol. 1.** 2002. America's Best Comics, ISBN 978156389857, 176p. ⓎⒶ
Heroes from 19th-century literature come to life and unite their intellectual and scientific powers to protect the British Empire on the brink of world war. Following the Dracula scare, British Intelligence assembles literary figures such as Captain Nemo, Allan Quartermain, Dr. Jekyll, and the Invisible Man as a sort-of superhero team to obtain cavorite (H. G. Wells's gravity substance blocker) from villain Fu Manchu, who will use it to build an airship that will destroy England. Moore and O'Neill team up to create a stunning portrayal of turn-of-the-century obsessions with science and sexuality and paint a fine superheroed steampunk version of the Victorian Age.

Murai, Sadayuki
Steam Boy. 2006. Viz Media, ISBN 1421504944, 192p.
Ray Steam has invented a "Steamball" that has the power of a small nuclear reactor and is caught between his grandfather, who wants to destroy his potent invention, and his father, who wants to promote the weapon for the glory of scientific progress. A nefarious corporation and the British government are also is trying to track down the Steamball for their own purposes. Featuring the Crystal Palace, built to showcase new technology from around the world, this visually enchanting portrayal of a Victorian era that has nuclear power addresses important questions that have yet to be answered: what sacrifices need to be made for scientific progress, and what is the best use of technology?

Talbot, Bryan
The Adventures of Luther Arkwright. 2008. Dark Horse, ISBN 1593077254, 216p. ⓎⒶ
Luther Arkwright is womanizing secret agent who can travel at will between multiple parallel Earths. Based in the parallel "zero-zero," a stable

high-tech world, Arkwright maintains peace in the multiverses by monitoring the activities of the villainous "Disrupters." Arkwright must save the universe when the Disrupters activate Firefrost, a legendary doomsday device, in a dark alternate England ruled with Puritan fervor by Cromwell's descendants since the mid-1600s defeat of the monarchy in the English Civil War. British cartoonist Talbot weaves mythological, historical, and political references into a healthy dose of outlandish inventions, machinery, and plot twists to produce this dense sci-fi yarn, which originally began serialization in 1978.

Tardi, Jacques
Arctic Marauder. 1972, 2011. Fantagraphics Books, ISBN 1606994352, 64p.

While exploring the Arctic Ocean in 1899, young Jerome Plumier and his crew see a mysterious derelict vessel perched high on an iceberg immediately before his ship, L'Anjou, inexplicably explodes. After a stint in the hospital, Plumier's search for his missing inventor uncle, Louis-Ferdinad Chapouties, leads him to the North Pole. There he contends with nefarious scientists, a death machine, a giant octopus, and futuristic underwater and aerial machines. French cartoonist Tardi was influenced by Jules Verne and florid pulp escapades in this over-the-top yarn whose magnificent art nouveau, faux-wood-cut style drawings perfectly illustrate the fin-de-siècle mechanical wonders that populate this steampunk "icepunk" world.

Way, Gerard, and Gabriel Ba
Apocalypse Suite, <u>**The Umbrella Academy**</u>. 2008. Dark Horse, ISBN 9781593079789, 192p. ☃ Y A

Forty-three exceptional babies are simultaneously and spontaneously born to single women in some unknown place and point in time. Entrepreneur Dr. Reginald Hargreeves, inventor of modern mechanical marvels including "The Televator, The Levitator and The Mobile Umbrella Communicator," uses his past-revealing monocle to locate seven of these oddly powered children. He aloofly trains his adopted motley crew to fight evil forces, beginning with a flying Eiffel Tower, manned by a robotic Gustave Eiffel. Award-winning Brazilian artist Ba illustrates Way's fun and eccentric superhero/family-saga/alternate-history with delightful Victorian steampunk embellishments.

Beyond the Family Circus: Dysfunctional Families

While the title of the long-running cartoon "The Family Circus" acknowledges a dash of chaos inherent in family life, the family in the cartoon remained stalwartly cheerful in its midst. Family life has always been a deeply mined subject in movies and film, but realistic presentations of dysfunctional family life are fairly new to the comics medium. The following titles are all moving, if sometimes disturbing, portrayals of life outside the well-adjusted family circus.

Bagge, Peter

The Bradleys. 2007. Fantagraphics Books, ISBN 1560975768, 160p.

The Bradleys are caricatured, loose-limbed misfits. Slacker Buddy Bradley, insecure teenage Babs, and gullible preadolescent Butch are always at one another's necks while trying to avoid their belligerent dad, Brad, and martyred mom, Betty. This disconcerting and hilarious satire on the torments of being part of a dysfunctional New Jersey family in the 1980s includes a venomous mother-daughter face-off, a tirade about an intolerably annoying little brother, and a darkly uproarious family holiday scene in "Merry F***king Christmas." Bagge finds humor in the dark side of suburban family torment in this stunning collection.

Kleid, Neil, and Nicholas Cinquegrani

▶ *The Big Kahn.* 2009. Comics Lit, ISBN 9781561635610, 176p. ⚥

At the funeral of the well-respected Rabbi David Kahn, his unheard-of brother, Roy Dobbs, shows up, revealing to the family and the whole congregation that not only was his brother a con man, but he wasn't even Jewish. The mourning family has to grapple with broken trust and maintaining faith, while being ostracized from their community. Finely, shaded drawings capture the turmoil as this family falls apart. This graphic novel presents a significant meditation on a family struggling to find new identities when their sense of integrity is abruptly uprooted.

Ono, Natsume

Not Simple. 2006. Viz Media, ISBN 9781421532202, 316p. ⚥

Ian is a wandering soul, always searching for the love and emotional connection he knows should exist in a family. Sold into prostitution as a young boy by his mother for drinking money and disowned by his father, he searches for his sister (who may be his real mother) from Australia to England and to the United States. In a clever narrative device, Ian's life history is told in reverse by a novelist friend, skillfully illuminating Ian's sadness and dissociation from his broken and dysfunctional family.

Powell, Nate

Swallow Me Whole. 2008. Top Shelf Productions, ISBN 9781603090339, 216p. ⚥ Ⓨ Ⓐ

Like all adolescents, stepsiblings Ruth and Perry are trying to make sense of their internal lives, family, and high school. Where they differ from others is that each has hallucinations. Ruth can talk to and hear insects that are swarming around her much of the time. Perry has a little wizard who sits on the top of his pencil, commanding him to draw for hours at a time. When their grandmother comes to stay with them, they find out that she is also schizophrenic. This mysterious and painful story of a loving family struggling to keep it together in the midst of mental illness resonates long after you turn the last swirling page.

Sandell, Laurie
Imposters Daughter. 2009. Little, Brown and Company, ISBN 9780316033053, 247p. Nonfiction. ☹

This phenomenal memoir explores one family's experience of revolving around a charismatic, lying, dictatorial father. Sandell's use of candid, engaging narrative with vivid, moving panels enriches her transformation from adoring daughter, to the adolescent subject of her father's rage, to her adult discovery that her father was no more than a conman, which shakes her to her core. She struggles with addiction, is unable to trust men, and must come to terms with her mother and sisters, who hid from the truth and enabled her father's lies. Investigating and writing about his past, coupled with a trip to rehab, allows Sandell to come to peace with the wounding abyss between the fictions and realities that had shaped her family's life.

White, Shane
North Country. 2005. ComicsLit, ISBN 0781561634354, 95p. ☹

Having moved across the country to flee his violent family life, Shane White is going home to visit after years. While traveling, he shares his memories of his childhood, when he lived in constant fear of his alcoholic, violent father. His only escape from terrifying attacks and nightmares was drawing and walking through the stunning nature of the North Country. When the family is reunited at home, there is happiness all around, bringing hope that they can perhaps lay the weighty family baggage to rest.

All Come to Look for America: Immigrant Tales

A ship filled with immigrants being welcomed by the Statue of Liberty is an iconic image in the melting-pot culture of the United States. While immigrants arrive in many ways, their experiences remain a compelling theme widely explored in literature and film. The following graphic novels grapple with the hopes and challenges of immigrants and their children.

Baker, Kevin
Luna Park. 2009. Vertigo, ISBN 9781401215842, 158p.

Alik, a recent Russian immigrant, works for a small-time loan shark in Coney Island and finds solace in heroin and his girlfriend. Her connection to a rival Russian gang puts Alik in a precarious position, resulting in flashbacks to his time as a soldier in Chechnya. This compelling illustration of the immigrant history cycles through misguided loyalties, betrayal, loss, and death. The vivid, dark art and compelling narrative depict most of the Russian wars and immigrant life in New York throughout most of the 20th century.

Eisner, Will
A Life Force. 1983. Kitchen Sink Press, ISBN 0878160396, 139p.

Jacob Shtarkah, an aging, Depression-era immigrant and carpenter, deals with poverty, intermarriage, and fear of the increasing fascism in Europe. Like his neighbors, he struggles to stay afloat and feed his family. Jacob philosophizes about the meaning of life by comparing humans with the cockroaches that are rampant in his Bronx tenement, where Eastern European Jews, Sicilian mafiosi, and Protestant immigrants coexist.

Kalesniko, Mark
Mail Order Bride. 2001. Fantagraphics Books, ISBN 9781560974109, 261p. Ⓨ Ⓐ

Kyong comes to Canada looking for change from her life in Korea. What she gets is an antisocial, cowardly husband who is looking for an Asian stereotype: traditional, hard-working, domestic, and a sex goddess to boot. Feeling objectified by her new husband and isolated by small-town values, she befriends a group of artists, models in the nude, and defies her husband. The evocative drawings reflect her journey to find herself and her place in her new country, a process that is fraught with ambiguities.

Kiyama, Henry (Yoshitaka)
The Four Immigrants Manga. 1931, 1999. Stone Bridge Press, ISBN 1880656337, 152p.

Four young Japanese immigrants, freshly remade with their Western names, Henry, Fred, Frank, and Charlie, struggle to achieve their dreams in early-20th-century San Francisco. They deal with obstacles such as cultural differences and outright prejudice, along with historical events, including the 1906 earthquake, the 1918 influenza pandemic, and World War I. Throughout their acclimation, they maintain a sense of humor that lightens their immigrant experiences. Initially published in 1931, this cartoony primary source on Japanese immigration is also historically significant as the first autobiographical graphic novel.

Lemelman, Martin
Two-Cents Plain: My Brooklyn Boyhood. 2010. Bloomsbury, ISBN 9781608190041, 320p. Nonfiction.

Lemelman's portrait of growing in the 1950s and 1960s, living in the back of his family candy store in Brooklyn, mixes the old-country influence of his immigrant parents' generation with the new-world experience of first-generation Americans. Anecdotes about the simple joys of childhood, including soda fountain egg creams (recipe included), early TV, and painting are set against the bigger narrative arc of the fallout from his parents' experience in the Holocaust, anti-Semitism, poverty, and the changing demographics of the neighborhood. Lemelman's humor and honesty balance nostalgia in the spare pencil drawings, supplemented with photos, documents, and artifacts that build this story of an immigrant family.

Novgorodoff, Danica
Slow Storm. 2008. First Second, ISBN 1596432500, 173p. ⚇
During tornado season in Kentucky, lightning strikes the horse stables that illegal immigrant Rafi has been living in. Awkward firefighter Ursa finds him in the ruins. Initially, their interactions are based on fear and distrust, but later they find common emotional ground as outsiders. In broken English, Rafi tells of crossing the border in search of a better life, being attacked by the smuggler and his homesickness. Ursa identifies with his sense of alienation and his conflicted feelings about homeland. Novgorodoff's powerful watercolors and expressive line evoke deep emotions of hope and despair, enriching this fragmented immigrant story.

Tan, Shaun
▶ *The Arrival.* 2006. Arthur A Levine Books, ISBN 0439895294, 128p. ⚇ Ⓨ Ⓐ
A nameless man packs his suitcase and walks with his family through empty streets to a boat packed with other immigrants. Greeted by the Statue of Liberty, he arrives in a strange new city and finds work, befriends other immigrants, and waits for his family to join him. Fantastical mutating creatures, bizarre monuments, and incomprehensible pictographic symbols abound, surreal elements that are rendered in the familiar warm sepia tones of antique photographs. Australian illustrator Tan tells a classic story in a powerful, wordless style that transcends the personal, capturing the essential experience of alienation in a new land.

Tran, GB
Vietnamerica. 2011. Villard Books, ISBN 0345508726, 288p. Nonfiction. ⚇
Tran's parents left Vietnam in 1975, three days before the fall of Saigon, and brought up their children in South Carolina. Tran wrestles with his identity, leading to a trip to Vietnam to learn about family history from relatives there, an honest exploration of his parent's adaptation to life in the United States, and a depiction of the conflicts of assimilation. Beautiful, detailed art enriches this fascinating meditation on the boundaries between memory and myth, moving between the past and the present to weave a profound intergenerational immigration story.

Wondrous World Building: Epic Fantasies

From early on, comics have been prone to extensive world building, from superhero to fantasy worlds. The titles on this list are examples of fantasy sagas whose inventive mythologies drive their far-reaching plots.

Civiello, Emmanuel
A Bit of Madness. 2005. Checker Book Publishing, ISBN 0975380893, 192p.

Igguk, an erudite elf, is summoned by the divine Queen of Faeries to recover the "Heart of Crystal," an artifact that will protect Faerieland from Oberon, a satanic demon. A stuttering troll and an elderly human sorceress join Igguk in battling outrageous monsters on the quest to save his world. The dialogue is spotty (translated from its original French), and at times the plot is hard to follow, but Civiellio's layered painted art creates a lush world, and the significant conclusion makes this epic a worthwhile read for fantasy fans.

Gaiman, Neil, Sam Keith, and Mike Dringenberg
▶ *Preludes and Nocturnes*, <u>Sandman</u>. 1993, 2010. Vertigo, ISBN 1401225759, 240p. ☿ Ⓨ Ⓐ

The first book of 10 stories introduces the main characters who populate British author Gaiman's exceptional world, including the Sandman (aka Morpheus or Dream) and his immortal siblings, Death, Destiny, Delirium, and Despair. Sandman escapes his 70-year imprisonment to find his dream-domain in shambles. People have been driven to insanity by insomnia or fallen into dream comas as a result of abused powers. To correct this situation, Dream needs to retrieve the objects of his powers. His quest sends him on a journey in which he crosses paths with Lucifer and an omnipotent madman. Gaiman's brilliant epic, a blend of his own glorious invention and elements culled from mythology, folklore, and literature, has been recolored in this new edition.

McNeil, Carla Speed
The Finder Library. 2011. Dark Horse, ISBN 1595826521, 616p. Ⓨ Ⓐ

Jaeger Ayers is a "Finder," a hunter/tracker, and a "Sin-eater," a ritual scapegoat. Orphaned in his teens, he travels with a nomadic clan in a far-future Earth in which humans, cybernetic animal-humanoids, and possible aliens form various sophisticated clans and cultures. Jaeger settles in the doomed city-state of Anvard, where he protects his lover, Emma, and her children from her abusive husband. Jaeger's loyalties are conflicted because he is obligated as a Sin-eater to help the disturbed man. McNeil is an expert world builder, creating complex characters on quests and in challenging situations in a detailed, fully formed civilization that is a compelling blend of aboriginal and technologically advanced urban beings. This Dark Horse collection presents the first three self-contained storylines of this previously self-published "aboriginal science fiction" fantasy series. (http://www.strangehorizons.com/2001/20010212/jaeger-hurt.gif.)

Moebius (Jean Giraud)
The Airtight Garage. 1987. Marvel, ISBN 9780871352804, 120p.

This mend-bending cult classic, first serialized in 1976, loosely follows the adventures of the immortal French explorer Major Grubert as he travels through multiple universes populated with strange species and surreal mysteries, perpetually chased by another immortal, Lewis Carnelian, for some unknown crime.

Grubet and Carnelian must eventually join forces against a malicious alien, the Bakalite, to save the titular hermetic multidimensional world that exists within an immense asteroid. French master cartoonist Moebius's epic space world is disjointed like an absurd and funny surreal dream, overflowing with whole civilizations, bizarre life forms, and conspiracies that are never explained.

Pini, Wendy, and Richard Pini

Wolfrider, <u>Elfquest</u>. 1981, 2003. DC Comics, ISBN 1401201326, 152p. ⑧ Ⓨ Ⓐ

When the humans decide to set the forest on fire, Cutter, chief of the Wolfriders, leads his elf tribe and their wolves on a journey across a desert to find another tribe of desert elves. Cutter tells tales of feats of past generations, saves the village from stampeding horses, and finds his soul-mate, a step in melding the two tribes. Book One of the Pinis' epic Tolkienesque storyline ends on an optimistic note, but there are many more twists and turns as these magical, life-respecting beings challenge the humans, the trolls, and the disappointments that come with high ideals.

Sim, Dave

High Society, <u>Cerebus the Aardvark</u>. 1986, 1994. Aardvark-Vanaheim, ISBN 0919359078, 512p. ⑧

Cerebus, an aardvark, began as parody of Conan the Barbarian, but he comes into his own in this second volume of Sim's sprawling opus. Astoria, a member of high society, uses promises of riches to manipulate Cerebus into campaigning to become prime minister of Iest, a medieval city-state in the imaginary world of Estacion. Astoria knows that Cerebus is not concerned with power, so Astoria will be the authority behind the office. Award-winning cartoonist Sim has crafted a unique fantasy epic, chock full of political and religious intrigue.

Smylie, Mark S.

Artesia, <u>The Book of Dooms</u>. 1999, 2003. Archaia Entertainment, ISBN 9781932386004, 192p.

Artesia, a sorceress and lover, rises from refugee to commander of the army in her matriarchal kingdom of The Known World in a time of ideological and territorial conflict. Artesia leads many battles, accompanied by the war deities, leading to a complete paradigm shift in this dark fantasy world. In this first book, Smylie avoids clichés of fantasy epics with his blend of well-realized spirit and human characters and his gorgeous, sweeping medieval landscapes.

Graphic Grief: Stories of Loss and Alienation

As in all theme-driven graphic stories, the blending of text and word is a potent combination in graphic novels for expressing feelings of loss and alienation. The titles on this list permit the reader to relate to poignant stories of sadness, grief, and isolation that will resonate long after the final page.

Gottlieb, Daphne, and Diane DiMassa
Jokes and the Unconscious. 2006. Cleis Press, ISBN 9781573442503, 113p.

As her oncologist father slowly dies in the hospital he worked in, Sasha alleviates the overwhelming sense of confusion and sorrow she feels with sexual encounters, drinking, and jokes. The expressive art, full of symbols and raw emotions, takes the reader on a ride that switches back and forth between periods of his dying and the aftermath, when Sasha gets a summer job at the hospital. This potent look at loss and mortality mines the unconscious for material that confronts the reader with its severe honesty.

Kim, June
12 Days. 2006. Tokyopop, ISBN 1598166913, 191p.

Jackie is heartbroken when her long-time lover, Noah, leaves her for a man. Soon after, Noah is killed in a car accident, leaving Jackie devastated. Noah's brother Nick brings Jackie Noah's ashes, which she uses in an unusual ritual to help her release her pain and let go of her memories. This heartfelt story focuses on grieving and the power of relationships in the process of mourning.

Kindt, Matt
3 Story: The Secret History of the Giant Man. 2009. Dark Horse Books, ISBN 9781595823564, 290p.

Craig Pressgang has a tumor that is putting pressure on his pituitary gland, resulting in continuous growth. His history is told through the three generations of women in his life: his distant mother, his wife, and his daughter. As he grows, he attains worldwide celebrity as "The Giant Man," works as CIA spy, and eventually grows too large to even hear or see other human beings. Kindt's evocative art adds a deeper dimension to this stunning story of alienation and loss.

Linthout, Willy
Years of the Elephant. 2009. Fanfare Ponent Mon, ISBN 9788492444304, 162p.

On a mundane day, the police come to the door to tell Charles Germonprez (Linthout) that his only son has jumped off the roof of their building. This tragic story follows the challenge he faces in accepting his son's absence and the irreparable chasm it creates in his marriage. Alcohol, therapy, and prescription drugs don't stop Charles from communicating with his son through bizarre, yet hear-trending methods.. Lost in a world of grief, Germonprez finds the seeds of healing in creating a book of poetry, just as Belgian author Linthout, who lost his son Sam, sought solace in writing this painful graphic novel.

Lutes, Jason

▶ ***Jar of Fools.*** 1994. Black Eye Productions, ISBN 9780969887423, 70p. Y A

Ernesto is a washed-out magician who is mourning his escape-artist brother, who killed himself by jumping off a bridge in a straitjacket, a ball and chain around his leg. His inability to accept his brother's death erodes Ernesto's relationship with his girlfriend, adding deep sorrow to his anguish. When his mentor, Al, escapes from the nursing home where he lives in and contacts him, Ernesto starts to thaw from the warmth of human contact. Readers who relate to this superb, lyrical tale should read on to Part Two, where Ernesto comes to terms with his grief.

Shadmi, Koren

In the Flesh. 2009. Villard Books, ISBN: 9780345508713, 145p.

A man has a love affair with a woman who carries her own decapitated head. A survivor of a nuclear bomb grows ever stronger as her boyfriend weakens, losing his hair and more. A morning after a one-night affair finds the man falling in love, while the woman doesn't give him a second thought. The short stories in Israeli Shadmi's collection range from surreal to allegorical, but they intersect in their subject matter of isolation, loss, and the darker side of love.

Sievert, Tom

That Salty Air. 2008. Top Shelf Productions, ISBN 9781603090056, 110 p.

Hugh and Maryanne are a young couple who are just eking out a living in a shack on a deserted beach. Two letters arrive on the same day, one with good news of Maryanne's pregnancy, the other with the shocking news of Hugh's mother's untimely death by drowning. In his despair, Hugh rages against the sea that he once revered. Their heartbreak leads to a dramatic ending that teaches much about accepting change and loss.

Earth-Friendly Ecosystems: Green Graphics

Beginning in the 1960s underground comics period, many causes were championed, including environmental issues, which were represented in the anthology *Slow Death Funnies.* These concerns continued to be expressed in superhero comics such as *Swamp Thing*, science fiction titles, and environmental apocalyptic stories. The following cautionary or motivational titles all raise awareness about the relationship between human beings and nature.

Chadwick, Paul

▶ ***Think Like a Mountain,*** **<u>Concrete</u>.** 1997. Dark Horse Comics, ISBN 1569711763, 1v. (unpaged). 🎖

Concrete became superpowered when aliens transplanted his brain into a massive concrete body. He lives in the real world, and his "villains" are contemporary moral issues. In this story, members of the ultra-environmental group Earth First! convince him to look at a clear-cut area of old-growth Northwestern forest. The appalling destruction forces Concrete to consider his arm-chair environmentalism through the lens of Edward Abbey's statement "Belief without action is the ruin of the soul." Concrete gets involved in a campaign to stop deforestation, the reader gets an education in logging, the politics of environmentalism, and the philosophies and history of Earth First!, all while enjoying the beauty of the natural world in award-winning Chadwick's art.

Coe, Sue

Pit's Letter. 2000. Four Walls Eight Windows, ISBN 1568581637, 1v. (unpaged).
Pit's life is told through an illustrated letter to his last living littermate. Abandoned as a pup, he is adopted by a boy, who is learning to injure the weak from his abusive father. Abandoned because of his incompetence as a fighter and hunter, Pit goes from being on the street, to living in a pound where he witnesses the callous killing of dogs, to an animal testing laboratory. Coe's illustrations; from Boschian visions of an animal apocalypse to simple pen-and-ink cartooning, combine with Pit's story to produce a strong political anticruelty message and a plea for empathy for all living beings.

Dysart, Joshua, Cliff Chiang, and Dave Stewart

Neil Young's Greendale. 2010. Vertigo, ISBN 9781401226985, 1v. (unpaged). �
Sun Green is maturing and learning what it means to be in a long line of powerful Green women. Her strong, humane beliefs are informed by the threat of the Iraqi war, political unrest, and environmental issues. The appearance of a strange man that only she can see and a visit with her lost female ancestors propels Sun to respond with an act of political protest. She rails against the corrupt corporate culture over the needs of the Earth, prompting hundreds of young activists to travel to Alaska to protest oil drilling with her. This beautifully drawn story about a young woman finding her voice instills a call to action in the viewer, as well.

Jensen, Derrick, and Stephanie McMillan

As the World Burns: 50 Simple Things You Can Do to Stay in Denial. 2007. Seven Stories Press, ISBN 9781583227770, 220p. �
Just when they thought they were sitting pretty, with the humans brainwashed into thinking they could have all their "things" *and* save the world by buying more energy-efficient light bulbs, the Corporations have their rights to plunder usurped by a race of Alien machines intent on consuming the planet. This turn of events accelerates the rate of ecocide, motivating a one-eyed bunny and two young girls to join forces and promote real change. *As the World Burns* is a radical environmental polemic and call to action, offering an entertaining story, humor, dogged honesty, and endearing, simple cartooning.

Kochalka, James
Monkey vs. Robot. 2000. Top Shelf Productions, ISBN 1891830155, 1v. (unpaged). ୪

Robots have set up a factory right in the middle of a forest full of contented monkeys. They are collecting large rocks to put into their machines, which produces toxic sludge. When a monkey is killed by the pollutants, they wage war against the robots. Award-winning cartoonist Kochalka's minimalist brushwork captures equally the range of emotional expressions that the monkeys experience and the cold metallic essence of the robots. This beautiful, virtually wordless story evokes both fear and hopefulness in the conflict between technology and nature and questions the connection between progress and extinction.

Miyazaki, Hayao
Nausicaa of the Valley of the Wind, **Vol. 1.** 1983, 2004. Viz, ISBN 1591164087, 130p. ୪ Ⓨ Ⓐ

A thousand years ago, an industrial society destroyed Earth's ecological system through pollution, creating a lethal new world, vastly depleted of natural resources. The Valley of the Wind, protected by crosswinds from the ocean, is in danger of being submerged by the Sea of Corruption, an ecosystem that hosts giant insects and fungi and gives off a mist of lethal spores. Princess Nausicaa has an empathic ability to communicate with all living creatures, including the brutal Ohmu, giant-sized insect guardians of the poisonous forest. Nausicaa holds the key to bringing nations together to work toward greater understanding and healing the planet.

Moore, Alan, Steve Bissette, and John Totleben
Saga of the Swamp Thing, <u>Swamp Thing</u>. 1987. DC Comics, ISBN 0930289226, 1v. (unpaged). ୪

Swamp Thing is captured and put on ice for an autopsy by Floronic Man, another DC plant/human hybrid. When he discovers that Swamp Thing was not essentially human as formerly thought, he assumes Swamp Thing will shed his human ethics and team up with him to inflict nature's revenge on humanity. Moore's hero diverges from the original 1970s series by Les Wein and Bernie Wrightson in his belief in the mutual dependence between plants and animals and in his role as a defender of both humanity and the environment.

Morrison, Grant, and Frank Quitely
We3. 2005. Vertigo Comics, ISBN 9781401204952, 104p. ୪ Ⓨ Ⓐ

Three household pets, a dog, a cat, and a rabbit are stolen for a top-secret military cybernetics project. Linked to mechanical metal armor, these simple animals are transformed into killing weapons, capable of horrifyingly gory destruction. When the military orders them to be decommissioned to make way for a mastiff machine, their emotionally attached trainer releases them into the wild. The animals are trained to kill but want only to make their way home, although they can't really understand what that means. This moving medita-tion on humanity's treatment of animals and displacement is beautifully illus-trated by award-winning artist Quitely.

Hindsight and Foresight: Personal Time Travel

Time marches on, and what has been done can't be undone. But what if a per-son could overcome the linear quality of life? What if we could relive our pasts with hindsight or face the rest of our lives with foresight? This age-old question has resulted in stories that use personal time travel as a plot device that allows characters the chance to alter perceived mistakes or to learn important lessons from their futures.

Kim, Derek Kirk

Good as Lily. 2007. DC Comics, ISBN 1401213812, 148p. ☒

At her 18th birthday party, insecure Grace Kwon gets hit in the head with a magical pig piñata. Suddenly she is confronted with three versions of her-self: 6-year-old Grace, 29-year-old Grace, and 70-year-old Grace. These other "selves" assist her with saving the school play, getting over a crush on her drama teacher, confronting her parents about her feeling lesser than her dead sister, Lily, and realizing the true nature of her feelings for a close friend. After each lesson, one of her incarnations disappears, leaving Grace with greater confidence with which to face her future and fulfill her dreams.

Kneece, Mark

Walking Distance, **Rod Serling's Twilight Zone**. 2008. Walker Books, ISBN 0802797156, 72p. ☒

Marc Sloan takes a drive into the country to escape the stresses of his hectic New York ad agency career. When his tire blows, he discovers that he is just a two-mile walk from his idealized childhood town, Homewood. When he arrives, he finds that the town is exactly how it was 20 years before. In fact, he comes face-to-face with a younger version of himself. Can he say something to his younger self that will change the emptiness he currently feels? This excellent adaptation of an episode from *The Twilight Zone* captures the double-edged denial of longing for childhood happiness.

Moon, Fabio, and Gabriel Ba

Daytripper. 2011. Vertigo, ISBN 9781401229696, 248p.

Bras de Oliva Domingos is a 32-year-old Brazilian obit writer who wishes to escape the long shadow of his father's literary fame. On his way to a cer-emony honoring his father, he stops at a bar to ruminate on his conflicted feel-ings about attending, but it becomes a moot point when he is caught in the crossfire of a robbery. Brazilian award-winning twins Moon and Ba capture many events in Bras's charmed life, moving back and forth in time from age 21, when his heart is broken, to age 11, when he has his first kiss, to age 38, when he meets his wife, with each day ending in death. The beautiful art and the lyrical storytelling shape this time-traveling device into a thoughtful meditation on the importance of appreciating each moment in the face of the fragility of life.

Moore, Alan, and Oscar Zarate
A Small Killing. 1995. Dark Horse, ISBN 9781878574459, 80p. Y A
Timothy Hole is soaring in the 1980s yuppie fast lane with a plum job advertising the latest diet-cola craze in post-*glasnost* Russia. One night, he nearly runs over a small boy who appears to be chasing him. The resulting paranoia uncovers the moral emptiness at Hole's core, leading him on a trip to turning points in his past where his actions killed off pieces of his childhood innocence. Zarate's expressionist art, a tumultuous blend of wild colors, perfectly complements Hole's stream-of-consciousness journey to his past.

Robinson, Alex
▶ *Too Cool to Be Forgotten*. 2008. Top Shelf Productions, ISBN 9781891830983, 128p. ੪ Y A
From nicotine patches to going cold turkey, nothing has helped smoker Andy Wicks kick the habit until his wife convinces him to try "mumbo-jumbo"— hypnotism. Andy freaks out when he goes under and finds himself back in high-school, once again an awkward, hesitant sophomore but with a 40-something mind. After much confusion, he lets himself go with the flow, even using his middle-age self-assurance to finally ask out his high school crush. When Andy passes on his first cigarette, he finds there is more to explore in the emotional roots of his compulsion to smoke, leading to a moving and painful conclusion.

Taniguchi, Jiro
A Distant Neighborhood. 2009. Ponent Mon, ISBN 9788492444281, 200p.
On his way home from a business meeting, Hiroshi Nakahara, a Tokyo family man, inexplicably finds himself on a train to his childhood hometown. When he gets there, he faints at his mother's grave, and, when he wakes up, he is his 14-year-old self. He retains his 48-year-old consciousness, giving him the opportunity to alter events that led to his father's abandonment, tearing the family apart. Taniguchi's detailed art captures the frustrating dilemmas and regret that come with reliving one's past with full awareness of the painful future but being unsure how changing it will play out.

Sweet Revenge: Tales of Retribution

Vengeance is a complicated affair and a popular theme in graphic novels. The plots in the following titles are driven by the need of the protagonists to right wrongs through the settling of scores.

Azzarello, Brian
First Shot, Last Call, <u>100 Bullets</u>. 2000. Vertigo Comics, ISBN 9781563896453, 127p. [Y][A]

All the protagonists in this series are visited by a mystery man, Mr.Graves, who offers them a briefcase containing 100 untraceable bullets, a gun, and a load of evidence about the people who wronged them. The recipients can use them to exact revenge without consequences. While in jail, Dizzy Cordova's husband and son are killed, supposedly by opposing gangbangers. Mr. Graves visits her when she is released, giving her information about who really killed her family. She struggles with which path will make things right, sorting through complicated gang politics and their endless cycle of payback.

Collins, Max Allen
▶ *Road to Perdition.* 1998. Paradox Press, ISBN 9780743442245, 294p. ☺

Michael O'Sullivan, an upright Catholic family man, is also known as the "Angel of Death" to the Looney family, his Rock Island gangster employers. When one of his sons witnesses a shoot-out, a hit is put out on him and his family. O'Sullivan escapes with one of his sons and travels through little Midwestern towns, seeking vengeance with a brilliant plan that involves the Capone gangsters. The relationship with his son, reminiscent of that in the landmark vengeance tale *Lone Wolf and Cub*, catapults this wonderfully illustrated graphic novel out of the ranks of 1930s gangster tales and into a class of its own.

Hubert & Kerascoet
Miss Don't Touch Me. 2008. NBM Publishing, ISBN 1561635448, 96p.

Modest maid Blanche sees her sister shot in the head by "The Butcher of the Dances," a serial killer in 1930s Paris. Armed with a single clue, she searches for revenge and lands in a high-society brothel, where she gains access working as the virginal dominatrix "Miss Don't Touch Me." Blanche learns about class privilege, police corruption, and human perversion as she follows the twists and turns that lead her to her sister's murderers. The use of brilliant colors deepens the unlikely combination of lighthearted and darkly lascivious moods that this juicy revenge tale achieves.

Jung and Jee-Yun
Kwaidan. 2001, 2004. Dark Horse, ISBN 1569718415, 144p. ☺

In 12th-century Japan, the lovely lady Orin turns away all suitors, waiting for her beloved Nanko to return from war. Her plain sister, Akane, also loves Nanko and, consumed with jealousy, throws acid in Orin's face. Orin drowns herself in a lake inhabited by ghosts. When Nanko learns of her suicide, he blinds himself by the river. For more than 200 years, their spirits remain in limbo until they embody a disfigured young woman and a blind man. The stunning art is computer generated but evokes delicate Japanese watercolors and skilled fantasy anime. The readers will be enthralled as this haunting revenge story unfolds like a beautiful, ethereal movie.

Koike, Kazuo

Assassin's Road, Lone Wolf and Cub. 2000. Dark Horse Comics, ISBN 9781569715025, 306p. 🅈🄰

Set in feudal Japan in the 1600s, this book tells of the shogun's assassin who is ordered to kill both himself and his infant son as a result of a perceived insult to the Emperor. Ogami Itto takes his baby and escapes, traveling the country roads, a sword for hire, hungry to settle the score. This tale of samurai sword fighting, both historical fiction and thriller, is the start of an epic journey, spanning 28 volumes, that is composed of vignettes of Itto and his son's exploits on the road.

Marcele, Philippe, and Thierry Smolderen

Colere Noire: For Justice. For Revenge. For Each Other. 2003. Humanoids Publishing, ISBN 9781030752750, 144p.

In the first of a series of supermarket attacks by masked murderers, Marielle loses her son and Stella loses her husband and unborn child. When their paths cross, they share their grief and explore taking matters into their own hands. A chance car accident brings Marielle face to face with the leader of the murderous gang, pushing them into the first step in their winding and occasionally surprising journey toward exacting what they see as a just revenge.

Moore, Alan, and Daniel Lloyd

V for Vendetta. 1998. Vertigo Comics, ISBN 140120841X, 296p.

In an alternate history Germany won World War II, and England is now a fascist country. The omnipotent ruler and his minions have created surveillance (à la *1984*) to curtail the liberties of its people. Crazed poet V hides his face with a Guy Fawkes mask, both to cover the wounds he sustained during imprisonment at a government relocation camp and as a symbol of his intention to overthrow the government and free the country from the evil grip of the totalitarian regime. This suspenseful, philosophical depiction of the potential abuses of government made possible by the complacency of the people is a mind-blowing, gripping read.

Trauma Deconstructed: Transformative Events

The titles in this list are a perfect demonstration of the command of the graphic form in depicting transformative stories. Readers act as witnesses to the traumatic events revealed within, producing a powerful healing effect for both the authors and their audience.

Bouchard, Herve, and Janice Nadeau

Harvey. 2009, 2010. Groundwood Books, ISBN 9781554980758, 1v. (unpaged). 🅈🄰

It's 1950s Quebec, the beginning of spring, and Harvey and his younger brother are racing toothpick boats in the gutters filled with rivers of melted snow. They happily return home to find neighbors gathered around with their heads down, hugs from the priest, an ambulance. Their mother is lost in her own world of grief and worry. Nobody explains what happened to the boys, and they struggle to understand that their father is gone. Harvey finds himself becoming invisible as he comes face to face with his dead father at his funeral. Nadeau's beautiful, muted illustrations are full of expression and visual images of emotional states, a powerful combination with Bouchard's ability to relate heartbreaking trauma through the eyes of a child.

Drechsler, Debbie
Daddy's Girl. 2008. Fantagraphics Books, ISBN 9781560978947, 86p. Nonfiction.

Lilly's father visits her in the night, forces himself on her sexually, telling her that she provoked it. This raw look at parental abuse illustrates how a child takes on the responsibility for her parent's actions, judging herself harshly while maintaining the guise of normalcy and keeping the dirty secret, whatever the expense to her self-esteem. Drechsler's ornate, undulating black-and-white art brings Lilly's crazy-making experiences to life. Readers beware, the abuse is not hidden on the page; it is frank and graphic, which makes this a disturbing read.

Gloeckner, Phoebe
A Child's Life. 1998. Frog Ltd., ISBN 9781583940280, 151p.

Minnie is about eight when this story opens with a description of the neglect and inappropriateness of her mother and her boyfriend. As she comes into adolescence, she has already been abused by a number of her mother's boyfriends, has been expelled from school, and has had indiscriminate sex for drugs. With her explicit drawings and honest detail, Gloeckner, recipient of a 2008 Guggenheim Fellowship, gives us a jarring look at psychological and physical abuse. This revised edition provides new material, which shows how Minnie overcame the abuse, becoming a professional medical illustrator, getting married, and having kids.

Ka, Oliver
Why I Killed Peter. 2008. NBM, ISBN 9781561635436, 122p. Nonfiction.

Ka explores his religious and sexual development from ages 7 to19, with a focus on his 12th year, when he is sexually abused by Peter, a populist priest and close family friend. At 34, when Ka enters a church, he finds that the memory of the trauma is triggered, and he becomes incapacitated. In a successful attempt to heal, Ka writes this powerful recounting, a process that leads him to confront a now old, frail Peter. The story and drawings are amazing, illustrating through bold color and poetic imagery the confused, burdened spaces where childhood trauma manifests itself in adult life.

Penfold, Rosalind B.
Dragonslippers: This Is What an Abusive Relationship Looks Like. 2005. Black Cat, ISBN 9780802170200, 257p. Nonfiction.

If you think strong, independent women can't end up in an abusive relationship, think again. Penfold's recounting of her 10 years in such a marriage will enlarge your understanding of spousal abuse. What starts as a whirlwind love affair with a widower with four children gradually turns into his crazy-making, disorienting abuse of her and the children. The images capture the slippery signs of abuse, the loss of a sense of self, and the shame that keeps suffering women quiet. With the help of her friends and a therapist, Penfold is able to extract herself from this toxic relationship and build her self-esteem once again.

Talbot, Bryan
▶ *Tale of One Bad Rat.* 1995. Dark Horse, ISBN 1595824936, 136p. ♀ Y A

Helen Potter, running from her emotionally abusive mother and sexually abusive father, is alone in London, homeless and begging. She identifies with rats, an animal that is often blamed for a variety of societal woes. When her pet rat is killed by a cat, Helen's love of Beatrix Potter tales leads her to the setting of her stories, the Lake District. Here she is taken in by a loving couple and finds solace in the countryside. Helen starts reading self-help books, leading her to confront her parents, triumph over her painful childhood, and find self-respect and love

Rail at the Machine: Graphic Satire

Comics, being outside mainstream culture, are an ideal medium for livid commentary and expressions of dissent. Satire has remained an important category in graphic novels, questioning everything from politics to consumerism. The titles on this list scrutinize the state of the powers that be and their influence on what we think and how we live.

Chaykin, Howard
American Flagg. 1983–1988, 2006. Image Comics, ISBN 9781582404189, 1v. (unpaged). Y A

The year is 2031, and a series of global crises has sent the U.S. government and its corporate backers to rule from Mars. On Earth, gangs, murders, and indiscriminate sex have become the norm, education is defunct except for military training, and the population is drugged on nonstop reality TV shows. Randy ex-TV stud Reuban Flagg joins the Plexus Rangers, who protect the status quo politics and commerce at the Chicago Plexmall. Flagg develops a conscience when he notices the corruption of the ruling class, passive consumerism, and the merging of media and reality. Chaykin's prescience can be chilling, and his energetic pop art layouts were influential on subsequent comics.

Darnall, Steve, and Alex Ross
Uncle Sam. 1997. DC Comics, ISBN 1563894823, 1v. (unpaged). Y A

Uncle Sam, the symbol of American democracy, lies on the streets of a contemporary city, disheveled and homeless. He questions what happened to the ideals of the founding fathers as images fill his mind of corporate power, foreclosures, poverty, crime, apathy, terrorism, and unemployment. Enraged that the symbol he embodies has been perverted, he revisits incidents where blood was spilled: the Revolutionary War, the 1832 massacre of the Black Hawks, the Civil War, and the assassination of J. F. Kennedy. Uncle Sam's confusion is intense as he struggles with the awareness that the ideals he represented may have always been hollow and driven by greed. Darnall's potent portrayal of today's Uncle Sam, rendered convincingly by Alex Ross, arouses fury, fear, and sadness over the abuses of political power and patriotism.

Ellis, Warren
Back on the Street, <u>Transmetropolitan</u>. 1998. Vertigo Comics, ISBN 1401220843, 144p.

    After sequestering himself on a mountain top for 10 years, antihero Spider Jerusalem has succumbed to the gonzo Internet journalist in him and come back to his futuristic dystopian city. His need to report the truth, no holds barred, builds his popularity with the people but makes him an enemy to the government. Read on in this outrageous series to uncover the lengths mainstream media will go to keep people like Spider from exposing reality.

Hickman, Jonathan
The Nightly News. 2008. Image Comics, ISBN 9781582407661, 154p.

    John Guyton was married with kids, a financial manager who lost everything after he was unjustifiably indicted because of a journalistic error. Approached by a man who promises him vengeance, he soon becomes the "hand of the voice," the unseen leader of a cult that avenges media lies by committing mass murders of journalists. Jam-packed with quotations, intellectual discourse, and statistics about globalization, consolidation of the media, indoctrination through education, and media errors, award-winning cartoonist Hickman is challenging in the ideas he presents and in his breakthrough graphics.

McGruder, Aaron, Reginald Hudlin, and Kyle Baker
Birth of a Nation. 2004. Crown Books, ISBN 1400048591, 137p.

    The outcome of a close presidential election might have been different if the residents of impoverished East St. Louis had been allowed to vote. In response to this "error," activist mayor Fred Fredericks encourages the people to secede, creating the nation of "Black Land." Fredericks is the president, local gang lords become the law enforcers, and a newly established "off-shore" bank finances the new nation. Can a disenfranchised city use capitalism to achieve a utopian dream? Will conservative, mainstream America and its crooked government bring the city's residents down, or will they simply implode? This thought-provoking and funny "what if" scenario, complemented by Baker's cartoony send-ups, holds nothing sacred as it satirizes controversial issues, including politics, race relations, and African American pop culture.

Origen, Erich, and Gan Golan
▶ *The Adventures of Unemployed Man.* 2010. Little, Brown and Company, ISBN 97803160998823, 1v. (unpaged). ☟

Ultimatum, a corporate motivational vigilante, challenges the freeloading poor and homeless to pull up their bootstraps and blame themselves for the negative thinking that keeps them down and out. When he gets the boot for questioning the boss, he ends up in Cape Town, U.S.A, a tent camp filled with unemployed heroes, including Master of Degrees, Fellowman, and Wonder Mother. Reinvented as Unemployed Man, he joins the others to motivate Everyman to stand up to the Just Us League, corporate supervillains who include Pink Slip, the Invisible Hand, and Toxic Debt Blob as they release their new weapon, The Deregulater. The incredible is credible in this spot-on retelling of the economic meltdown, with excellent visual images that capture the complexities of the crises through hilarious superhero parody.

Venditti, Robert, and Brett Weldele
The Surrogates. 2006. Top Shelf Productions, ISBN 9871891830877, 158p.

The year is 2054, and even working-class people have surrogates, a perfect blend of cybernetics and virtual reality, who can smoke, drink, have sex, work, and eat for them, without consequence to their real bodies. When a few surrogates are rendered unsalvageable by powerful electrical currents, the cops have a readymade suspect, the rabidly antisurrogate leader of the Reservation, where no surrogates can even enter. This intelligent cautionary tale, with its innovative artwork, condemns the consumer and youth culture that could drive our society to desperate ends.

Wood, Brian
Channel Zero. 2000. AiT/Planet Lar, ISBN 0967684749, 144p.

The U.S. government, highly lobbied by right-wing Christians and Mothers for Censorship, has taken over all media sources with the passing of the "Clean Act" in order to package the news and control the citizens. Jennie 2.5, a performance artist prior to the Clean Act, hacks her way into a major New York TV station to broadcast revolutionary messages in an attempt to encourage people to fight the system. This hardcore commentary drives home how the media, in the hands of a few, shape who we are as a nation.

Chapter Two

Character

Comic books have historically centered on continuing characters, from Superman to Tintin, from Archie to Mr. Natural. Fans typically read the comics with their favorite character, following them through ongoing series. Some of these characters carry the story by themselves; others are part of a cast of characters. Some are stock characters; others are appealing for their uniqueness. The appeal of ongoing characters in comic books has carried over into their literary sibling, the graphic novel.

Graphic novels span all varieties of subject matter; consequently, the medium doesn't include as many defined character types as a fiction genre does. The traditional protagonists, superheroes and anthropomorphic characters, have survived. The comic-book universe was primarily white, male, and heterosexual until women, gays, and minorities, as part of a larger movement for equal rights, rebelled against these barriers. While some diverse characters were previously included in comics, they were commonly stereotyped. As graphic novels strive to represent the multiplicity of the world we live in, the characters, writers, artists, and readers continue to diversify.

Marginalized characters are emerging, and cartoonists seem particularly interested in developing autobiographical and biographical characters. Graphic novels have an inherent directness that breeds familiarity, allowing readers to identify with a character's personal development as they grapple with challenge and emotions.

When one reads a prose novel, the description of the characters fuels the reader's mental image of the character. The visual representation in graphic novels gives the reader a different layer of information. Expressions and body language may provide more information than narration or dialogue alone. Perspective is experienced differently in a graphic work, with multiple points of view possible as elucidated by the visuals. And a reader's feeling about a character can be influenced by how "well drawn" the character is, both literally and figuratively. The following lists contain graphic novels that have characters that drive the narrative arc.

"Autofictionalography": Exploring Their Pasts

The term *autofictionalography*, coined by cartoonist Lynda Barry, is an apt label for this graphic memoir trend. In the 1990s, during the prose-memoir publishing craze, cartoonists hopped on the bandwagon and looked in their mirrors for their protagonists. In these autobiographical works, the author offer firsthand narratives about a pivotal influence, theme, or event in their lives or their family history. The concept of memory is often explored as authors contemplate the past and walk a line between facts and fictions. The comic's medium, by its nature, brings in a certain level of imagination that blurs the lines further. Each of the personal stories on this list has a distinctive blending of text and image, offering intimate and insightful reads.

Bechdel, Alison

▶ *Fun Home: A Family Tragicomic.* 2006. Houghton Mifflin Company, ISBN 9780618477944, 232p. Nonfiction. ☿ Ⓨ Ⓐ

Bechdel's impressive memoir revolves around particular events in her family life and her exploration of her sexual orientation. Each member of the family is alienated from the others, and Bechdel longs for attention from her obsessive, distant, and volatile father. Bechdel often alludes to authors, including Proust, Joyce, and Wilde, finding it easier to perceive her family as fictional, rather than to face the truth. The drawings are incredibly detailed, including pages from her childhood journals, and family photos add realism to her efforts to comprehend her complex family history.

Fleming, Ann Marie

The Magical Life of Long Tack Sam. 2007. Penguin Group, ISBN 9781594482649, 170p. Nonfiction. ☿ Ⓨ Ⓐ

When Fleming, a Canadian filmmaker, began to wonder about the stories she had heard concerning her great-grandfather, a world-renowned Chinese magician and acrobat, she began a journey to fill in the numerous "blanks" that remained three generations later. Meeting with magicians, family members, and magic experts all over the world, Fleming fleshes out his wondrous story and learns a great deal about herself, her family, and memory. This is both a magical memoir of a gifted, cosmopolitan man and a history of race, mixed marriages, and a family spread the world over.

Katin, Miriam
We Are on Our Own. 2006. Drawn & Quarterly, ISBN 9781896597201, 136p. Nonfiction. ⚇

In 1944, in Budapest, when Jews were sent to Auschwitz, Katin's mother, Esther, faked her and her daughter's deaths, and, disguised as peasants, they fled to the country. To keep her two-year-old daughter safe, Esther endured being the mistress of a Nazi commandant and being raped by Russian soldiers. Katin depicts scenes from the war in somber, impressionist pencil drawings. Bright pastel drawings portray scenes from 30 years later, as Katin grapples with the fallout from her early childhood experience, struggling with belief in God and how to make a Jewish life for her own daughter.

Kuper, Peter
Stop Forgetting to Remember. 2007. Crown Publishers, ISBN 9780307339508, 208p.

Kuper takes a break from his powerful wordless graphic novels to create this humorous and honest autobiographical work. Speaking directly to the reader from his studio, Kuper's self-professed alter ego, Walter Kurtz, sheds light on his daily life as a cartoonist, his marriage, his experiences of becoming a first-time parent, and his friendships. Confessional aspects appear in stories of sex and drugs in his adolescent years, but for the most part this mature memoir deals with the challenges of balancing family, work, and friends while paying attention to world politics, with personal responses to events such as 9/11 and to the Bush administration. This sincere memoir brings both everyday realities and the author's vivid imagination to life.

Potts, Phoebe
Good Eggs. 2010. Harper Collins, ISBN 0061711462, 272p.

Potts feels her biological clock ticking as her friends become parents while she and her devoted husband, Jeff, have only their cat to shower with love. The quest for a baby is besieged with heartaches and frustrations that are tempered by Potts's insight and humor. She explores infertility in the context of her search for meaningful work, religious identity, and her struggle with depression. Phoebe and Jeff, their family, and their friends are affectionately depicted in cozy, cartoony art that amplifies their warmth and humanity.

Thompson, Craig
Blankets. 2003. Top Shelf Productions, ISBN 1891830430, 582p. Nonfiction. ⚇ Ⓨ Ⓐ

The titular blankets are Thompson's symbol of human connectedness. As a child, Craig shared a bed with his brother, and they fought over blankets and hid under them for safety from a punitive father, an abusive babysitter, and bullying classmates. As a teenager, he meets his muse and first love, Raina, at Bible Camp and again feels deep connection and shelter with her under the quilt she has sewn for him. Craig's belief in heaven gives him solace, but, when this blissful relationship ends, he begins to doubt the Christian fundamentalism he grew up with. Craig's sensitivity and experience of beauty in nature and relationships develops into a humanist embrace of life that is reflected in his gorgeous, graceful artwork.

Tyler, C.

You'll Never Know: Book One: A Good and Decent Man. 2009. Fantagraphics Books, ISBN 9781560971442, 1v. (unpaged). Nonfiction.

Tyler marries pictures to stories in this photo-album format, recounting her father's World War II experience. Tyler's rich characterization of her father as a distant parent, an adoring husband, a competent jack of all trades, and a lively crackerjack allows the reader to reflect, along with the author, on how the atrocities of war shaped him. Blended into her father's story, are award-winning cartoonist Tyler's own difficult circumstances—becoming a single mother to a young teen when her husband leaves her for another woman. Wonderfully gentle illustrations reflect perfectly the way a person's life is molded by the experiences she has and the people around her.

Yang, Belle

Forget Sorrow: An Ancestral Tale. 2010. W. W. Norton, ISBN 039306834X, 350p.

Yang, in her early 20s, moves back into her parents' home to escape an abusive boyfriend. Her father blames her for this situation but also shows compassion. Curious to know about her history, her father shares stories of how his grandfather, the patriarch, and his four sons fared through the Communist takeover of China. Patterns in the inherited family dynamics help Yang to rebuild confidence, move ahead, and "forget sorrow," both the meaning of her name and a phrase from ancestral lore.

Kid's Stuff: From a Child's Point of View

While the teen years and the 20s are popular subjects in adult graphic novels, there are few examples of child protagonists. The following titles create strong characterizations of children's experiences.

Azuma, Kiyohiko

Yotsuba &! 2008. Yen Press, ISBN 0316073873, 208p. ☻ Ⓨ Ⓐ

When Yotsuba, a little green-haired, supercurious girl, moves into the neighborhood with her adoptive father, the fun begins! She discovers cicadas and climbs up telephone poles, rings strangers' doorbells for the joy of seeing who opens the door, and runs amok in a "compartment" store, falling asleep in one of the display beds. The neighbors try to protect Yotsuba from herself, but her energy is contagious, leading them all into mischief of their own. As she splashes through a thunderstorm, her father comments, "She can find happiness in anything. Nothing in the world can get her down." This Eisner Award–nominated manga is an all-ages delight, with loads of funny predicaments that adorable, plucky Yotsuba gets into.

Barry, Lynda
▶ *One Hundred Demons*. 2002. Sasquatch Books, ISBN 1570613370, 216p. Nonfiction. ☃ Ⓨ Ⓐ
   Applying a 16th-century Japanese painting exercise called "One Hundred Demons," Barry has crafted a semiautobiographical look at her own childhood demons in this tender and amusing book. In addition to topics such as lice, lost blankies, angry parents, boyfriends, and popularity, she hits on many of the confusions and losses of childhood. The dancing demon explores how budding self-consciousness ends a child's liberty to move without restraint, the magic demon captures the crossing of a threshold when music replaces imaginary play, and the hate demon is a wonderful piece about how confusing forbidden words and their euphemisms are to children. Bold and colorful, this book captures the protagonist at this uncomfortable stage as she nears the end of childhood.

Forney, Ellen
Monkey Food. 1999. Fantagraphics Books, ISBN 1560973625, 144p. ☃ Ⓨ Ⓐ
   Forney's fun-loving, comical collection conveys the trials and fun of a liberal childhood in 1970s Seattle. The expressive cartooning highlights the emotional responses to visiting a nudist camp, realizing the potential for embarrassment because her name rhymes with the word "horny," and the thrill of reading Judy Blume's *Forever*. Loaded with 1970s kitsch, from shag rugs to the Bionic Woman, Forney's child's-eye view of growing up offers an affectionate depiction of a happy preadolescence.

Gaiman, Neil, and Dave McKean
Violent Cases. 1987, 2003. Dark Horse Books, ISBN 1569716064, 48p.
   Roughed up by his violent father, an impressionable four-year-old visits an elderly osteopath, once notorious gangster Al Capone's doctor, who shares tales about the violence he witnessed in 1920s Chicago. Gaiman reflects on the nature of memory as he pieces together this influential, frightening memory without glossing over the truths. He captures the perspective of a four-year-old, the novelty of experiencing things for the first time, the boy's fear of magicians, and the awe he feels about the adults around him. McKean's layered multimedia art speaks to the haziness of memory and the smallness of a child in a harsh adult world.

Hartman, Rachel
Amy Unbounded: Belondweg Blossoming. 2002. Pug House Press, ISBN 0971790000, 201p. ♂ Y A

    This enchanting tale is about imaginative and spirited Amy of the medieval town of Goredd during the summer of Amy's 10th birthday. The story is told from her eyes, as she plays with her buddy Bran, does chores, and listens in on the goings-on among the adults who surround her. She learns many difficult lessons, including that love doesn't conquer all, people we love move away, and women must work hard for their independence. Amy's optimism, along with a little help from her parents and friends, keeps her looking forward to her future adventures as she lets go of her days of pure childhood.

Matt, Joe
Fair Weather. 2003. Drawn & Quarterly, ISBN 1896597564, 116p. ♂

    Canadian Joe Matt depicts the typical events in the life of a devious comics-addicted kid and his friend Dave, who transports him round their suburban town on his banana bike. They engage in typical preteen behavior: watching horror movies, digging forts, viewing sunbathing woman through peepholes, and making fun of other kids. Matt renders the protagonist as mean, cheating, and lazy, but, despite his unpleasant traits, this is a glimpse into a kid's-eye view of interactions between friends spending a couple of lazy summer days together.

Myrick, Leland
Missouri Boy. 2006. First Second, ISBN 1596431105, 110p. Nonfiction. ♂

    These touching vignettes covering 10 years of Myrick's childhood evoke a sense of nostalgia for the simple moments in childhood; building and flying paper airplanes with his twin brother, getting buried in the fall leaves, putting off firecrackers on the Fourth of July. There are also the painful instances, such as getting unexpectedly teased by friends and the awkwardness of first crushes. Myrick relates these incidents from his own perspective, his sensitivity and perceptiveness imbuing the colorful illustrations with the shifting, partial quality of memory.

Ware, Chris
The ACME Novelty Library #16. 2005. Acme Novelty Library, ISBN 156097513, 64p.

    Rusty Brown, a bullied eight-year-old boy, fills the gaps in his isolated existence with love for Supergirl and fantasies about having special powers (thanks to his supersonic hearing, only he can hear his parents fighting). Chalky White and his older sister are scared and resentful, moving in with their grandmother and beginning a new school. Ware zeroes in on how these characters intersect over a few hours, from waking up to starting the school day, simultaneously portraying a profound sense of isolation from and connection with one another.

Superhuman, Superdark: Superheroes Deconstructed

Since the creation of Superman, superheroes have lived in a world where good always triumphed over evil, as they battled supervillains intent on harming the common man, fought the Axis powers, and became patriotic "Commie-bashers." Beginning in the 1960s, with Stan Lee's Fantastic Four, the Hulk, and Spider-Man, superheroes began to take on human complexity. As the perception of the world seen in black and white dissolved, superhero stories saw a shift from action to character, shedding light on their inner conflicts, shortcomings, and dark sides. This humanizing of the superhero mythos continues to draw in readers who can now identify with the darker, flawed superhero.

Ennis, Garth, and Darick Robertson

The Boys. 2007. Dynamite Entertainment, ISBN 9781933305738, 1v. (unpaged).

When Wee Hughie's girlfriend, an innocent bystander during a superhero battle, is killed, he joins The Boys, a special team of CIA-backed agents whose goal is to keep the superheroes in line. In this real-world setting, the superheroes are immoral and irresponsible. Beholden to those who back them financially, they need to get their job done, irrespective of collateral damage. But The Boys, led by a sociopath named Butcher, can match the superhero's brutality blow for blow. The original publisher, Wildstorm, a DC imprint, discontinued this series after six issues. Ennis's signature irreverence and violence are in full force in this scathing superhero satire, making this a bad choice for the faint of heart.

Miller, Frank

Batman: The Dark Knight Returns. 1986. DC Comics, ISBN 9781563893421, 199p. ☃ Ⓨ Ⓐ

Still plagued by visions of his parents' murder, an aging Batman ends a 10-year retirement when Arkham Asylum releases two heinous villains: Two-Face and the Joker. The stakes have risen in Gotham City, and Batman finds himself reviled by politicians and the military, while a band of murderous mutants takes over the city and the threat of nuclear war is ever present. The reader is bombarded with images of violence and broadcasts from inane news stations as Frank Miller's revolutionary Batman retains the trappings of the old-style superhero while transforming into a darker vigilante, obsessed to a fault with fighting crime.

Mills, Pat, and Kevin O'Neill

Marshal Law: Fear and Loathing. 2002, 1990. Titan Books, ISBN 1840234520, 1v. (unpaged).

The U.S. government has become skilled at creating superheroes to send to war. The surviving supertroops have come back to San Futuro, corrupted by a failed war, to become mired in gang warfare. Supersoldier Marshal Law

manages to avoid their fate and enlists in the police force to fight these manufactured superheroes. Public Spirit, an original superhero, becomes his main
target when he suspects that this upright, beloved superhero is guilty of serial rape and murder. In this venomous antihero narrative, protagonist Marshal Law embodies a contemptuous viewpoint of superheroes as distorted and
twisted, supported by O'Neill's forceful art.

Morrison, Grant, and Frank Quitely
E is for Extinction, <u>New X-Men</u>. 2002. Marvel, ISBN 0785108144, 144p. ᵬ

Award-winning Scottish cartoonist Morrison creates a fresh take on the
X-Men, not only superficially, with their spandex traded in for hip leather,
but by shifting the basic premise and focusing on the relationship dynamics
between them. Humans will die out within four generations, and, as evolution forms new variants of mutating species, X-Men, a distinctive mutant species, are no longer representative of the "other," victims of racism. In addition,
X-Men characters are notable not merely for their strange powers but because
of their multifaceted emotional relationships in this mature, darker interpreta-
tion.

Rucka, Greg, and J. H. Williams
Batwoman: Elegy. 2010. DC Comics, ISBN 9781401226923, 1v. (unpaged).

Batwoman is a young Jewish woman in limbo, searching for relevance in
her life. In flashbacks, the reader learns that her soldier mom and twin sister
were murdered on her 10th birthday. A promising cadet student, Kane stood
up for herself as a gay woman and was booted out of the army as a result. Supported both emotionally and technologically by her colonel father, she wrestles
with an innate duty to serve and protect and the desire for revenge. When the
Lewis Carroll–quoting Goth Alice and her cultish Religion of Crime return to
extinguish Gotham City, Kane's ambivalence is forced. Kane harnesses all her
soldier energy and assumes her superhero identity to mete out her own brand
of moral justice. Williams's lush art deco splash pages and Rucka's compelling
plot portray a character who is superhero and fully human at the same time.

Straczynski, Michael, Peter David, and Reginald Hudlin
Spiderman: The Other. Evolve or Die. 2006. Marvel Comics, ISBN 0785117652,
144p. ᵬ

Spiderman is preoccupied with disturbing dreams, thoughts of his own
mortality, and assessing his motives as a superhero, when he starts to feel his
powers diminishing. Living in a superhero condo with his wife, MJ, and his
Aunt Sue, he tries every idea to save himself, to no avail. When the higher
spider authority that gave him his powers decides to grant Peter Parker a second chance at life, with his powers increased, it is conditional on his evolving,
looking deeply into his real, hidden self. Although he remains a joker and a
good guy, he gets in touch with a darker side in this interesting take on Spider-
man's origins.

Waid, Mark, and Alex Ross
▶ *Kingdom Come.* 1997. DC Comics, ISBN 1563893177, 228p. ☝ Ⓨ🄰
   The world is on the brink of nuclear war when an aging and defeated Superman comes out of hiding, looking for help from old-generation superheroes to fight against super-villains and the new breed of superheroes, who are lacking in morals and compassion. A broken Batman also reappears to try to prevent an apocalyptic war that is threatening. The old-time superheroes are fully fleshed out, dealing with grief and grappling with the need to use violence to prevent violence. Ross's gorgeous photo-realistic illustrations contribute to this futuristic tale that pits old-concept superheroes against new world antiheroes.

Famous Folks: Graphic Biography

   Biography is a very popular trend in graphic novels. While it's difficult to create a graphic biography, when an author succeeds, the added visual dimension can pack a powerful punch. The fact that there is significantly less text in this medium is a challenge in terms of choosing which life events to include. For a compelling read, the images must transcend the lives of the subject, rather than merely illustrating them. The following works effectively combine words and pictures to take advantage of the unique characteristics of graphic biography.

Anderson, Ho Che
▶ *King: A Comics Biography.* 2005. Fantagraphics, ISBN 9781606993101, 312p. Nonfiction. ☝ Ⓨ🄰
   Anderson's well-researched, interpretive retelling of Martin Luther King Jr.'s life succeeds in revealing the multifaceted man behind America's enduring icon and in transcending his life to illuminate the history of the civil rights movement. This is an excellent example of the use of the graphic-novel medium for biography. Anderson employs multiple storytelling methods, from straightforward narrative with simple line drawings to "talking head" characters who give their opinions of Dr. King. In doing so, he provides multiple points of view, using real photos in collage and splash pages of color to convey powerful emotional events such as the Birmingham riots or King's assassination. Anderson succeeds in building complex characters and creating compelling, multilayered biography in a visually beautiful style.

Baker, Kyle
Nat Turner. 2008. Harry N. Abrams, ISBN 9780810972278, 207p. Nonfiction. ☝ Ⓨ🄰
   Despite the fact that literacy is illegal for slaves, Turner learns to read at a young age, which opens his mind. Thought to have special markings as a baby and able to see events from the past, he has been brought up with a sense of special purpose. In response to the horrors of the slave trade, Turner instigates a violent and gory insurrection against slaveowners and their families. Emotionally

expressive illustrations join with quotes from William Styron's *The Confessions of Nat Turner* to reveal the drama and brutality of Turner's history from his family's capture in Africa to his hanging in 1831 at the age of 31.

Brown, Chester
Louis Riel: A Comic-Strip Biography. 2003. Drawn & Quarterly, ISBN 1896597637, 272p. Nonfiction. ☿ YA

In the late 19th century, the Canadian government took over the region that would later become Manitoba, and, because of his knowledge of English, Louis Riel became an advocate for his people, the mixed Indian and French Métis. Deception and the breaching of treaties were commonplace in the British and Canadian government's imperialist hunger for land. Riel led an 18-year rebellion for self-determination, many of which he spent in hiding, but ultimately the Métis were crushed and he was executed. Twenty-one pages of notes and a bibliography add many well-researched details that enrich Canadian cartoonist Brown's beautiful, perceptive line drawings biography of Canadian folk-hero Louis Riel.

Geary, Rick
J. Edgar Hoover. 2008. Hill and Wang, ISBN 0809095033, 102p. Nonfiction. ☿

Hoover is portrayed as a man with an obsessive need for power, devious in his allegiances and extremely secretive. His driving philosophy that anything outside the American-Christian "good versus evil" paradigm was dangerous to upright Americans drove him to push for the creation of the FBI, to undertake anti-immigrant and anti-Communist campaigns, and to reject the civil rights movements and the Kennedy Administration. Geary not only creates a picture of the man but also provides the reader with a bird's-eye view of the events of the 20th century. While this account of Hoover's life does not go into depth, it does explore the events in his life, his motivations, and the larger political context of which he was a part.

Jones, Sabrina
Isadora Duncan. 2008. Hill and Wang, ISBN 0809094975, 129p. Nonfiction. ☿

The stunning brushwork in this graphic biography fully captures the liberated movement that was the essence of Isadora Duncan. Jones recounts her revolutionary life with an economy that fully conveys her passions and vulnerabilities and the progression of her ideas and ideals, which made her so ground-breaking and suspect to Victorian society. All aspects of her life are covered with humor and grace, from her professional life to motherhood and from her teaching to her notorious string of lovers. Her tragic death ended the life of this amazing woman, a free-thinker whose ideas lived on in her pupils and facilitated the founding of modern dance.

Mairowitz, David Zane, and Robert Crumb
Kafka. 2007. Fantagraphics Books, ISBN 9781560978060, 176p. Nonfiction. ☿

This compelling description of Kafka's life and writings focuses on the great writer's crushing fear of his father, his low self-esteem as a Jew, and his feeling of being lost. Born in the Prague ghetto, he felt restricted throughout his life and was timid, with a self-deprecating humor that Mairowitz claims is often overlooked in his writing. This compelling graphic biography uses prose to enhance the comics, which are aptly created by a similarly neurotic and self-hating artist, Robert Crumb. His life circumstances are juxtaposed chronologically with the plotlines of his writings and the political events surrounding them. A brilliant, enlightening read that delves into the psychology of this often misunderstood writer.

Redniss, Lauren
Radioactive: Marie and Pierre Curie: A Tale of Love and Fallout. 2010. It Books, ISBN 0061351326, 205p. Nonfiction. ☿

Using an impressive array of sources, Redniss builds a detailed montage of the Curies' early lives, their profound love affair, and their collaboration in the discovery of radioactivity and its contemporary applications from nuclear weapons and energy to medical radiation. This radiant portrait of the passions and intellects of these famous Nobel Prize winners melds lyrical words and resonant images. Redniss created print process that presents images in negative, deepening the metaphors and the sense of mystery with which this radiant, haunting biography is infused.

Teen Angst: Coming of Age

These graphic novels follow a long line of teen comics starting with Archie Comics in 1941. The medium is extremely popular with young adults, and a great deal of quality material has been produced. The following stories delve into the complexities of the awkward and sometimes painful searching of the teen years, placing them light-years away from the All-American Riverdale of Archie and into the heart of the confusing teen world.

Brown, Chester
I Never Liked You. 1991. Drawn & Quarterly, ISBN 1896597149, 185p. Nonfiction. ☿

Canadian award-winner Brown's poignant memoir illustrates, through minimalist line drawings, some of the basic experiences of adolescence, including the cruelty of peers and self-absorption. Brown's teenage self is artistic and funny but also a little peculiar and withdrawn. He struggles mostly with his inability to say the things he wants to say, to his sickly mother and to a number of girls he likes. Once he is able to share his thoughts with a girl, he suffers from his inexperience about how to follow feeling with action.

Clowes, Dan
▶ *Ghost World.* 1998, 2008. Fantagraphics Books, ISBN 9781560974277, 80p. ☿

Cynical outcast Enid Coleslaw and her naïve best friend, Rebecca, are in limbo during the summer after high school ends. They avoid facing the impending realities of separation and entering adulthood by talking about sex, playing pranks, and ridiculing the residents of their suburban town. Award-winning cartoonist Clowes's striking portrayal of the insecurities, frustrations, and headiness of these well-realized 18-year-olds is captured in emotional dialogue and sensitive drawings. The eerie green shading over crisp black-and-white line work articulates the limbo world and the haunting conclusion of the last summer of youth.

DeMatties, J. M., and Glenn Barr

Brooklyn Dreams. 2003. Paradox Press, ISBN 1401200516, 384p.

Middle-aged Vincent Carl Santini opens his account of his senior year in high school by reflecting on the subjectivity and the faultiness of memory and truth. He proceeds to weave a story about the angst and rebellion that lead him to drug use, arrest, and, ultimately, spiritual enlightenment, in his rundown Brooklyn neighborhood, circa 1970. Balancing humor, sympathy, and sentimentality, Santini's depiction of his dysfunctional family's antics and the characterization of his adolescent self are greatly enriched by Barr's elastic, caricature-prone art, memorable expressions, and interesting use of perspective.

Miss Lasko-Gross

A Mess of Everything. 2009. Fantagraphics Books, ISBN 9781560979562, 223p. ୪

This semiautobiographical retelling of adolescence is a common story: an intelligent, off-beat, rebellious character encountering mean-spirited peers, coming to grips with an anorexic friend, going through a phase in which she tries drugs and cuts school, and her confusion about boys. What makes this story unique is that Lasko-Gross has a gift for articulating her thoughts and expressing emotion visually, conveying her world outlook in her smoky palette. The reader will likely relate to her as she tries to find her place in her world while sticking to her values and doing it her own way.

O'Malley, Bryan Lee

Lost at Sea. 2005. Oni Press, ISBN 1932664164, 159p. ୪

From page one, the reader knows that Raleigh, a shy 18-year-old, has a lot on her mind as she travels home to Vancouver after visiting her Internet boyfriend in California. While the car is filled with music and the chatting of three hip classmates, Raleigh moves through her interior landscape, from memories to dreams to internal monologues about the loss of her best friend, her parents' divorce, and her subsequent belief that a cat stole her soul. Eventually her blossoming connection with her traveling companions and their earnest attempts to find her soul lifts her sense of being alone in her melancholy and confusion. Award-winning Canadian cartoonist O'Malley's simple, manga-influenced art beautifully captures the awkwardness and the hopefulness of the teenage experience.

Tamaki, Jillian, and Mariko Tamaki
  Skim. 2009. Groundwood Books, ISBN 9780888999641, 144p. ☿ ⓎⒶ
     Sixteen-year-old Skim ("not slim") is having difficulty fitting in at her preppy all-girls Catholic school. She is playing with her identity, looking for refuge in the Goth subculture and practicing Wicca with a group of grown-up women. When a popular cheerleader gets jilted and kills herself, Skim finds herself reluctantly drawn into the collective mourning, leading her to change in unexpected ways. Between Skim's frank diary entries and Mariko's wonderfully communicative drawings, this sophisticated coming-of-age story truly offers a nuanced depiction of a teenager's internal life.

Weinstein, Lauren
  Girl Stories. 2006. Henry Holt, ISBN 0805078633, 237p. Nonfiction. ☿
     These edgy, humorous, semiautobiographical vignettes about social life during eighth and ninth grade will bring back memories for adult readers. The protagonist is obsessed, in all her new adolescent glory, with getting into the "in" crowd. Her antics include a bellybutton piercing, wearing punk clothing, pining over the rock band The Smiths, getting a skateboarding boyfriend, and making fun of less popular kids. On the other hand, she still plays imaginary games with her Barbies, struggling to move out of childhood. Written over seven years, award-winning cartoonist Weinstein produces an assortment of styles, fleshing out her characters and revealing the embarrassments of becoming a teenager.

Animal Farm: Serious "Funny Animals"

Animals have traditionally been used as characters not only for the comic aspects but also because of the visual shorthand of the cultural and social stereotypes associated with different species and breeds. In adult graphic novels, animal characters are often employed as metaphors for situations where the humane is left out of humanity. The cartoonists' use of animal characters to portray serious situations is particularly ironic because it plays with the historically goofy "Funny Animals" genre, which took off in the 1940s with Disney and Warner Brothers cartoons. George Orwell's use of anthropomorphized animals in his scathing social commentary, *Animal Farm*, brought his point home in a way that had a visceral impact akin to that of the following titles.

Alanguilan, Gerry
  Elmer. 2010. SLG Publishing, ISBN 9781593622046, 144p.
     Jake Gallo, a down-on-his-luck writer, is enraged by incidents of racism he perceives around him. In his alternate 21st-century world, chickens suddenly developed human consciousness in 1979 and, after a bloody revolution, were given full human rights by the United Nations. Jake's journey to

self-acceptance is interwoven with his parent's experiences in the revolution, both narratives building complex, engaging characters. The ludicrousness of Alanguilan's choice of chickens as the new minority softens the edge of the serious issues of race and prejudice that his characters wrestle with.

Diaz Canales, Juan

▶ *Blacksad.* 2010. Dark Horse, ISBN 159582393X, 184p. Ⓨ Ⓐ

Blacksad is a moral black bear P.I. who is working on finding a missing child in a town whose prosperous heyday has been destroyed by white supremacists and crime. The Spanish authors instill a large amount of humanity through appropriate choices of animals to represent various types of people, along with spot-on dialogue and lush, sensitive illustrations. Embedded in this compelling crime story is commentary on human racism, clearly portrayed as contemptible through the anthropomorphic characters.

Dorkin, Evan, and Jill Thompson

Beasts of Burden. 2010. Dark Horse, ISBN 1595825134, 184p. ☧ Ⓨ Ⓐ

A motley crew of pets and strays fights off supernatural menaces in the seemingly idyllic town of Burden Hill. A wise dog, a member of a group of professional canine occult warriors, aids them in clearing a haunted doghouse, expelling a coven of cat-loving witches and exorcising a zombie dog. Each dog and the lone stray cat have distinctive personalities, further developed through Thompson's wonderful painted art. Humor, horror, and engaging animal characters create a winning brew in these emotionally resonant stories.

Hines, Adam

Duncan the Wonderdog. 2010. AdHouse Books, ISBN 0977030490, 1v. (unpaged). Ⓨ Ⓐ

Pompeii, a Barbary monkey who is the head of a guerrilla organization, detonates a bomb at a California university. Voltaire, the wealthy CEO of Muir Industries, is an animal-welfare advocate in a mixed mandrill-human romance. Connected in their quest to fight for equality, these colorful characters are two among many fully realized talking animals that are rising up against human sovereignty. The narrative is told in clear line cartooning that is frequently mixed with tangential anecdotes depicted in abstract painting, photorealism, and collage, creating a complex, massive meditation on what the world would look like if animals could speak, understand, and rise up against human cruelty.

Kerschbaum, John

Petey & Pussy. 2008. Fantagraphics Books, ISBN 9781560979791, 126p.

Petey, a female-chasing dog, and his partner-in-crime, Pussy, a caustic cat, are animals with balding, middle-aged human heads. While Pussy is busy taunting the mice behind the wall, their owner, a senile old woman, torments her parrot, Bernie, driving him to plead for death. Meanwhile, Petey and Pussy wander the streets of New York, talking dirty and drinking in Joe's dive while getting into shady misadventures. While Kerschbaum may be commenting on the plight of pets, as well as human depravity, there is no sentimentality here. His wonderful illustrations are as disturbing as they are enjoyable in these twisted "funny animal" vignettes.

Onstad, Chris

The Great Outdoor Fight. 2008. Dark Horse Books, ISBN 9781593079970, 104p.

Multimillionaire entrepreneur Ray and his buddy, Roast Beef, are a couple of tight cats who sign up for the Great Outdoor Fight (GOF) after they discover that Ray's father was the 1973 grand champion. Three thousand men, in an enclosed three-acre field, are left for three days to fight one another until only one remains standing. Onstad's simple line drawings and funny dialogue and his use of anthropomorphized men diminish the rampant violence and amplify the underlying disturbing premise of the GOF, a narrative from Onstad's award-winning webcomic, *Achewood.*

Talbot, Bryan

Grandville. 2009. Dark Horse Comics, ISBN 978159582397, 98p.

Grandville is an alternate-history Paris in a steampunk world populated by animals (humans, referred to as "doughfaces," still exist as a servant minority). France has dominated the world since Napoleon defeated Britain and its allies. Britain, an insignificant little country, rebelled and gained independence a few decades before the story begins. Detective Archibald LeBrock of Scotland Yard, a big bruiser of a badger, is sent to a sleepy English village to investigate the ostensible suicide of Raymond Leigh-Otter, a wanted anarchist in Grandville. This case leads the tenacious LeBrock right into the heart of political intrigue and Grandville's elite secret societies. Talbot's beautifully illustrated anthropomorphic thriller is an action-packed political satire.

Vaughan, Brian, and Niko Henrichon

Pride of Baghdad. 2006. Vertigo, ISBN 1401203140, 136p. ☙ Y̲Ａ

In 2003, during Operation Iraqi Freedom, American bombs fell on the Baghdad Zoo, "freeing" a pride of lions from their confines. Vaughn tells the story from their perspective, as if they were a human family, cast out from the safety of their homes, trying to survive in the war-torn city. While searching for food, they come in contact with tanks, with other wild animals, and with guns, as their dreams of freedom transform into the unfamiliar nightmare of war. Through the lions' powerful fictionalized story, the well-written dialogue, and the stunning watercolors, the reader experiences the devastating ripple effects of war on the environment, the inhabitants, the soldiers, and the animals.

Navel-Gazers: Cartoon as Confessional

This memoir subgenre was especially popular in the "tell all" climate of the 1990s, but its roots are in the "let it all hang out" culture of the 1970s.

Justin Green wrote his underground comic classic *Binky Brown Meets the Holy Virgin Mary* with the self-professed intent to "purge" himself of his Catholic guilt. There is a great deal of purging as the authors in this category seem hell-bent on sharing their every quirky habit and uneasy secret with their readers. So steer clear of these graphic novels if this sounds like "too much information" (as we say in the 2000s). Fortunately, they all have their saving graces and their audience. If you like a character that is young, self-reflective, and unself-conscious, you will enjoy any of the following titles. Compelling content balances the navel-gazing found in some of these autobiographical works.

Readers beware: these titles may contain text and images of a sexual or disturbing nature.

Brunetti, Ivan

Misery Loves Comedy. 2007. Fantagraphics Books, ISBN 9781560977926, 1v. (unpaged). Nonfiction.

Award-winning cartoonist Brunetti takes self-loathing and misogynist misanthropy to new heights in this collection of his twisted autobiographical comics. He presents himself contemplating suicide, homicide, and rape, along with a host of other x-rated, demented thoughts and urges. This pessimistic confessional is almost painful to read, the nihilist stories mercifully broken up with laugh-out-loud bits.

Crumb, Robert

My Troubles with Women. 1992. Last Gasp, ISBN 0867193743, 78p. Nonfiction.

Labeled as "Graphic Angst" or, as Crumb comments in one story, "comics therapy," this collection delves into the development of Crumb's kinky sexual attraction to women. Irate about his inability to attract a woman, he feels his frustration grow into sexual hostility. Once he becomes a famous underground cartoonist, women flock to him, and he breaks all the taboos, living out his most perverse fantasies. His troubles with women eventually move beyond the sphere of sex, with stories concerning the ups and downs with his long-time wife and his doting relationship with his daughter. In this tell-all history, award-winning cartoonist Crumb exposes his deepest desires, despite others' opinion that he is a misogynist, and gives the reader a glimpse into his complex, profligate mind.

Doucet, Julie

My New York Diary. 1999. Drawn and Quarterly, ISBN 1896597246, 85p. Nonfiction. Ⓨ Ⓐ

In this collection, Doucet, a Canadian cartoonist, illustrates a period of her life in her own superb idiosyncratic style in this book, which is split into three sections: her loss of her virginity, her stint as a student in a junior college in Montreal, and the six months she spent living in New York City. She portrays herself as a naive Catholic school girl eager to experiment and to absorb new experiences. While there is a fair amount of sex, jealous boyfriends, and drugs, this memoir doesn't have the sympathy-seeking tone of some confessionals. Her illustrations are more neurotic than she appears to be, and it's easy to identify with Doucet as she makes mistakes, learns from them, and easily moves on.

Green, Justin
Binky Brown Meets the Holy Virgin Mary. 1972, 1995. Last Gasp, ISBN 0867193328, 92p. Nonfiction.
    Justin Green created this comic out of a great internal need to work through the intense neurosis he developed from the conflict between his sexual urges and his Catholic upbringing. Green felt that his "impure thoughts" were so strong that they could emanate from his body as rays and spoil anything holy in his proximity. In response, he developed compulsive rituals to protect the sacred from the profane. His story of the misery of living with these disruptive fantasies evokes a deep sympathy in the reader, and for that reason this comic has endured.

Heatley, David
My Brain Is Hanging Upside Down. 2008. Pantheon, ISBN 9780375425394, 1 v. (unpaged). Nonfiction.
    Heatley divides this frank retelling of the incidents of his life into five thematic chapters; his history with "Sex," "Race," "Mom," "Dad," and "Kin." The majority of the vignettes are given equal weight through his format of 48 small panels per page, leading to a glut of retelling of embarrassing incidents. The full-color, beautifully illustrated surreal dreams with which Heatley begins each chapter provide thematic and emotional resonance that are lacking in all but the family history. Heatley is basically a likable character, although his visceral material might feel self-indulgent and make for an uncomfortable read for some.

Kominsky-Crumb, Aline
▶ *Need More Love.* 2007. MQ Publishing, ISBN 101846011337, 383p. Nonfiction.
    Kominsky-Crumb makes use of her powerful creative force, with paintings, photos, prose, and comics in her huge graphic memoir. She tells the story of growing up in post–World War II Long Island, with her parents fighting nonstop and her father struggling to keep his con games running. Kominsky-Crumb portrays her feelings about her lack of popularity and self-esteem in her frank and humorous style. She illustrates her life with her bold and colorful cartooning developed from working in underground comics, describing her marriage and the daughter she had with Robert Crumb, their move to France, and the development of her art. Her self-indulgence and self-flagellation don't mar her wild tales of sex, funny shopping sprees, and the search for love.

In Full Color: Diversity Rocks!

Minority representation was meager in comics' history, with a sprinkling of minor characters that were pigeonholed into existing societal preconceptions. Starting in the 1990s, there was an increase in the number of multicultural minority artists creating authentic characters. These characters were breaking through stereotypical characters: the Asian kung-fu expert, the spiritual Native American, the African American embroiled in ghetto violence. The characters of color in the following titles show how the minorities' representation in comics has expanded to include depictions of three-dimensional characters dealing with their own realities.

Aaron, Jason, and R. M. Guera
Scalped. 2008. DC Comics, ISBN 978140121912, 166p. ⓎⒶ

Undercover FBI agent Dashiell Bad Horse returns after 20 years to the Lakota reservation. Working as a cop, he is under orders to frame Chief Lincoln Red Crow, the greedy head of the res who was once a radical nationalist involved in a protest that saw two FBI agents killed. Dash is caught up in a series of events that force him to confront where his loyalties lie, with the Lakota or the FBI. One of few representations of Native Americans in graphic novels, this American Indian noir creates a picture of life on a poor reservation, with rampant crime, murder, gambling, and drug and alcohol use, juxtaposed with the strength and beauty of traditional Lakota lifestyle.

El Rassi, Toufic
Arab in America. 2007. Last Gasp, ISBN 978986719673–3, 117p. Nonfiction. ☿

El Rassi, of Lebanese and Egyptian descent, grew up from the age of one in the United States. From the time he sees that he is the only dark face in the crowd on a video of a school play, he struggles with being different. This identity crisis gained urgency in the post-9/11 climate, where all Arabs became suspect. In his heavily narrated graphic novel, El Rassi grows proud of his heritage and acknowledges the sad truth that, although he has lived his whole life in the United States, he will always be an outsider here.

Hernandez, Gilbert
Luba in America. 2001. Fantagraphics Books, ISBN 1560974672, 169p.

Luba, a psychotherapist, flees her fictional Central American town to end a perceived political threat to her family. As she tries to acclimate to the United States and to learn English, she interacts with her sisters, Fritz and Petra, their children, and the many men who come in and out of her life. Peppering her tale with magic realism and touches of Mexican soap opera, award-winning cartoonist Hernandez bring to life a Latino community, held together by the women who populate it, fully exploring both their internal, psychological development and the daily external events that make up their lives.

Kawaguchi, Kaiji
Eagle: The Making of an Asian American President, Book 1. 2000. Viz, ISBN 1569314756, 415p.

A very charismatic third-generation Japanese American senator, Kenneth Yamaoka, is an underdog on the campaign trail to win the 2000 Democratic presidential candidacy. He is a Vietnam vet, a Yale graduate, and a well-respected lawyer who married into an elite banking family. Yamaoka's self-confidence and flair for public speaking, combined with his calculated strategizing, are moving him up in the race. But he has a skeleton in his closet—a Japanese wartime love-child, Takashi Jo, a young reporter whom he has invites on the campaign trail. When Jo finds out that Yamaoka is the father he has been wondering about his whole life, he struggles with a confusing array of emotions. Japanese award-winning mangaka Kawaguchi builds his compelling story and characters through lively dialogue and expressive art.

Morales, Robert, and Kyle Baker
Truth: Red, White & Black. 2004. Marvel Comics, ISBN 0785110720, 1v. (unpaged).

Inspired by the Tuskegee experiments, this comic explores African American soldiers in World War II with a twist. The super-serum that created Captain America is here injected involuntarily into black troops to create "Super Soldiers" who are sent into Germany to prevent the Nazis from getting the formula. Only one survives, and he is given Captain America's uniform, becoming a black superhero soldier. Morales's dark tale brings issues such as racism, eugenics, and human experimentation into real-life situations at the same time that he humanizes Captain America, who is searching for answers once this controversial use of his serum becomes declassified.

Tomine, Adrian
Shortcomings. 2007. Drawn & Quarterly, ISBN 1897299168, 104p. Ⓨ Ⓐ

Ben, the gloomy, passive-aggressive Japanese American protagonist, is always at odds with his beautiful Japanese American girlfriend, mostly around issues of sex and race. When she finds his stash of all-white porn, she leaves him. Ben's isolation and sense of alienation are broken up only by his pursuit of cute blondes and time spent with his sassy Korean American lesbian friend. Tomine's crisp drawings and realistic characterizations explore the role that race plays in romance, with characters who question the saying that love is blind.

Tooks, Lance
Narcissa. 2002. Doubleday, ISBN 0385503423, 1v. (unpaged).

Narcissa, a highly spirited African American filmmaker, is making a feature film about the young, radical black theater group she is a part of. The producer, an overbearing white man who specializes in making "black" films, wants to make her project into a stereotypical "gangsta"-type movie. Suffering from overwork and stress, Narcissa collapses and finds out she is dying. The introspective tale of Narcissa's adventure to Spain and her return home again is told primarily through Narcissa's thoughts and award-winning cartoonist Took's stylized, animated illustrations.

Wang, Gene
▶ *American Born Chinese.* 2006. First Second, ISBN (9781596432086), 233p. ☿ Ⓨ Ⓐ

Three stories are interspersed within this endearing and sophisticated minority character study. Ancient Chinese tales of the Monkey King follow his longing to be something he is not and his thwarted attempts to become human. Jin Wang, a second-generation Chinese American, has strong ties to his Chinese identity and is alienated and bullied in his Caucasian elementary school. Teenage Danny, a white, assimilated Jin stand-in, is painfully embarrassed when his heavily stereotyped cousin visits from China. The stories in this American Book Award nominee are woven together into a beautiful, clever lesson about coming to terms with one's racial identity when it is at odds with mainstream ideals.

Slouching toward Adulthood: Slackers, Hipsters, and Other 20/30-Something Characters

Characters in their 20s often have one foot in childhood and the other foot moving all too rapidly into the adult world. They struggle with finding love, fleshing out their identities, and balancing their passions with the need to work. This is a very popular character in graphic novels, particularly as many young cartoonists are writing about the world they inhabit.

Abel, Jessica
La Perdida. 2006. Pantheon Books, ISBN 0375423656, 256p. ☿

On a whim, Carla, a 20-something Mexican American, moves to Mexico to find her roots. Initially, she lives with her ex-lover, frat-boy Harry, but, given her Mexican blood, she feels above the expatriate community. Carla's desire to experience the "real Mexico" clouds her judgment as she falls in with a group of native petty thieves, leading to disastrous consequences. Award-winning cartoonist Abel is expert at depicting Carla's acceptance of her folly and her loss of innocence.

Bagge, Peter
Buddy Does Seattle. 2005. Fantagraphics Books, ISBN 1560976233, 336p.

This collection of award-winning cartoonist Bagge's *Hate* comic books follows slacker Buddy Bradley and his eccentric pals as they fall into wild shenanigans in Seattle's 1990s grunge scene. Buddy is portrayed as egotistical and pathetic but endearing as he faces his inadequacies and struggles with translating thought into action. Bagge's characterization of this stage in life is not only laugh-out-loud funny but so apt that readers will see people they knew in their 20s—that is, if they don't see themselves!

Gran, Meredith
Octopus Pie. 2010. Villard Books, ISBN 9780345520432, 252p. ☿

The first two years of this popular webcomic are now collected in print, presenting the escapades of two Brooklynites: Eve, a surly, smart Chinese American who works in the local vegan coop, and her roommate, childhood friend Hannah, a bubbly stoner who makes her own line of baked goods with her laid-back boyfriend. Gran's cartoony style and great sense of humor contribute to constructing fun characterizations of the romantic antics, work issues, and identity shaping that occupy young adults in their the postcollege years.

Inio, Asano
Solanin. 2008. Viz, ISBN 9781421523217, 412p. ☿

Meiko is 24 years old, longing to find meaning in her life while trying to adjust to her humdrum job as an office assistant. When she quits her job, she finds that doing nothing doesn't fulfill her, either. Her boyfriend decides to get his band together again as an alternative to an everyday job, but he too finds disappointment with the struggle to succeed. Japanese cartoonist Inio's simple drawings and emphasis on relationship dynamics truly capture the characters' personalities and the difficulty of saying goodbye to their childhoods and entering the adult working world.

Kim, Derek Kirk
Same Difference and Other Stories. 2004, Top Shelf Productions, ISBN 1891830570, 139p. ☿ Ⓨ Ⓐ

Simon and Nancy, two nerdy, Korean Americans living in Oakland, California, are both looking for their place in life. Nancy admits to Simon that she has been replying to a man who has been sending love letters to a woman who no longer lives at her address. When they go to spy on the writer of the letters, they both learn lessons that elevate them out of their self-absorbed 20s. Kim's complex characterizations of these two free-floating friends offer an animated depiction of this tender period in life.

O'Malley, Bryan Lee
Scott Pilgrim's Precious Little Life, <u>Scott Pilgrim.</u> 2004. Oni Press, ISBN 1932664084, 168p. ☿ Ⓨ Ⓐ

Scott Pilgrim is a 23-year-old Canadian slacker, drifting through life playing bass in his rock band, Sex Bob-Omb, playing Super Mario Brothers, and hanging with his platonic younger girlfriend, Knives. When he becomes obsessed with rollerblading Amazon delivery girl Ramona Flowers, he learns that, in order to win her heart, he must defeat her seven evil ex-boyfriends. Love, rock n' roll, kung fu fighting, and hilarity all come together in award-winning Canadian cartoonist O'Malley's expressive, manga-inspired series.

Robinson, Alex

▶ *Box Office Poison*. 2001. Top Shelf Productions, ISBN 1891830198, 602p. [Y][A]
With its multiple storylines of romantic love, betrayal, and friendships, this meaty graphic novel could veer into a soap opera of post-art-school grads in 1990s New York, if it weren't for Robinson's quirky and candid portrayal of his characters. Insecure Ed still lives with his parents and works in their store, while assisting a forgotten Golden Age comic's creator and pining for a girlfriend. His pal Sherman has his heart set on being a writer as he whiles away his days clerking in a bookstore and managing an unhealthy relationship. Their daily lives interweave with their friends, workmates, and love interests, providing the reader with a peek into the seemingly real lives of compelling 20-something characters.

Wang, Jen

Koko Be Good. 2010. First Second, ISBN 9781596435551, 304p. 𝄞
Jon and Koko are both aimless, early-20-somethings, but that's where the commonalities end. Staid Jon has cast aside his dreams of being a musician to follow his older girlfriend to work in a Peruvian orphanage. Koko is wildly impulsive and into minor scamming to get what she needs. When the two meet by chance, they connect and complement each other, leading each of them to reflect on what to do with their lives. Wang's energetic, fluid line is enhanced by her beautiful watercolors, primarily a range of honeyed browns that carry the emotion with subtlety and create a deep sense of place, making this ordinary coming-of-age story a noteworthy debut.

Wertz, Julia

Drinking at the Movies. 2010. Three Rivers Press, ISBN 9780307591838, 122p.
When she lost her job and boyfriend, award-winning cartoonist Wertz decided to move from hometown San Francisco to New York. Slice-of-life vignettes from the big city describe seven jobs, four apartments, innumerable bottles of whiskey, and wacky interactions with a variety of unsavory types. With her chunky, expressive drawings and bawdy sense of humor, Wertz looks at her drinking habit and her troubles maintaining relationships and establishing herself professionally. Ultimately, she makes decisions that help reduce her confusion and move her forward in her quest to "really grow up."

Friendship Frolics: Comic Buddies

With society becoming more and more transitory and traditional ties weakened by life changing events such as divorce, moving, changing jobs, having kids and caring for aging parents, adults are challenged in maintaining precious friendships. The titles in this list articulate what is often felt but seldom written about in graphic novels: the ways friendships play on the human heart.

Bordeaux, Ariel
No Love Lost. 1997. Drawn & Quarterly, ISBN 1896597084, 52p. ☃
  This slice of life opens with Gwen talking to the reader about what it means to have a "problem friend" like Emma, her self-involved co-worker whose conversations focus exclusively on her boyfriend problems. We see scenes of Emma with her tepid boyfriend Jed, whom she clings to despite their lack of chemistry. Gwen chats with common friend Mira as they vent and psychoanalyze Emma's unhealthy relationships. In the end, Emma learns some lessons and tries to correct the imbalances with her girlfriends.

Larson, Hope
Salamander Dream. 2005. Adhouse Books, ISBN 0972179496, 97p. ☃ YA
  Hailey, a young girl who is enchanted by nature, walks through the woods accompanied by her friend Salamander (a nonhuman) as she observes animal tracks, sounds, and plants. He tells her of his adventures with other critters. Adolescent Hailey loses track of Salamander but runs into him during a game of hide-and-seek with her friends, and they share both their happiness at being reunited and the awkwardness of waning friendship. This whimsical story is an interesting study of the process of outgrowing childhood friends.

Mills, Scott
Big Clay Pot. 2000. Top Shelf Productions, ISBN 1891830163, 1v. (unpaged). ☃
  Sun Kim arrives in Japan circa 200 BCE as an immigrant from Korea. Her klutziness gets her off to a bad start when she spills a mother's stew and breaks another villager's pot. She runs for protection from the angry insults to an isolated old man's tent. His patience helps her learn to overcome her clumsy mishaps, and she brings sunshine into his life as he mourns for his long-dead wife. This beautiful tale teaches a quiet lesson about people who are out of the mainstream but who connect and create deep bonds that take the place of family.

Orff, Joel
Waterwise. 2004. Alternative Comics, ISBN 1891861822, 116p. ☃
  After a breakup, Jimbo leaves the city to take time off in a forest where he vacationed as a child. There he unexpectedly finds an old friend, Emily, who just got divorced and is stopping off on her way to her new home. The two of them easily slip into the comfort of childhood friends, sharing bits about their lives, talking about various subjects, playing in the lake, building sand people, playing Ping-Pong. Orff is an expert at expressing both motion and quiet moments, which enhances the connection the reader feels in this unexpected meeting of old friends.

Swain, Carol
  Food Boy. 2004. Fantagraphics Books, ISBN 156097575X, 72p.

      Ross and Gar grew up together in a bleak, isolated town in Wales. Ross has always been an outsider, but an event at an Evangelist tent show pushes him to reject human society. He lives on the outskirts of town around a large reliquary of a crucifix. Gar comes to check on him and to bring him food. He watches as Ross slides beyond the margins of civility into a feral state. Gar, the titular "foodboy," continues to bring Ross food and watches from afar as his friend becomes too wild to be approached directly. This unsettling story is rich in its depiction of the deep sense of loyalty that Gar feels.

Thompson, Craig
  ▶ *Good-Bye, Chunky Rice.* 1999, 2004. Pantheon Books, ISBN 0375714766, 125p. ☿ Ⓨ Ⓐ

      Chunky Rice, a quiet, Motown-lovin' turtle, is parting ways with his best friend, Dandel, a sweet philosophical mouse, to pursue his innate wanderlust. They spend their last night camping out, feeling their love and sharing the sadness of their loss, before Chunky departs on a ship to cross the ocean. Dandel fills the gap, sending out wordless notes in bottles she collects, while Chunky misses her. Thompson creates a tender story about two very different characters experiencing the "delicate frolic o' friendship" and the poignancy of separation.

Varon, Sara
  Robot Dreams. 2007. First Second, ISBN1596431083, 208p. ☿

      Dog is overjoyed when he assemblies his mail-order kit and finds that he and his new friend, Robot, get along famously. They take a trip to a dog beach where Robot gets rusted and Dog can't get him home. Dog tries to reduce his loneliness with other fleeting friends; he strikes up friendship with a duck family that soon flies south and a snowman that soon melts. Meanwhile, Robot is spending the changing seasons dreaming of happiness with Dog. This lively, heartfelt wordless book captures these characters' strong bonds and their sorrow when friendship is lost.

Out of the Closet and into the Comic Book: LGBT Folks

      Howard Cruse began creating gay characters in the 1970s underground scene. Alison Bechdel followed with her 1980s strip, *Dykes to Watch Out.* These comics where published primarily by gay and lesbian publications. After the Comics Code was overhauled, mainstream cartoonists began to move from stereotypical representation toward a positive approach in depicting homosexuals. X-Men's Rictor and Shatterstar, a decade after their controversial outing, were the first same-sex couple to kiss in 2009 mainstream comics. The characters in the following titles will speak to readers looking for affirmations of homosexuality.

Baillie, Liz
My Brain Hurts. 2007. Microcosm Publishing, ISBN 1934620033, 128p. ⚥

Kate Callahan is a Mohawk-sporting, punk-activist, nonmonogamous dyke struggling to get finish high school before she gets thrown out. Kate's circle of queer outcasts includes Joey, flamboyantly queer-positive, and Desi, her charismatic Latina activist love. Baillie's cartooning is fun and detailed, resulting in authentic depictions of the New York youth punk scene and of Kate's experiences with first loves, promiscuity, substance abuse, and bullying. Kate is a compelling character developing self-respect and exploring her sexual identity.

Bechdel, Alison
Essential Dykes to Watch Out For. 2008. Houghton, Mifflin Harcourt, ISBN 9780618968800, 392p.

Award-winning cartoonist Bechdel follows six lesbian friends and the people who enter and exit their lives in this radical collection of previously published strips spanning 20 years. Mo is the central character, a neurotic whose tirades keeps her friends—Lois, Ginger, Sparrow, Toni, and Clarice—on their feminist, pacifist, progressive feet. Bechdel's characters are fully realized as they mature from young adults to middle-aged women. With the politics of the day as the backdrop of their ongoing stories and conversations, Bechdel creates a moving representation of an intelligent and witty community of lesbians.

Camper, Jennifer (editor)
Juicy Mother: Celebration. 2005. Soft Skull Press, ISBN 1932360700, 86p.

A fun anthology of stories that explore sexuality, identity, and societal acceptance, *Juicy Mother* not only has male and female gay cartoonists but is also racially and ethnically diverse. Camper's contribution, *Ramadan*, conveys the conflicted emotions and memories that its Muslim, Lebanese American, lesbian protagonist feels when she decides to fast for Ramadan, a tradition she hasn't followed since her closeted teens. Other stories feature a young African American man experiencing first love and racism simultaneously, a gay Latina teenager's meeting with extraterrestrials, and two older men who get married before gay marriage was legalized anywhere in the United States. While this collection is somewhat uneven, as a whole it presents a wonderful diversity of experiences and people, a little bit of something to satisfy all readers.

Cruse, Howard
▶ *The Complete Wendel.* 2011. Universe Press/Rizzoli, ISBN 9780789322166, 280p.

Easygoing Wendel Trupstock dreams of becoming a novelist and finding love when he moves to the big city after college. When he meets Ollie Chalmers, an aspiring actor, the attraction is instantaneous and deep. Published in *The Advocate* throughout the 1980s, these collected strips follow the ups and downs of daily life in this couple's relationship and their community of friends and family. It also captures the tumultuous sexual politics of the decade, including issues such as gay liberation, AIDS, homophobia, and the growing right-wing conservatism of the Reagan-Bush years. Award-winning cartoonist Cruse's expressive cartooning creates fully formed characters, which drive a narrative that is as entertaining and relevant today as it was revolutionary in its time.

DiMassa, Diane
The Complete Hothead Paison: Homicidal Lesbian Terrorist. 1999. Cleis Press, ISBN 1573440841, 428p.

Hothead is revolted by the violence of men toward women, both straight and gay, and decides to take justice into her own hands. This quintessential lesbian antihero loses control and lashes out, with equal sadism, at men who abuse women and men who are contemptuous of lesbians. This subversive character satirizes the brutality in the real world, with only her cat, her nonviolent best friend, and, finally, a lover to temper her wrath. DiMassa's cartoony style and insane humor places this narrative clearly in the fictional realm. While many readers will find this revenge fantasy a cathartic salve, its violence will be disturbing for numerous others.

Schrag, Ariel
Potential. 2008. Touchstone, ISBN 1416552359, 232p. Nonfiction. ⚥

The second volume of Schrag's High School Chronicles tells the story of her junior year. While her parents are going through a divorce, Schrag is focused on her identity crisis and subsequent coming out. In pursuit of understanding her sexual orientation, she attempts to have sex with a boy, explores her fantasies, and has her first relationship with a girl. Blessed with living in progressive Berkeley, California, Schrag achieves gay pride fairly early and doesn't have to cope with some of the typical hardships of other GLBT teens. Stylistically diverse, Schrag uses a detailed, mature style to depict events and a ragged, minimal line to illustrate emotional states in this insightful queer coming-of-age story.

Takako, Shimura
Wandering Son. 2011. Fantagraphics Books, ISBN 978–1606994160, 192p. ⚥

Shuichi is a painfully shy boy starting fifth grade at a new school. He strikes up a friendship with tomboy Yoshino. Innocent experimentation with wearing one of Yoshino's girly dresses begins Shuichi's slow acknowledgment of his deep desire to be a girl. Yoshino shares his atypical gender identity, but her path is more anguished because of the interest of the boys in their class and the biological realities of menstruation. Takako presents a sensitive portrayal of friends supporting each other in their evolving transgender identities during the awkwardness of puberty.

What's It All About? In the Midst of a Midlife Crisis

A generation of cartoonists has been creating middle-aged characters and describing their experiences as they age. The challenges that they find at this stage of life include feeling the weight of responsibilities to others, assessing what they have done with their lives, and coming to a deeper acceptance of who they are and who they want to be. The following graphic novels' protagonists are middle-aged characters dealing with these and other questions of middle age.

Ames, Jonathan, and Dean Haspiel
The Alcoholic. 2008. Vertigo, ISBN 9781401210564, 136p.

The middle-aged protagonist of this story takes a long look at himself and his past after he awakens in a garbage bin following a night of drug and alcohol abuse. He traces the history of his substance abuse to its roots to high school, drinking with his best buddy, a friend he lost. His parents die in a car accident, and he longs for a woman who doesn't love hm. As the losses multiply, along with guilt and self-loathing, his drinking becomes his solace, although it undermines his behavior and his health. Award-winning cartoonist Haspiel's angular, heavily shaded illustrations complement the protagonist's deep delving into his internal life; his self-awareness swells as he mines his past, hoping to make a different life for himself in the present.

Clowes, Daniel
Wilson. 2010. Drawn & Quarterly, ISBN 9781770460072, 77p.

Wilson is a middle-aged misanthrope. He continuously engages strangers in conversation, yearning for real connection, only to ramble on in a fatuous, demeaning manner. Wilson looks for meaning in his relationship with his dog, in searching out his ex-wife, and in kidnapping the daughter he didn't know about from her adoptive parents. Award-winning cartoonist Clowes structures the book as a series of one-page stories, using many different styles and color schemes to slowly build a deep picture of the emotional life of this unpleasant but all too human middle-aged character.

Feiffer, Jules
Tantrum. 1979, 1997. Fantagraphics Books, ISBN 1560972823, 120p.

Feiffer's wonderful fantasy of chucking the burdens and responsibilities of middle age truly hits the nail on the head for people entering this age. At 42, Leo is a good man who has taken care of his wife and children. He slips into a depression, feeling his life is all give and wondering where the excitement has gone. In response, he throws such a huge tantrum that it brings him back to the age of two. He no longer has obligations, just wanders from one adult he knows to the next; looking for someone to bathe him and to give him piggyback rides. Award-winning cartoonist Feiffer's full-page panels and his squiggly line style perfectly convey the "what about me" tantrum at the heart of a midlife crisis.

Kanan, Nabiel
   Birthday Wishes. NBM/ComicsLit, ISBN 1561632996, 64p. ☙
      Max Collins lives in a country house with his family and commutes to London, where he is a campaign adviser for a ruthless mayoral candidate while there are riots in London over laws to eradicate the homeless and gypsies. Exposure to homeless kids his daughter's age sends Max on a journey to his past, when he was an activist and a professor of socialist theory. This moving story portrays a middle-aged man who is reassessing his current beliefs in an effort to bridge the gap between who he was and who he has become.

Mahler, Nicolas
   Lone Racer. 2006. Top Shelf Productions, ISBN 9781891830693, 92p.
      Lone Racer was a champion car racer as a young man. Now his wife, practically catatonic, lives in the hospital, and he goes out drinking with old racing buddies every night. He continues to dream about racing and hangs out at the track, only to be scorned by the younger generation of drivers. He feels his world shrinking in middle age, so he sets out to accomplish his dream of competing in one last race, a goal that will bring him to peace with the realities of his age.

Ollman, Joe
   ▶*Mid-Life.* 2011. Drawn & Quarterly, ISBN 9781770460287, 172p.
      John, an alcohol-swilling curmudgeon, is facing 40 with two grown daughters, a younger second wife, and an infant son. His saggy body, mediocre job performance, and invisibility to attractive young women are adding up to a midlife crisis that spirals out of control when he develops a crush on a children's performer, Sherry. John's mind is nimble as he swings between believing the lies he tells himself, blaming himself or others, and realistic self-appraisal. Award-winning Canadian cartoonist Ollman's hilarious and uncompromisingly honest characterizations expose both the mortifications and the hard-earned lessons of entering middle age.

Fractured Comics: Fairy-Tale and Nursery-Rhyme Characters Redux

Fairy tales were originally passed down as oral stories. Charles Perrault was the first to record European fairytales, including those of the Sleeping Beauty, Cinderella, and Mother Goose, which were later revised and added to by the Brothers Grimm. Before the fantasy genre classification was established, many novels, including *The Wonderful Wizard of Oz* and *Alice's Adventures in Wonderland*, were termed fairy tales. The inclusion of traditional fairy-tale characters in contemporary literature makes use of their powerful archetypes and allows for comic contemporary twists (usually nonsexist) on fractured fairy tales. The titles on this list will delight fans of modern spins on fairy-tale characters.

Avery, Ben, Mike S. Miller, and Hector Sevilla
Wisdom Seeker, Lullaby. 2005. Alias Enterprises, ISBN 1933428627, 98p. ☿
  Buxom Alice, now an army general second in power to the Queen of Hearts, sets off with her Cheshire cat to investigate dark forces that have come to Wonderland. On the way, she is joined by a foxy Little Red Riding Hood, a furtive Pied Piper, Pinocchio, and others who form a quirky fellowship. Traveling through sweeping landscapes, they forge friendships, battle over betrayals, and carry deeply felt hopes of finding what they are each looking for in their destination of Oz. This wacky blend of childhood literary characters is given a new life in this fun and magically illustrated tale.

Beddor, Frank, Liz Cavalier, and Ben Templesmith
The Looking Glass Wars, Hatter M. 2008. Automatic Pictures Publishing, ISBN 9780981873701, 176p. ☿ [Y][A]
  Mad Haddigan, the white queen's devoted bodyguard, flees Wonderland to protect Princess Alyss. Escaping through the Pool of Tears, they become separated. A 13-year search through Victorian Europe pits Haddigan against the imagination killers and sundry dark forces. In this grisly graphic adaptation of Beddor's 2006 novel, the characters go through unexpectedly dark transformations, existing in a world devoid of imagination and wonder.

Cammuso, Frank
Max Hamm, Fairy Tale Detective. 2005. Nite Owl Comix, ISBN 0972006141, 208p. ☿
  Porcine P.I. Max Hamm, of the famed Ham and Eggs Detective Agency, is in hot pursuit of the culprit who felled his now splattered partner, Humpty Dumpty. In the naked city of Storybookland, the go-to boss is Mother Goose, who guides Hamm's investigation from Little Bo Peep to Little Boy Blue. The hard-boiled detective is caught up in back-alley intrigue involving gun-toting dwarves and evil stepmothers after Snow White's own stepmother calls him with an ugly secret. Cammuso's amusing version of fairy-tale and nursery-rhyme characters results in a clever noir gem where there is no happily ever after.

Medley, Linda
Castle Waiting. 2006. Fantagraphics Books, ISBN1560977476, 457p. ☿ [Y][A]
  The titular castle is the same that Sleeping Beauty slumbered in and left abandoned when she married the prince. Over the next century, the castle becomes a safe haven for lesser-known misfit fairy-tale characters. Into their

midst comes courageous Jane, a pregnant lady who comes to the castle to escape her abusive husband. Medley reinvents traditional fairy tales and mixes them with a strong dose of feminism and wry humor to build an honorable and fun world within the legendary castle walls.

Simon, Kristen Koerner (editor)
Fractured Fables. 2010. Image Comics, ISBN 1607062690, 160p. ☸
Cinderella, a bossy, trendy teenager, is frustrating her old fairy godmother as she tries to organize Prince Charming's big bash. Rumpelstiltskin is demented, Little Miss Muffet is an arachnophile, and the Little Mermaid is having an emotional breakdown. Anything goes in the colorful collection of revamped classics where beloved childhood characters are updated with contemporary sensibilities and a comical spin without losing their sense of enchantment. The varied cartoonists include Terry Moore, Bryan Talbot, Doug TenNaple, and Ben Templesmith, resulting in a clever and fun collection of fractured fables.

Willingham, Bill, and Lan Medina
▶ *Legends in Exile*, Fables. 2002. DC Comics, 1563899426, 119 p. ☸ Ⓨ Ⓐ
When the fairy-tale homelands of legends such as Jack (of *Jack and the Beanstalk*), Bluebeard, Prince Charming, and Beauty and the Beast are conquered by "The Adversary," the immortals, from lords to peasants, escape into contemporary New York City, where they live according to their own government. In this first book of the series, Snow White's sister, Rose Red, goes missing, and her apartment is found strewn with blood. The Big Bad Wolf works with Snow White to investigate the case, shedding light on this society of legends living among the "mundane." The art melds the two worlds into a place where "mundanes" (us mortals) and this splendid cast of compelling characters live together.

Willful and Wonderful: Realistic Female Protagonists

Wonder Woman, the first female superhero, created in 1941, was ensnared in narrow conventional roles dictated by a male-dominated medium. By the early 1970s, influenced by the women's liberation movement, female cartoonists were becoming disenchanted with women's depiction in comics. With the advent of underground comics, ground-breaking feminist comics were produced including *Wimmen's Comix* and *Twisted Sisters*, which portrayed female characters confronting the real issues that women were grappling with. In the 1990s, the merging of feminist energy with a riot-grrl power produced strong political messages and ordinary women who rule!

Davis, Vanessa
Make Me a Woman. 2010. Drawn & Quarterly, ISBN 9781770460218, 176p. Nonfiction. ౘ

Award-winning cartoonist Davis interweaves multipaged, boldly colored narratives with sketchy penciled bits from her diary covering the mundane moments that add up to a fascinating portrait of a girl growing into womanhood. For Davis, this means exploring her Jewish identity, her complicated relationship with her mother and her sister, her romantic involvements, her art, and the bigger questions about life. She infuses her pictures of zaftig women with beauty and grace that reflect her comfort in her own feminine body. Dramatic watercolors and charming compositions filled with skewed perspectives reveal Davis's development into a candid, well-balanced and humorous woman.

Hernandez, Jaime
▶ *Locas in Love.* 2000. Fantagraphics Books, ISBN 1560974125, 120p.

In this collection of interwoven tales, award-winning cartoonist Hernandez returns to his fully realized characterizations of Latina women from the revolutionary series *Love & Rockets.* Characters include Maggie, the bisexual mechanic; her close friend and sometimes lover, Hopey; Norma, struggling with her daughter Negra; beautiful bon vivant Penny Century; and Izzy, struggling with her mental health. Hernandez's classic line, sense of playfulness, and deep insight into women result in meaningful characters of multiple generations who struggle with daily life, love, lust, friendships, mothering, aging and gaining weight!

Satrapi, Marjane
Embroideries. 2005. Pantheon Books, ISBN 0375714677, 144p.

When their husbands go off for an afternoon nap, a group of Iranian women takes advantage of their freedom to share afternoon tea and talk. This opportunity allows this multigenerational group of beautiful woman to let loose and share stories of sexual exploits. A number of these bawdy tales involve the "embroideries" of the title, which refers to a surgical procedure that women can undergo to have their virginity restored, an important thing in a repressive society where loss of virginity prior to marriage can result in death. The perks of being a mistress, rather than wife, of pursuing lovers, and of poorly treated wives' comeuppances all combine to show how these strong female characters live with passion and strong bonds with other women in the face of cultural gender subjugation.

Tyler, Carol
Late Bloomer. 2005. Fantagraphics Books, ISBN 1560976640, 135 p. Nonfiction.

This lovely collection of stories covers Tyler's life from childhood to middle age. As a cartoonist, she put off her professional ambitions to care for her child and to be a housewife, like so many women have done. Issues covered include how motherhood changes a woman, troubles with men, frustrations of daily life, and the joys of blooming creatively in middle age. Award-winning cartoonist Tyler is a strong female protagonist whose honesty and warmth permit the reader to relate to her experiences.

Wood, Brian, and Ryan Kelly
Local. 2008. Oni Press, ISBN 9781934964002, 376p. ⚇

Defiant Megan McKeenan runs from problems, traveling to 12 cities over the course of 12 years in which she ages and matures into a confident woman. Stuck in a cycle of running from self-destructive boyfriends, Megan eventually establishes a career and a relationship. Moving back home, she begins the process of exploring the deeper sources of confusion from which she had been running. This involving collection of stories, with realistic black-and-white heavy inks, presents a portrait of the development of a real and sympathetic female character as she comes into her own over a 12-year stretch.

Yoshinaga, Fumi
All My Darling Daughters. 2003, 2010. Viz Media, ISBN 9781421532400, 204p.

Yukiko is 30 and still lives with and fights with her mother, Mari. After a bout with cancer, Mari decides to marry a man who is younger than her daughter. Yukiko has mixed feelings and decides to move in with a co-worker. Five interconnected stories about Yukiko's friends and family follow, exploring the misunderstandings between women, attitudes about work, and various ways that women make peace with the limitations of their histories. Award-winning mangaka Yoshinaga creates complex, mature female characters whose inner thoughts and interactions with each other ring true. Readers looking for unique women in comics will find many within these pages that will surprise and touch them in this insightful, emotional manga.

Sunset Years: Senior Citizens Can Be Comics Characters, Too!

Considering that, for a long time, the demographic for comics readers consisted mainly of white men, 20 to 30 years old, there wasn't a great deal of interest in stories about the aging process. As readership diversifies, so, too, do the range of characters and the content. Old age is a stage where people take stock of their lives, sometimes leading to uncustomary actions or ruminations. Elders are dealing with grief as their family and friends die and as they consider their own mortality. The following titles give various perspectives on the final stage in the life cycle.

Bilal, Enki, and Pierre Christin

Black Order Brigade. 2000. Humanoids Press, ISBN 9780967240183, 84p.

When a group of old fascists from the Spanish Civil War massacres a whole village for electing a Communist mayor, their former opponents, a now geriatric group from the International Brigade, is smuggled into Spain, where the two foes fight once again. Award-winning French cartoonists Bilal and Christin combine realistic dialogue and wonderfully detailed drawings to reveal larger themes of coming to terms with the limitations of aging and how the past shapes the present, demanding a high price for avenging the past.

Farmer, Joyce

Special Exits. 2010. Fantagraphics Books, ISBN 9781606993811, 200p. Nonfiction.

Lars and Rachel are dealing with issues of physical decline, caretaking, and memory loss as they come into their early 80s. Their daughter, Laura, tells the poignant story of their fight to maintain their independence as they become housebound in their increasingly rundown home. Their sorrow as their mobility decreases and their daily lives get smaller and smaller is balanced by their good spirits and enduring relationship. This award-nominated memoir of aging and death, based on Farmer's experiences taking care of her father and her stepmother, eschews sentimentality while embracing pronounced compassion and heart.

Greenberger, David

No More Shaves. 2003. Fantagraphics Books, ISBN 1560972572, 159p. Nonfiction.

Greenberger interviewed residents of a men's nursing home, respectfully recording their words in their own distinctive cadences in his zine, *Duplex Planet.* This collection presents the musings, fluctuating in their coherence, of six elderly men on everything from science to sex to sports and politics. Comic artists, including Daniel Clowes, Jason Lutes, Tim Hensley, and Ron Rege, illustrate their stories in a multiplicity of visual styles. Greenberger offers the reader an unaffected portrait of the unique voices of these ordinary aged men, in moments of humor, insight, and confusion.

Lemire, Jeff

Ghost Stories, **Essex County**, Vol. 2. 2007. Top Shelf Productions, ISBN 9781891830945, 224p. ☃ ⓎⒶ

The second in a trilogy of stories that focus on life in Lemire's native Essex County, Ontario, *Ghost Stories* explores the history of two brothers, Lou and Vince. At 80, Lou lives alone, deaf and apparently suffering from dementia. These factors result in an isolation that lends itself to rumination over decisions he made that hurt his brother and family. Almost a pro hockey player in his youth, he compares his choices with his brothers' as he recognizes the harsh reality that he did not live the life he wanted to live. Both sadness and compassion are palpable in the communicative drawings, resulting in an perceptive portrait of the human experience of aging.

Osborne, Rob

Sunset City. 2005. Ait/Planet Lar, ISBN 1923051414, 80 p.

After retiring and losing his wife to cancer, Frank moves to Sunset City, a retirement community in Arizona. Bored, Frank keeps to himself, talking to his dog, going through his daily routine, waiting for phone calls from his daughter. At the funeral of a bigger-than-life neighbor, another resident advises Frank that he needs to live life to its fullest. Shaken out of his monotony, Frank swerves radically out of character to bring a murderer to justice, vigilante style. *Sunset City* reflects the concerns and worries of aging and the variety of attitudes about life in a retirement community.

Seth

Clyde Fans. 2004. Drawn and Quarterly, ISBN 189659784X, 156p. Ⓨ Ⓐ

This nostalgic look at mid-20th-century Canada begins with a day in the life of Abraham as he wanders about the premises of his now defunct business, Clyde Fans, going through his daily routine and talking about his existence. Abraham tells the reader about the business in its heyday, his life as a salesman and manager, his outlook on his isolated brother, and how he prevailed over his own fears. The second part of the book is a flashback to his brother's failed experiences as a salesman. This nuanced characterization beautifully represents the kind of life review an elderly person engages in, coming to new understandings as he questions the meaning of his life.

Chapter Three

Setting

Setting is a vital element in the visual medium of graphic novels, whether it is a geographic location, a period in time, or a "world" in which a story is framed. Readers may prefer unknown or familiar places, copious historical details, visions of the future, or a chance to get lost in a world that connects to their interests. A sense of place is created through backgrounds, clothing, architecture, dialogue between characters, plot elements, and the inclusion of culture-specific details. Cartoonists depend on research, experience, and imagination to create this element, which prose leaves to the reader's imagination. The following lists contain graphic novels in which setting, or frame, is critical to the reader's reading experience.

Familiar Tales: Exotic Locales

The titles in this list have basic plots that readers are familiar with, from coming-of-age stories to stories about the quest for a missing parent. What sets them apart and gives each its own unique flavor is that they are set in less-traveled international locations. This list contains graphic novels that reaffirm that humanity shares basic experiences in places as varying as the Ivory Coast, Hawaii, Seoul, and Turkmenistan.

Abouet, Marguerite, and Clement Oubrerie
▶ *Aya.* 2007. Drawn & Quarterly, ISBN 1894937902, 96p. ☽ Ⓨ︎Ⓐ︎

Set in the Ivory Coast during the Golden Age of the 1970s, this tale of teen intrigue revolves around three beautiful high school girls: Aya and her best friends, Adjoua and Bintou. Aya keeps herself out of trouble with her studies and dreams of becoming a doctor. Her friends spend their time dancing, flirting, and fooling around with boys, imagining marriage and beauty shops. Abouet's story reflects the free spirit of the optimistic Ivorian working class, their daily life, and the realities of teenage behavior. This French wife-and-husband team offer humorous dialogue and radiant, beautiful drawings that bring the reader into the lively world of Yop City.

Aristophane
The Zabime Sisters. 2010. First Second, ISBN9781596436381, 80p. ☚

French comic artist Aristophane portrays life on the Caribbean island of Guadeloupe, where he grew up. This simple series of vignettes depicts three young sisters on their first day of school vacation as they play in the woods, watch a schoolyard fight, and suffer the consequences of a forbidden sip of rum. Teasing, arguing, having fun—the simple activities that make up childhood sibling relationships are all depicted through expressions and simple truthfulness. Aristophane's bold textured brushwork makes the lush, wild surroundings prominent, the island environment almost a character in this understated slice of life.

Byun, Byung-Jun
Run, Bong-gu, Run. 2007. NBM/ComicsLit, ISBN 1561635014, 111p. ☚

Bustling Seoul feels huge and impersonal to Bong-gu and his mother, who have traveled from their seaside village by boat and train to search for his father, who disappeared into the big city. Bong-gu befriends a homeless girl, searching for food in a garbage can, who illuminates the danger and hardship of city living. Her grandfather recognizes the missing father from a photograph and reunites them. Shamed by his inability to make money in the city, the dad joins the family in returning to the relative ease and comfort of village life. Korean Byun's deft line work and coloring contrast the bustling old city with the warmth of the village in this touching manwha.

Johnson, R. Kikuo
Night Fisher. 2005. Fantagraphics Books, ISBN 1560977191, 144p. ☚ [Y][A]

The Hawaiian Islands formed and reformed over billions of years, but it took only hundreds of years for the introduction of myriad foreign species to upset the indigenous balance of the ecosystem. Loren has always felt that he sticks out like a sore thumb ever since he moved to Hawaii with his dad six years ago. As he anticipates the end of high school, he is in a rut, passive about applying for college and watching as his best friend, Shane, drifts away. Shane wakes up when they get arrested one night for stealing a generator to trade for batu (crystal meth), but what will happen to shake Loren's apathy? Johnson's wonderful black-and-white inking portrays the beaches, mountains, tropical plants, and various neighborhoods of Maui and unites the geography and botany of the Hawaiian Islands with this realistic coming-of-age story.

Lonergan, Jesse
Joe and Azat. 2009. NBM Comics Lit, ISBN 9781561635702, 101p. ☻
Joe is in post-Soviet Turkmenistan for two years, teaching through the Peace Corps program, and he becomes fast friends with Azat, a warm, ambitious dreamer. Azat pumps Joe incessantly with naïve questions about democracy, capitalism, and women. Joe attends festive weddings and is inundated with photos of local woman for an arranged marriage. This is a peek into a traditional country that has its own particular logic, where a river is created in the main city while people have no water, 50 percent are unemployed, and modernity is something on TV. Lonergan based this story loosely on his own Peace Corp experiences, his minimalist style illustrating Joe and Azat's moving friendship as it transcends cultural differences.

Moon, Fabio, and Gabriel Ba
De: Tales: Stories from Urban Brazil. 2006, 2010. Dark Horse, ISBN 1595825576, 112p.
Award-winning Brazilian twins Moon and Ba collaborate on these slice-of-life stories about two 20-something brothers, bar-hopping, picking up girls, and just hanging out with each other. Self-reflective scenes and a touch of magical realism add meaning to these stories. The twins' love for their city, Sao Paulo, shines through the many details of cityscapes, buildings, and the feeling for the scene that they create.

History before Your Eyes: Bygone Eras

Graphic novels have proven to be a wonderful medium for representing history. The illustrations develop the settings, and the stories are enhanced with period dialogue and narratives that are chock full of information that is bound to please fans of historical fiction.

Abadzis, Nick
Laika. 2007. First Second, ISBN 1596431010, 205p. ☻ Ⓨ Ⓐ
This historical novel beautifully interweaves the destinies of a released gulag prisoner, Sergei Pavlovich Korolev, who becomes the chief designer of Sputnik, and a beloved, curly tailed dog, Laika, that was sent into space to die in that vessel. Abadzis's well-researched graphic novel provides a detailed picture of the early Soviet space program, dealing with politics, science, and the vagaries of the heart with equal skill.

Bogaert, H. M. van den, George O'Connor, and Hillary Sycamore
Journey into Mohawk County. 2006. First Second, ISBN 1596431067, 144p. Nonfiction. ☻
In 1634, Dutch trader H. M. van den Bogaert and two others left Fort Orange (now Albany, New York), with Indian guides to travel north into

Mohawk territory. Their goal was to ascertain why the popular beaver pelt trade, the primary source of interaction between Mohawks and Europeans, had slowed down. Bogaert kept a journey, detailing the landscape and describing features of Mohawk living and their traditions. O'Connor, employs Bogaert's words to bring this slice-of-history to life, producing a colorful depiction of life for both the natives and the traders in 17th-century America.

Chantler, Scott
Northwest Passage. 2007. Oni Press, ISBN 9781932664614, 267p. ☻

The legendary British New World explorer Charles Lord has been governing a frontier trading post in 1775 Canada. On the eve of his retirement, the fort is invaded, and the brutal Frenchman Montglave takes Lord's son as a hostage. The survivors run off into the wilderness, where they come up with a plan to take back the fort and free Lord's son. Historical fiction readers will not only take pleasure in reading this gripping multi-award-nominated adventure story but also revel in the in-depth annotations that reveal the history behind this thriller.

Geary, Rick
The Borden Tragedy, <u>Treasury of Victorian Murders</u>. 1997. NBM, ISBN 1561631892, 1v. (unpaged). Nonfiction. ☻

Told from the point of view of one of Lizzie Borden's friends, this well-researched reconstruction brings up all the questions left unanswered about the notorious 1892 double murder of Andrew and Abby Borden in small-town Massachusetts. The reader gets a sense of what family and society were like in a repressed New England Victorian town and will delight in award-winning cartoonist Geary's amazing detail in depicting everything from clothing to interior design, down to the wallpaper, the dresser pulls, and the implements of daily life.

Jackson, Jack
Indian Lover: Sam Houston and the Cherokees. 1999. Mojo Press, ISBN 1885418205, 120p. Nonfiction.

Sam Houston, Texas's first president, was brought up by Cherokees and held his relationship with them dear. Jackson, a well-respected Texan historian and underground commix artist, brings to light the complexities of the relationships among the Indians, the whites, and the Mexicans in the development of Texas. Jackson's wonderful illustrations bring this piece of American history to life, as does the copious research that went into the telling of this tale.

Kubert, Joe
Yossel: April 19, 1943. 2003. Ibooks, ISBN 074347516, 121p. ☻

In 1926, at the age of two months, award-winning cartoonist Kubert came with his family to America from a small town in Poland. This is his take on what might have been had they not left. Yossel and his family are forced to march to the Warsaw Ghetto, where he is separated from his parents and sister in a selection. He grows close to Mordecai, one of the leaders in the Warsaw Ghetto uprising. As long as Yossel has a bit of paper and a pencil to draw the comic characters he loves, he can handle the atrocities he sees and hears about. He becomes a key player in the Ghetto uprising, a collective effort by Jews to fight back against the Nazi soldiers' brutality.

McColloch, Derek, and Shepherd Hendrix
Stagger Lee. 2006. Image Comics, ISBN 9781582406077, 231p.
   The setting is 1895, St. Louis, Missouri. The pivotal event happened in a saloon when Stagger Lee killed Billy. Lee had friends and enemies in high places, making for a complicated legal battle, drenched in racism and politics. Beyond that, it's hard to separate fact from layer upon layer of folklore, a task that the authors have undertaken with great detail and skill. A blend of historical fiction, from court procedure to romance, mixed with an examination of the songs that have been written about Lee results in a compelling portrayal of the growth of a legend.

Moore, Alan, and Eddie Campbell
From Hell. 2000. Top Shelf Productions, ISBN 0958578346, 572p. Ⓨ Ⓐ
   This story takes place in 1888 in London, where the newspapers are filled with the gory details of Jack the Ripper's ritualistic murders. Moore's research is incredible (pages are annotated with historical detail), and he looks at the killings from various points of view, landing with the premise that Queen Victoria's doctor, William Gull, was insane and had Masonic delusions that drove him the murder. Campbell's scratchy ink drawings create a dark, moody Victorian London, and Moore's dialogue brings the Victorian sensibilities to life.

Sturm, James
▶ *James Sturm's America: God, Gold and Golems.* 2007. Drawn & Quarterly, ISBN 9781897299050, 191p. ⌛ Ⓨ Ⓐ
   This montage of the roots of America starts in 1801 at a huge religious revival meeting in Cane Ridge, Kentucky, where a family seeks healing for their daughter. Next, Sturm depicts a murderous takeover of a gold mine from a group of Chinese miners in the mining town of Solomon's Gulch, Idaho, in 1886. The third part is Sturm's award-winning story of a Jewish minor-league baseball team's struggles with anti-Semitism as they travel around 1920s small-town America. Each story is illustrated in a style reflecting the different periods in history that come together to provide a bigger picture of the harsh building of this country.

Vollmar, Rob, and Pablo Callejo
The Castaways. 2002, 2010. NBM Publishing, ISBN 156163493X, 80p. ⌛
   Like many others during the Great Depression, Tucker Freeman's father was a hobo who didn't return home. His family becomes dependent on the pity

of his mean aunt, who quickly gets fed up with all the mouths she has to feed and suggests that Tucker leave. Tucker jumps a train traveling through his small Southern town, making the acquaintance of Elijah, an old hobo who shows him the ropes and teaches him an important lesson. This well-researched, award-nominated story gives a glimpse into hobo life, racial relations in the South, and rural life during the Great Depression.

They Got the Beat: Set in the Music World

The connection between music and comics has been strong since the days when underground comics counterculture overlapped with rock and roll and, later, with the punk and rap scenes. Many contemporary cartoonists are also musicians or have illustrated CD covers and concert posters. The following titles, set in the world of music, reveal musicians lives, musical history, and perspectives on various types of music and sure to engage the music-loving reader.

Amos, Tori (editor), and Rantz Hoseley

Comic Book Tattoo. 2008. Image Comics, ISBN 1607060310, 480p. YA

Eighty comics artists interpret or illustrate more than 50 Tori Amos songs, resulting in a beautiful mix of poetry, music, and comics. Amos's lyrics, included with each comic, tell stories, sometimes straightforward, sometimes obscure. The cartoonists had complete freedom to depict their songs literally, to flesh out the lyrics, or to use them as a springboard to their own flights of fancy. This anthology showcases a wide variety of artistic styles, most in color, some wordless, some poetic, some silly. This interesting application of the graphic-novel format to create a beautiful publication will appeal to Amos fans and graphic-novel lovers alike.

Brunner, Vincent

Tunes: A Comic Book History of Rock and Roll. 2010. Rizzoli Books, ISBN 0789322005, 240p. Nonfiction.

Brunner, a past editor of *Rolling Stone France*, assembled 33 French artists to visually represent significant moments, personalities, or bands in rock and roll history. This fine overview offers stories on subjects ranging from Elvis, Little Richard, and the British Invasion to punk, heavy metal, and grunge. Subjects covered include the Ramones playing on stage and Janis Joplin's death. This engaging read has informative text accompanying the comics and a discography for every musician and band.

Carey, Percy and Ronald Wimberly

Sentences: The Life of MF Grimm. 2007. Vertigo, ISBN 9781401210472, 128p.

Relating a powerful cautionary tale, Carey tells the story of his life, his involvement with the roots of the hip-hop movement, drug dealing, and shoot-outs, including the one that left him in wheelchair-bound. After he spends time in jail for dealing, his gritty rhymes catapult him to the top echelon of emcees in the hip-hop industry. This insightful account tells the history of the first generations of hip-hop artists, including Tupak and Dr. Dre.

Crumb, Robert
R. Crumb Draws the Blues. 1993. Last Gasp, ISBN 0867194014, 1v. (unpaged).

This collection of comics created between 1975 and 1985 focuses on Crumb's love for old-time traditional American music, including blues, jazz, and bluegrass. Three biographical pieces stand out: an homage to Charley Patton, jazzman's Jelly Roll Morton's struggle with a voodoo curse, and the story of Kansas City's Frank Melrose. Crumb also includes autobiographical pieces about his lifelong collection of 78s, rants about modern music (anything from the swing era to now), and offers diatribes about the profit-driven music industry that has eclipsed the traditional, community-based creation of music.

Davis, Mike, Mark Davis, and Brandon Schultz
Blokhedz. 2007. Pocket Books, ISBN 9781416540731, 112p. ♻

Blak is an up-and-coming rapper, with a gift for rhymes and powers that are as yet unknown to him. When his older rapper brother is killed following Blak's run-in with a gang, he realizes the challenges he faces if he is to overcome the gang rivalries and street life and become the artist he is meant to be. The energy is high in this realistic depiction of ghetto rapping, from showing your rhymes on the street to battling for supremacy and getting a label.

Dawson, Mike
Freddie & Me: A Coming of Age (Bohemian) Rhapsody. 2008. Bloomsbury, USA, ISBN 1596914679, 405p. Nonfiction. ♻

Dawson states that when he thinks of Queen, he remembers his whole life and places his family's timeline against Queen's discography. During his childhood in 1980s England, he was the band's "#1 super-fan" and belted out "Bohemian Rhapsody" at a talent show. Dawson's adolescence in the United States is buoyed by his turning his school friends onto Queen, and he is jolted by a deep sense of loss when singer Freddie Mercury dies. As an adult, he finally gets to see the band in a reunion concert in England while attending the funeral of his grandma. Dawson's hero fantasies and dreams are beautifully worked into his memoir as he literally illustrates the way that songs that we identify with can stir up memories, like guideposts in our lives.

Derf
Punk Rock and Trailer Parks. 2009. SLG Publishing, ISBN 1593621353, 1v. (unpaged).

Otto, an overgrown junior in high school, calls himself "The Baron" and is a total dork. Akron, his home town, is a boarded-up wasteland where the only culture is found at a closed bank turned punk club. Happenstance leads Otto to become the unofficial tour guide of early punk bands, beginning when he takes the Ramones to get the best burger in town and when the Clash dedicate a song to him. Otto's confidence increases in response to the sense of transcendence he experiences with punk music, and he starts a band of his own. This graphic novel offers a humorous, perceptive look into how small-town punk counter-culture impacted the youth of the late 1970s.

Kleist, Reinhard
▶ *Johnny Cash: I See a Darkness*. 2009. Abrams ComicsArt, ISBN 0810984636, 224p. Nonfiction. Ⓨ Ⓐ

German cartoonist Kleist presents the spirit of Cash here, rather than his complete life history. Included are Cash's Depression-era childhood, his early success, his struggle with drugs, the disintegration of his first marriage, his Folsom prison concert, and his later years working on *American Recordings*. Beyond the events, the book is framed by dynamic narratives of famous Cash songs, "Folsom Prison Blues" and "Ghost Riders in the Sky," so evocative that the reader can almost hear them. The potent black-and-gray illustrations and the symbolism Kleist uses capture psychological truths about the "Man in Black."

Vollmar, Rob, and Pablo G. Callejo
Bluesman Complete. 2008. NBM/ComicsLit, ISBN 1561635324, 208p. ☿

Traveling musicians Lem Taylor and "Ironwood" Malcott walk the roads from Oklahoma to Arkansas, looking for juke joints to play some mean blues. God-fearing folks kept clear of the blues in the early days. Lem coaxes those they meet to give them food, booze, and a bed and tries to keep his rakish part-ner out of trouble. When they land in a town named Hope, a traveling salesman who doubles as a talent scout offers to get them a chance to record a couple of songs in Memphis, awakening their yearning for the big time. But this is the world of the blues, so, as quickly as optimism flares up, trouble finds them big-time, and Lem is on the run to Arkansas to escape in this moody, beautifully drawn graphic novel.

On the Battlefield: Graphic Combat Zones

Superheroes, particularly Captain Marvel, crossed over the fictional historic divide and went to war against the Nazis in World War II. In these battles, the difference between good and bad was clear-cut, and the outcome was predes-tined to be for good. As weapons gained in sophistication, flag-waving dimin-ished, and cynicism trumped idealism, graphic novels began to address the gray areas that are the reality of war. Like literature and films, comics are a medium that communicates the events and costs of war on a human scale, evoking sym-pathy, rage, and grief in these cautionary tales.

Aaron, Jason, and Cameron Stewart
The Other Side. 2007. DC Comics, ISBN 1401213502, 123p. ☺

In September 1967, Billy Everette, accompanied by blood-spattered ghosts of soldiers past, leaves Alabama for Vietnam to save the free world from the "commie gooks." At the same time, Vo Binh Dai says his farewells to his North Vietnamese village to become a sage warrior and liberate his country from the "animals," the American imperialists. Their fates of these misled, blameless young men are intertwined, for they are destined to meet in a stand-off at the besieged base Khe Sanh. This unique, balanced, and potent depiction of the Vietnam War demonstrates the overwhelming dread and the horrifying realities that young men had to face in the jungles of Vietnam.

Dysart, Joshua, and Alberto Ponticelli
Haunted House, <ins>Unknown Soldier</ins>. 2009. Vertigo, ISBN 9781401224240, 144p. ☺ Y A

Lwanga Moses was seven years old when his family fled the Amin regime in Uganda for America. Armed with an Ivy League medical degree, his Ugandan wife, Sera, and a staunch pacifist philosophy, Dr. Moses returns in 2002 as a healer to run a displaced-person's medical clinic. Northern Uganda is appallingly brutal, with abducted children soldiers waging guerrilla warfare for the Lord's Resistance Army (LRA) against their own people. During a violent confrontation with child rebels, Moses feels an aggressive fighting spirit erupts in him. With his disfigured head wrapped in bandages, he launches a violent one-man war against the LRA. This well-researched and violent story revives popular DC World War II character the Unknown Soldier to confront readers with the complex and painful realities of the child-led battlefields of Uganda.

Goodwin, Archie
Blazing Combat. 2009, 1965. Fantagraphics Books, ISBN 9781560979654, 207p. ☺

In this uncompromising anthology of war comics, writer Archie Goodwin's realistic portrayals of multiple wars depict the gory over the glory, spanning the years from the Revolutionary War to the Vietnam War. Various artists, including greats such as Wally Wood and Alex Toth, illustrate the moral dilemmas and often pointless loss of life in stories about the Vietnam War, the Civil War, the Korean War, both World Wars, and the legendary battle of Thermopylae. Goodwin's ardent antiwar stance was radical at a time when war comics were colored by blind patriotism, and, after just four issues in 1965–1966, *Blazing Combat* was unapologetically censored by the military.

Kubert, Joe, and Brian Azzarello
Sgt. Rock: Between Hell and a Hard Place. 2004. DC Comics, ISBN 1401200540, 144p. ☺

Supplies are short and forces are diminishing for infantrymen on the German-Belgium border as they press on to conquer Berlin near the end of

World War II. During a patrol, the incomparable Sgt. Rock and his Easy Company capture four S.S. officers. When the carnage subsides, they find that three of the prisoners have been shot point blank and one has vanished. While untangling the events, they come face to face with the moral ambiguities of war. Award-winning cartoonist Kubert revisits one of his signature characters from the 1950s and 1960s, when war heroes were larger than life. Azzarello's writing of this contemporary script leaves Easy Company's camaraderie intact while revealing the despair and the gruesome realities of war.

Lomax, Don

Gulf War Journal. 2004. Ibooks, ISBN 0743486692, 216p. ☻

When "Journal" Neithammer learns that his daughter is in Israel, under threat of Scud missile attacks and chemical warfare, he abandons his reclusive life in the mountains to cover the 1991 Persian Gulf War. Journal's impressions of war, politics, and the culture of war journalists are interspersed with reportage about the power of U.S. weaponry, the devastating bombings of Iraq and the Kuwaiti border, and ground-troop maneuvers in the desert sands and the burning of the oil fields. Lomax, himself a Vietnam veteran who wrote the acclaimed *Vietnam War Journal*, begins this in-depth account of Operation Desert Storm with a story about the 9/11 terrorist attack and the beginnings of the second U.S. war in Iraq.

Miller, Frank, and Lynne Varley

300. 1999. Dark Horse Comics, ISBN 1569714029, 1v. (unpaged). ☻ ⟦Y⟧⟦A⟧

In 480 BCE Sparta, a messenger arrives to proclaim the Persian King Xerxes' supremacy over Greece. The reserved and wise King Leonidas kills the messenger, provoking the autocratic Xerxes to attack. The old-fashioned oracles won't allow a war, so Leonidas takes his 300 bodyguard warriors to march across Greece into a three-day battle, leading tens of thousands of Persians to the deaths. Their illustrious sacrifice inspires the Greeks to join forces, outnumbering Persian fighters three to one, to fight to preserve reason and enlightenment in Greece. Miller's depiction of the ancient battle points to the glory and honor of the Spartan warrior.

Mills, Pat

Charley's War. 2004. Titan Books, ISBN 1840236272, 1v. (unpaged). ☻

Sixteen-year-old Charlie Bourne lies about his age to join the British Army during the First World War. Simple and friendly, Charlie goes to France a few weeks before the Battle of the Somme, bright-eyed with patriotism and ready to valiantly defend his country. This idealism fades as the realities of war set in: the mix of terror and boredom of the trenches, generals and a despicable captain who blithely send soldiers to their deaths. Award-winning British cartoonist Mills began this weekly series in 1978; it was pioneering in its break from sanitized, patriotic depictions of war and was censored because of its challenging depiction of the appalling truths of the Great War.

Murphy, Justin, and Al Milgrom
Cleburne: A Graphic Novel. 2008. Rampart Press, ISBN 9780979957901, 1v. (unpaged). ♻ Ⓨ Ⓐ

Irish immigrant turned Confederate general Patrick Cleburne is a respected leader, but he creates waves of dissent when he proposes to bolster the Confederacy's embattled ranks by enlisting slaves to fight in exchange for their freedom. In retaliation, another general takes the troops into their final fight, the Battle of Franklin, which ends up a gory, futile attempt to retake Nashville. While Cleburne was not the only one to fight for this unpopular idea, his story brings the reader onto the bloody battlefields of the Civil War, where bayonets and cannons left the fields strewn with dead.

Shanower, Eric
Age of Bronze: A Thousand Ships. 2001. Image Comics, ISBN 9781582402000, 208p. Nonfiction. ♻ Ⓨ Ⓐ

In retelling the epic legend of the 10-year war between Troy and Greece, Shanower synthesizes an impressive number of sources, including mythology, literary sources, and archeological evidence. This first volume introduces the key characters and depicts the events that led up to the Trojan War. Shanower's classic pen-and-ink drawings provide copious details that create a strong sense of place and time, and the bibliography speaks to the in-depth research that went into this sweeping, poetic portrayal of war.

Tardi, Jacques
It Was the War of the Trenches. 2010. Fantagraphics Books, ISBN 9781606993538m 118p. Ⓨ Ⓐ

This powerful, fury-inducing World War I portrayal places the reader next to Privet Binet, a misanthropic Frenchman, in his daily life in the filth and gore of the trenches, firing across the hell of a no-man's-land at the Germans. Disgust and anger emanate from French cartoonist Tardi's well-researched depiction of the rotting corpses, mud, huge rats, and debris left by dead men. His characters' expressions are ones of horror, depression, and paranoia, whether they are French, German, Algerian, Vietnamese, or Sikh. Tardi's text conveys the futility and injustice of war and the absurdity of the loss of life from the first to the last page.

Biblio Graphics: In the Book Realm

Authors are frequently interested in everything book-related and have produced many wonderful novels set in bookstores, libraries, and the rare-book world. Increasingly, graphic novels have also been set in the book world. Some of these titles take advantage of the comics' ability to illustrate imaginary settings and speak to our book-related fantasies. Others are bibliomysteries or literary riffs that are bound to please the bibliophiles among us.

Arikawa, Hiro, and Kiiro Arikawa

Love & War, <u>Library Wars</u>. 2010. Viz Media, ISBN 9781421534886, 200p. ☃

    Through the Media Betterment Act, the Japanese government has taken control of the media, allowing rampant censorship of "offensive" books. Libraries have become the champions of free speech and access to information, running the Library Defense Forces (LDF) to oppose the regime. Iku Kasahara has dreamed of joining the LDF since an agent saved a desired fairy-tale book during a bookstore raid when he was a child. In this first volume, she trains to become a member of the dangerous elite Library Task Force. This manga mixes a developing love story with gung-ho action in the stacks, making for a light read on a serious library topic.

Carey, Mike, and Peter Gross

Tommy Taylor and the Bogus Identity, <u>The Unwritten</u>. 2010. Vertigo Comics, ISBN 9781401225650, 1v. (unpaged). ☃

    A little bit of Harry Potter magic, a dash of conspiracy thriller, and a large dose of literary references make for a super start to a series about the power of stories. The best-selling author of the *Tommy Taylor* fantasy series disappears, leaving his son, Tom Taylor, dependent on the proceeds of the books and merchandise tie-ins. Tom protests that he is not the title character, but, when characters from the book start to appear in his life, he must reassess his belief. This story within a story uses its visuals well, switching between present and past, reality and fantasy. The first volume of this award-nominated series ends with an alternate history of Rudyard Kipling's work, which begins the fantastical spin into mythologizing literature.

Niffenegger, Audrey

Night Bookmobile. 2010. Abrams, ISBN 9780810996175, 40p. ☃ Ⓨ Ⓐ

    Wandering the streets of Chicago during the wee hours of the night, Alexandra comes upon a shabby Winnebago that beckons her to come in with the sounds of a favorite song. Greeted by Mr. Openshaw, the librarian of "The Night Bookmobile," Alexandra discovers that the collection is composed of everything she has ever read, including novels, textbooks, the backs of cereal boxes, and even her diary! Alexandra is possessed by the desire to be a Night Bookmobile librarian, sacrificing everything else in her life to reading. This tale of obsession and supernatural bookmobile events will elicit delight and fright in library lovers.

Perker, M. K.

Insomnia Café. 2009. Dark Horse Books, ISBN 9781595823571, 79p. ☃

    Peter Kolinsky, a rare-book expert in handwritten books, loses his job at a top auction house when he secures a buyer for a stolen book for a hoodlum, Oblomov. He escapes serving prison time by turning in Oblomov's brother. Fearful of revenge, Peter is unable to sleep, and he discovers the all-night Insomnia Café. One of the employees there brings him to "The Archives," a secret library which houses the world's incomplete works of fiction, from Stephen King's current title to all the secret, half-done works of J. D. Salinger. When Oblomov reappears, Peter slowly spirals into insanity, leading him to rash actions in "The Archives."

Shiga, Jason
Bookhunter. 2007. Spark Plug Comics, ISBN 9780974271569, 1v. (unpaged). ♀ ⓎⒶ
    When the Oakland Public Library finds that the rare 1838 Caxton Bible, on loan from the Smithsonian, has been replaced with an expertly bound fake, the library police are the ones for the job. They conduct forensic science on the fake, perform deep detective work into circulation records, and even have a swat team to make the arrests. This cleverly constructed mystery is both funny and informative. No violence here, the book is a wonderful choice for readers looking for light mystery.

Stamaty, Mark Alan
Alia's Mission: Saving the Books of Iraq. 2004. Alfred A. Knopf, ISBN 03759321678, 30p. ♀
    Real-life superhero Alia is the chief librarian of the Basra Public Library in 2003 as the likelihood of war between Iraq and the United States grows. When she arrives at work one day to find soldiers with anti-aircraft guns stationed on the roof of the library, she understands why her request to the governor to move the books before the impending invasion was declined. She and her husband begin moving the collection out in carfuls, as dedicated volunteers join them in saving 30,000 books that record the history and traditions of their people. Based on a real story, this gratifying graphic novel may be shelved in your library's children's department, but it will touch and educate adult readers about the ravages of war on institutions that preserve culture.

Turner, James
I, Librarian, <u>Rex Libris</u>. 2007. SLG Publishing, ISBN 9781593620622, 184p.
    Superlibrarian Rex Libris has been defending access to knowledge since he began working at the Great Library of Alexandria. His autobiography opens when a samurai warrior, wielding his sword, attempts to check out a book without a library card. Just in time, Rex makes it to the mythology section in Middleton Public Library, where he finds a book on vanquishing samurais. Rex answers only to the ancient ranting god Thoth, who sends him on missions to retrieve overdue books from villains throughout the cosmos. Turner's unique style is text heavy and chock full of mythology, history, philosophy, and adventure.

Vicarious Journeys: Graphic Travelogues

The travelogue has the power to catapult readers to faraway settings where they participate in vicarious encounters with unknown cultures. Comics are a wonderful way to both tell and show readers what the traveler sees and experiences. Graphic-novel travelogues, through the intimacy and immediacy of their images, make for some very effective armchair traveling.

Delisle, Guy
Pyongyang: A Journey in North Korea. 2003, 2005. Drawn & Quarterly, ISBN 1896597890, 176p. Nonfiction. ☃
    Arriving in North Korea, French-Canadian animator Delisle is met by his guide and translator, who will accompany him daily during his eye-opening and slightly surreal two-month work stint. The first stop on every foreigner's agenda is to leave flowers at the base of a 22-meter high bronze statue of Kim Il-Sung, the deceased but still supreme president. He and his son's photos are everywhere (including on standard-wear jackets), and all broadcasts, music, and movies are propaganda for the glory of the Communist dynasty in their valiant fight against imperialist America and Japan. The reader is allowed a peek into this highly regulated society as Delisle depicts the bleak, monotonous showcase city and observes the poverty and hardworking lives of the brainwashed and depressed population.

Knisley, Lucy
French Milk. 2007. Epigraph Publishing, ISBN 978978942755, 179p. Nonfiction. ☃
    Paris through the eyes of a 21-year-old art student offers fun things to buy, delicious food, art museums galore, and the most delectable, nourishing French milk! Knisley and her mother lived in a small apartment for a month to celebrate her mother's 50th birthday. There are days when she gripes and groans, homesick for her boyfriend and fearful about her future as a cartoonist, but Knisley journals the day's events, soaking in the Parisian culture and sites. Light, descriptive pages full of little details about the cafes, the scrumptious food, and the art, parks, and markets balance the young-adult angst that permeates the book.

Martinson, Lars
Tonoharo: Part One. 2008. Pliant, ISBN 9780980102321, 128p. ☃ Y A
    Following graduation from an Ivy League school, Dan Wells travels to a fictional rural Japanese town, Tonoharu, to work as an English teacher's aide. Instead, the teachers rarely use him, so he finds himself bored sitting at his desk all day. He is alienated, a social klutz of sorts, and unable to connect with his co-workers or the rare Westerners whom he meets. Using his personal experiences with working abroad as a base for this fictional account of life in small-town Japan, Martinson creates elegant illustrations that reflect a Japanese aesthetic in this attractive graphic novel.

Neufeld, Josh
▶*A Few Perfect Hours.* 2011. Alternative Comics, ISBN 1891867792, 128p. Nonfiction. ☃ Y A
    Josh and his wife, Sari, backpacked through Southeast Asia, spent a year in the Czech Republic, and traveled through parts of Central Europe. In this

pioneering 2004 graphic travelogue, Josh depicts an anxiety-producing climb through the Cave of Fear in Thailand, working as extra's in a Singaporean TV show, witnessing a cremation ceremony in Bali, and volunteering on an isolated Malaysian organic farm. While living in Prague, the couple travel to Turkey by train and have unsettling incidents in Serbia related to wartime paranoia and nationalism. Neufeld covers all the bases with his intelligent observations, from depicting the landscapes and cities to covering the dynamics between the traveling companions and offering hot travel tips on how to manage squat toilets, showers, and packing.

Schwieger, Dirk

Moresukine: Uploaded Weekly from Tokyo. 2008. NBM/Comics Lit, ISBN 1561635375, 1v. (unpaged). Nonfiction. ☿

Schwieger, a German ex-pat working as a Japanese software translator, put out a challenge to readers of his blog to submit "assignments" for him to explore various aspects of Tokyo. The results include a ride on a zany mall rollercoaster, visits to the Studio Ghibli Museum of anime master Hayao Miyazaki and to an origami museum, a night spent in a pod hotel, and a hike up Tokyo's gorgeous Mount Takao. Other missions focus on culture, seeking out motorcycle gangs (Bosozoku), recording outrageous fashion trends, giving impressions of gender roles, and eating the potentially deadly fugu. Schweiger recorded his experiences and impressions in his moleskin journal (the title is the Japanese pronunciation) and posted them as weekly webcomics, resulting in a unique depiction of contemporary Tokyo that will appeal to young, hip readers.

Thompson, Craig

Carnet de Voyage. 2004. Top Shelf Productions, ISBN 1891830600, 224p. Nonfiction. ☿

Thompson spent two months traveling in France, Morocco, and Spain while promoting his graphic novel and using this sketchbook journal to record his experiences. In France, he captures the feeling of the neighborhoods of Paris, the seaside in Toulouse, and the Alps near Lyon. In Morocco, a land of sensory overload, Thompson captures the tumult, the desert, and culture shock, physical discomforts, and homesickness. He goes gaga for Gaudi and is drawn to the yucca trees in Barcelona, where he meets a kindred spirit. His amazing sense of place and his energetic brushwork bring the places he saw to life, creating a most pleasurable vicarious journey for the reader.

Survivalist Landscapes: Post-Apocalyptic Visions

The creation of the atom bomb brought the realization that humans are capable of destroying the earth we inhabit. As threats such as chemical and biohazard weaponry, global warming, and the use of virtual technology increase, writers and artists confront the specter of apocalypse. While mass destruction is the premise for these popular stories, they are about surviving under harsh circumstances in landscapes plagued with Mad-Max-like technologies, environmental ruin, and moral ambiguities.

Endo, Hiroki
Eden: It's an Endless World, **Vol. 1**. 2005. Dark Horse, ISBN 1593024069, 216p. ☹

> A horrific plague that hardens flesh to stone while internal organs waste away has wiped out much of the population. Three survivors on an island, two teens and their afflicted mentor, are trying to determine if they must repopulate the earth and questioning evolution, God, and humanity. Jump forward 20 years to Elijah, the teens' son as he wanders the earth with a robot, looking for girls and balancing power plays in a world of scheming, cybernetically enhanced humans, mechanized beings, and the rare survivor. Endo's keen sense of place brings the reader into this post-apocalyptic setting with overgrown cities, sophisticated weapons, artificial intelligence and high levels of violence.

Ennis, Garth, and Jacen Burrows
Crossed, **Vol. 1**. 2010. Avatar Press, ISBN 1592910904, 240p.

> The United States is hit by a virus that corrupts the conscience, transforming ordinary people into savage psychopaths. The Crossed, named for the cruciform scars on their foreheads, roam the earth rejoicing in finding fresh blood to eat and people to rape and to mutilate. In their midst are small groups of unafflicted humans who band together, trying to make it through another day in the face of such depravity. The in-your-face violence forces the reader to grapple with a common post-apocalyptic moral quandary: is it worth surviving if the cost is one's humanity? Ennis and Burrows's post-apocalyptic horror story will appeal to those who can stomach extreme gore and violence to get to the commentary at its core.

Johnston, Antony, and Christopher J. Mitten
Cities in Dust, <u>Wasteland</u>. 2007. Oni Press, ISBN 1932664599, 160p. ☹

> This series begins 100 years after "the big wet," a cataclysmic event that left the earth a barren desert lacking rainfall. Sand eaters, mutated beings with supernatural powers, attack the illiterate nomads roaming the deserts, following them as they seek sanctuary in the city of Newbegin. Newbegin resident Jakob joins the Council to find ways to defend against the imminent threat to life as they know it, in this introduction to a seven-part series that melds paranormal dilemmas, political conspiracy, and racial tensions into survivalist tactics.

Kindt, Matt
Revolver. 2010. Vertigo, ISBN 9781401222420, 192p. ☹

> Every night at 11:11 P.M., Sam leaves his petty daily concerns, his dead-end job, and a society overtaken by media and consumerism to enter an apocalyptic

world: millions killed by Avian flu, cities bombed out by the government, and armed vigilantes roaming the streets, ready to kill for food. As he attempts to unravel his existence in parallel world, Sam matures, taking on the responsibility to protect those he loves and eventually saving the world. Kindt presents a bleak contrast between a United States where headlines focus on celebrities, insider trading, and sports and a country facing worldwide power and food shortages, natural disasters, nuclear bombs, and the death of millions daily. The chaos is visually palpable, forcing people to become survivalists, despite murky moral and ethical questions.

Kirkman, Robert, and Tony Moore
Days Gone Bye, <u>The Walking Dead</u>, **Vol. 1.** 2004. Image Comics, ISBN 1582403589, 144p. ♒ [Y][A]
   Police officer Rick Grimes wakes up from a shotgun wound–induced coma to find that zombies have taken over his now vacant rural town. Horrified and confused, he makes his way to Atlanta in search of his family and government aid. There he hooks up with a disparate group of humans living in the forest outside the zombie-infested city. Kirkman creates strong characterizations of the survivors as they struggle to maintain their humanity in a post-apocalyptic world overrun with desperate zombies.

Lemire, Jeff
Out of the Deep Woods, <u>Sweet Tooth</u>. 2010. Vertigo Comics, ISBN 9781401226961, 124 p. ♒
   Gus's dad has taught him never to leave the woods because of the dangers that lurk outside, where most the population has died because of a pandemic. Only hybrid animal-human kids have been born since then, such as Gus, who has deer ears and antlers, and there is a high price on their heads. When his father dies, Jess is tempted by chocolate bars into the arms of bounty hunter Mr. Jepperd, who promises to take him to a safe "preserve" for hybrid children. Jess retains his trust in the goodness of his new guardian, despite the savage violence he is exposed to. In this first volume of a trilogy, award-winning Canadian cartoonist Lemire gives us a startling look (like a deer in the headlights) at innocence in a survivalist world where death is always imminent.

Rapp, Adam
Ball Peen Hammer. 2009. First Second, ISBN 9781596433007, 134p.
   Imagine a contemporary Black Plague, corpses strewn through the streets, coupled with unrelenting darkness, acid rain, and perpetual food and water shortages. Add to that a disturbing mysterious Syndicate that offers survival (food and lodging) to those who will carry out their ethnic cleansing, using as the weapon the ball peen hammer. Obie award-winning playwright and novelist Rapp portrays a few good people who continuously face the choice between inhumane brutality and survival in the claustrophobic world that they inhabit. Visceral artwork by O'Conner illustrates the horrors of such a world.

Tezuka, Osamu

Phoenix: A Tale of the Future. 1967, 2002. Viz Communications, ISBN 159116026X, 298p. ☿

The year is 3034. The universe is dying. Earth is barren because of a nuclear war. Mammals are extinct, except for the 25 million humans living in five underground metropolises run by huge god-like computers. Space patrolman Masuto chooses to flee to the surface rather than leave his alien love, a much maligned, shape-shifting species that retains its imaginations in a conformist culture. On the surface, they team up with a phoenix, an immortal guardian of the universal cosmos, to try to save the world. This volume is the second installment in award-winning mangaka Tezuka's groundbreaking 13-volume saga that follows the mighty phoenix back and forth from the past to the future.

Vaughan, Brian, Pia Guerra, and Jose Marzan Jr.

▶ *Unmanned,* **Y: The Last Man.** 2002. Vertigo/DC Comics, ISBN 1563899809, 127p. ☿ Ⓨ Ⓐ

All of a sudden, all male mammals except Yorick Brown, an amateur magician and recent college graduate, and his male pet monkey die from an unknown virus. City infrastructure is crumbling; transportation is near impossible because of the multitudes of abandoned cars left when the men died; and the majority of the world's women are in shock. As roving bands of Amazonian women fight to establish a new matriarchal society, the female members of the U.S. government scramble to try to reestablish order. All Yorick wants to do is find his girlfriend in Australia and make babies the old-fashioned way. Instead, he must flee from women with darker plans for him, protected by a special agent and a cloning expert, to figure out how to repopulate the next generation.

Comics, Comics Everywhere: Comics Heaven

The following graphic novels are set in the multifaceted world of comics—the lives of cartoonists, comic's critics, fanboys, and collectors. It's fun and revealing to see cartoonists spoofing and paying homage to their world in their depiction of life in cartoonists' studios, industry realities, comic conventions, and comics stores.

Campbell, Eddie

Alec: How to Be an Artist. 2001. Top Shelf Productions, ISBN 09577869637, 127p. Ⓨ Ⓐ

Scottish cartoonist Campbell's ongoing autobiographical series starring his alter ego, Alec MacGarry, focuses on the ups and downs of becoming a comic's artist and breaking into the industry. His sketchy, freewheeling line drawings portray his friendly, thoughtful character as he experiences marriage, birth, and his own professional development. Campbell's commentary on the 1980s comics history in the United Kingdom and the history of the graphic novel enrich this excellent study of becoming a comics artist.

Clowes, Dan

Pussey. 1984, 2010. Fantagraphics, ISBN 1560971835, 54p.

Dan Pussey (pronounced poo-SAY) is a typical nerdy fanboy who makes good when he accepts a job at a mainstream studio assembly line as a penciller for a line of superhero fantasy comics. His work rises above his co-workers and he achieves unexpected fame, experiencing what it's like to be on the other side of the comic's convention table. Pussey's adored creative writing teacher encourages him to create meaningful stories leading Pussey on an eye-opening journey through the "modern, avant-garde, neoexpressodecontructivist" com-mix world, only to realize superhero comics are where he belongs. Award-winning cartoonist Clowes's humorous, telling spoof on both mainstream and high-brow comics offers commentary on the industry's greed and the expendable quality of its workforce.

Dupuy, Philippe, and Charles Berberian

Maybe Later. 2006. Drawn & Quarterly, ISBN 1896597211, 128p. Nonfiction.

French comics artists Dupuy and Berberian resolve to keep solo journals about the making of one of their popular co-created *Monsieur Jean* graphic novels. They explore their unique collaborative effort (both write and draw equally) and offer insights into their personal styles of working. Berberian uses humor to disclose his struggles with procrastination (in the form of shopping for comics and CDs) and balancing family life with working. Dupuy's resistance to journaling, along with his emotional upheaval after a marital separation, is revealed through dream and fantasy sequences. This unique look into the creative process for these two master cartoonists also provides an interesting look into French comics publishing.

Horrocks, Dylan

▶*Hicksville.* 1998, 2010. Drawn & Quarterly, ISBN 1770460020, 264p. Ⓨ🅐

Cartoon critic Leonard Batts arrives in the remote New Zealand town of Hicksville to research the mysterious childhood of cartoon star Dick Burger. The locals and resident cartoonists won't talk about Burger, but everyone, from old to young, sure does love to talk comics. Batts is blown away by their library, which is composed of comics only, from contemporary Mongolian mini-comics to early superhero comics, including many copies of the super-rare *Action Comics* #1. While New Zealander Horrocks protests the loss of poetic potential in a vapid mainstream comics industry, he presents his devotion to comic art in all its forms, as reflected in the wide range of styles he uses to create the magical comic-loving haven of Hicksville.

Jason
Left Bank Gang. 2005. Fantagraphics, ISBN 1560977426, 46p. ⓎⒶ

This wacky alternative history is set in 1920s Paris with anthropomorphic ex-pats Ernest Hemingway, F. Scott Fitzgerald, James Joyce, and Ezra Pound desperately working on their comics. Fitzgerald is seen hunched over his drawing table working feverishly on his panels. Gertrude Stein is there giving them advice on how to be successful cartoonists. The four spend endless hours in cafés discussing comic art. This amusing depiction of cartooning as a respected high art unexpectedly evolves into a starving-cartoon-artists-deluded heist tale.

Seth
Wimbledon Green. 2005. Drawn & Quarterly, ISBN 1896597939, 125p.

The mysteries and character of Wimbledon Green are presented here in mockumentary fashion, through interviews with comic-book dealers, store owners, and top collectors. Green's adventures in hunting down rare comics are intertwined with first-person narration by the self-professed greatest comic-book collector in the world. Award-winning Canadian cartoonist Seth fully realizes this world through both image and text. and his sense of place and nostalgia pull the reader in. These interconnected stories about where Green came from and where he vanishes to both honor Golden-Age comics and spoof the world of comic-book collecting.

Tatsumi, Yoshihiro
A Drifting Life. 2009. Drawn & Quarterly, ISBN 1897299745, 855p. Nonfiction. ⓎⒶ

Tatsumi was a trailblazer in Japan's manga revolution with his introduction of "gekiga," an alternative style with darker themes and realistic narrative. In this biographical work, Tatsumi relays his part in Japan's postwar obsession with manga, his frustrations with the circumscribed limitations of the format, and his struggles to produce and publish more realistic comics. This substantial book not only tells his personal history playing with the manga iconography but also is an elemental history of the growth of manga, placing it in historical and artistic context. This is a beautiful, intelligent example of a cartoonist reflecting on his own art.

Fantastical Cities: Urban Imaginings

From Gotham City to Sin City, cartoonists have been creating urban settings, the gritty, crime-infested city being the most prevalent. The authors and artists of the following titles have taken this stereotypical comics setting and have recreated it to include fantastical elements that elevate them to something greater, which, like mysterious characters, may linger long after the graphic novel is finished.

Busiek, Kurt, Brent E. Anderson, and Alex Ross
Life in the Big City, <u>Astro City</u>. **1995,** 2011. DC Comics, ISBN 1401232612, 192p. ☿ Ⓨ Ⓐ

Astro City runs on a large dose of urban fantasy. Superheroes mingle with the unpowered residents, keeping the supervillains, monsters, and spirits that lurk beyond the modern city at bay. In this collection of stand-alone tales, caped Samaritan waxes eloquent about the beauty of free flight. Anxiety accompanies thrill when a regular Joe sees supervillain Jack-in-the-Box unmasked. A resident of unprotected Shadow Hill commutes to the luminous, art-deco downtown but is unable to leave her talismans and chants behind. Busiek and Ross have created a complete visionary, photorealistic city with distinct neighborhoods and provided 75 years of backstory to create their own universe to rival Gotham City.

Dalrymple, Farel
Pop Gun War. 2003. Dark Horse Comics, ISBN 1569719349, 134p. ☿ Ⓨ Ⓐ

When a tattooed angel falls to a gritty city, a construction worker saws his wings off and throws them into a garbage can. Sinclair, an isolated little boy, retrieves the wings and attaches them to himself, surprised when he finds he can fly. From the air, he watches the bizarre happenings in the city. A miniature man with a floating fish competes for attention with a corporate executive and his severed talking head. All the children are charmed by the shows of a creepy puppeteer who holds them hostage in a doll factory. Dalrymple expresses both the beauty and the ugliness of the city while telling stories laced with magical realism.

Katchor, Ben
Julius Knipl, Real Estate Photographer. 1996. Little Brown, ISBN 0316482943, 106p.

Knipl moves through a multilayered city, recording the factories, the retail stores, the headlines, people's stories. and his strange interactions in this decaying yet poetic urban setting. A Licensed Expectorator spits on him for undercutting his client on the "Rachmunis" (compassion) job, the Siren Query Brigade comforts callers whose worries loom large at the sight of a passing ambulance. Mundane moments are revered, and ubiquitous signs display the prosaic yet fanciful names of the establishments of the city. Katchor's crude drawings and the combination of narration and interwoven dialogue create a distinctive cadence that evokes a city where humor, Yiddishkeit, and nostalgia come together.

Mathieu, Marc-Antoine
Dead Memory. 2003. Dark Horse Books, ISBN 1569718407, 64p.

Building after building looms large over the people who walk in the deep valleys between them in this infinite city grid, all hooked into a huge computer that runs the people through programmed scheduling and keeps society moving blindly forward in response to big-brother platitudes displayed on huge monitors attached to buildings. When high brick walls begin to crop up, blocking streets, bungling officials meet, only to realize that their lawmaking is ineffective in the face of unexpected disruption. Mathieu's dramatic high-contrast black-and-white drawings perfectly represent this dystopian flight of fancy, as citizens grow to be immobilized, their memories evaporating when they are unplugged from technology and the familiar architecture of the city itself.

Matsumoto, Taiyo
Tekkon KinKreet. 2007. Viz Media, ISBN 1421518678, 614p. Ⓨ Ⓐ

Black and White, orphaned street boys, perch on roofs and telephone poles with the humongous crows, watching over their dreamlike, corrupt Japanese city, Treasure Town. When *yakuza* (mobsters) and alien real estate developers try to take over the city, Black fiercely defends his city, brutally fighting back as three assassins hunt them down. White, an addled visionary, is separated from Black and taken into police protection, leaving his "other half" to wrestle with his dark side. Matsumoto draws the city from unsettling cinematic perspectives where buildings curve and huge crows fly straight at the reader in this surreal and multilayered story of the power of the heart and the maintenance of innocence in the midst of urban upheaval.

Schuiten, Francois, and Benoit Peeters
▶ *Brusel*, <u>Cities of the Fantastic</u>. 1992, 2001. NBM, ISBN 1561632910, 120p.

Swept up in the marvels of new, early-20th-century utopian promises, a massive rebuilding project of Brusel is undertaken by inept bureaucrats and corporate oligarchs. The city is torn down to make way for massive skyscrapers with airborne highways. Tubercular florist Constance is conflicted; as a potential supplier of plastic plants, he is also trying to stop the bulldozers from destroying his home. When the ground below can't support the weight of the half-built city, it begins to sink into the groundwater, making it uninhabitable. Belgian artist Peeters's delicate line and soft palette perfectly depict French cartoonist Schuiten's idiosyncratic architectural vision in this humorous, cautionary tale.

Manga Munchies: In Japanese Kitchens

Starting with *Like Water for Chocolate*, readers' appetite for food-related literature has increased.

"Cooking manga" has long been popular in the Japan, beginning with the ongoing 1983 series *Oishinba* (Gourmet). Readers interested in cooking, Japanese food, or straight Japanophiles will find their mouths watering while reading the following fun graphic novels.

Hashiguchi, Takashi
Yakitate!! Japan, Vol. 1. 2006. Viz Media, ISBN 9781421507194, 208p. ☖
 Kazuma has created 55 variations of "Ja-Pan" since he was six years old in his quest to make unique Japanese bread, one that his village grandfather would consume with gusto equal to that he felt eating the traditional staple, rice. When he is old enough, he leaves home to compete for a baker position in a posh Tokyo bakery. His inventiveness and the gift of "hands of the sun," hands the ideal temperature to knead a perfect loaf, balance his complete lack of knowledge and his ignorance of the context of baking history and breads of the world, giving him a surprising edge over his highly trained competitors. Love of bread-making—the techniques, the science, and the pleasure of the finished product—shine through in the first volume of this engaging and fun manga series.

Kariya, Tetsu, and Akira Hanasaki
Japanese Cuisine, Oishinbo. 2009. VIZ Media, ISBN 1421521393, 272p. ☖
 A prominent newspaper is presenting a new series, "Ultimate Menu," reflecting the highest ideal of Japanese gourmet cooking. Yamaoka Shiro, a cynical slacker with a developed palette and a vast knowledge of Japanese ingredients and technique, is researching and writing the series. The visits to restaurants and the meals and food competitions with various gourmets and chefs are rich in dialog about Japanese cuisine. This humorous slice of life is spiced up by Shiro's rivalry with his father, who owns the exclusive Gourmet Club. This first translation of the grandfather of cooking manga, award-winning Japanese serial *Oishinbo* (1983–) leaves the reader salivating for subsequent volumes that focus on menu specifics such as vegetables, sake, and ramen and gyozo.

Komura, Ayumi
Mixed Vegetables, Vol. 1. 2005, 2008. Viz Media, ISBN 142151967, 196p. ☖
 Hanaya Ashitaba's father has a renowned bakery. One night, her fish-hating mother isn't home, so her father introduces her to sushi. So begins her secret dream to marry into a family that owns a sushi restaurant. She has her eye on just the boy in her high school culinary certification course; his father is a celebrated sushi chef. As he helps her with her knife skills, Hanaya unexpectedly starts to fall for him, without knowing that under his skills slicing sea bream and cucumbers lurks a dream to be a pastry chef! This is the first volume, setting the stage for a cute culinary series that offers up a light and fun read for foodies.

Saijyo, Shinji
Iron Wok Jan!, Vol. 1. 2005. ComicsOne, ISBN 158899256X, 190p. ☖
 Trained by his severe grandfather, the finest Chinese master chef in Japan, Jan Akiyama enters his first job with great culinary skill and an obnoxious attitude. His philosophy is "cooking is competition," so, when he is challenged by

a former chef at the restaurant he works in, he takes up the gauntlet with relish, creating a plotline that mimics *Iron Chef*, the popular competitive Japanese TV import. Sweet and sour pork with pomela and oranges and tilefish are some of the classic dishes through which they battle each other in this first volume. There is much here for the gourmand: in-depth exchanges about classic and inventive techniques, wonderful depictions of food made with rare ingredients, and information on the origins of various dishes.

Shimabukuro, Mitsutoshi
Toriko. 2010. Viz Media, ISBN 9781421535098, 203p. ೮

Toriko is a gourmet ingredient hunter whose bottomless appetite and desire for ever more rare eats leads him to face even the most dangerous or disgusting of creatures. Japan has entered the gourmet age, and the International Gourmet Organization, which has created a system for rating the hazards of catching a beast, is planning a feast for a group of international leaders at its Gourmet Hotel. The head chef searches out Toriko to catch the most exotic of ingredients, the 300-pound Garara gator, and decides to go along on the hunt to see Torika kill with his bare hands. This slightly gruesome cooking manga will appeal to those who enjoy *Kitchen Confidential*.

Yoshinaga, Fumi
Antique Bakery, **Vol. 1.** 2005. Digital Manga Publishing, ISBN 1569709467, 200p.

Crabby owner Tachibana wants only the best at his Antique Bakery. Lacking a sensitive palate, he hires sexy master pastry chef Yusuke and enthusiastic ex-boxer Eiji as his apprentice. Yusuke is gay and, once rebuffed by ex-classmate Tachibana, is always up for playful flirting. In-depth discussions about French pastries are coupled with award-winning mangaka Yoshinaga's signature sensitive portrayals of relationships between the protagonists and the bakery's customers.

The Hot War: From Ground Zero to the Middle East

Behind the headlines and the countless reports of the conflicts with and in the Middle East lie multitudes of stories that speak to the complex world of religion, war, oil, oppression, and politics. The following titles touch on these aspects and on North America's involvement with this region, examining the resultant conflicts and tragedies.

Folman, Ari, and David Polonsky
Waltz with Bashir: A Lebanon War Story. 2009. Metropolitan Books, ISBN 9780805088922, 128p. Nonfiction. ೮

Listening to a friend's repeated nightmares about the Lebanon war, Israeli filmmaker Folman begins to wonder why all he can recall about the war are his visits home. He meets with a specialist in posttraumatic stress disorder, fellow veterans, and friends to help jog his memory and piece together his wartime experience. What he finds is unrelenting fear of snipers, a shoot-or-die mentality, and memories of the Christian militia's massacre of Palestinians at the Sabra and Shatila refugee camps. Readers are pulled into the experiences of young soldiers, good boys in positions of moral ambiguity in this dreamlike meditation on memory, trauma, and the futility of war.

Glidden, Sarah
How to Understand Israel in 60 Days or Less. 2010. Vertigo Books, ISBN9781401222338, 206p. Nonfiction. ⅊

Progressive American Jew Glidden has many assumptions about the Israeli-Palestinian conflict when she goes to Israel on a "Birthright Israel" tour. At first she assumes that any pro-Israeli sentiments are propaganda, but, as she travels to Jerusalem, the Golan Heights, Masada, and other historic sites and confronts the everyday realities facing citizens, her beliefs are challenged. This emotional presentation of the beginnings of an understanding of the complexities of this controversial topic overlaps with Glidden's changing attitude toward her Jewish identity. Attractively presented with cartoony drawing and beautiful watercolors, award-winning cartoonist Glidden's honest, thoughtful journey will move readers.

Inzana, Ryan
Johnny Jihad. 2003. NBM Publishing, ISBN 1561633534, 20p. ⅊

Throughout his childhood, John Sendel's father, a macho Vietnam vet, belittles him and abuses his mom. He spends his teen years as an empty misfit until a Muslim co-worker's religious fervor provides him with a desire for faith for the first time. Before he knows what's happening, he is persuaded to become a soldier in an upstate New York Islamic terrorist training camp. He is captured by the CIA after executing an imam and, in lieu of prison, is sent to Afghanistan to spy on Al Qaida, which the United States previously funded and armed to fight the Soviets. This graphic novel is an eye-opening account of the possible effects of contemporary alienation and the complexities of allegiances in the murky war on terror.

Jacobson, Sid, and Ernie Colon
The 9/11 Report: A Graphic Adaptation. 2006. Hill & Wang, ISBN 0809057387 117p. Nonfiction. ⅊

This smart condensation of the 600-page federal report released by the National Commission on Terrorist Attacks upon the United States makes the emotionally charged material accessible to a wide audience. Simultaneous fold-out timelines follow the four planes on the morning of 9/11, providing a very clear narrative of what happened and the communication breakdown between agencies and the actions of the Islamic fundamentalists. The authors manage to distill the significant findings of the report, particularly its numerous recommendations. This graphic adaptation, a finalist for a National Book Award, does justice not only to the government document it's based on but also to the traumatic national events of 9/11.

Lappe, Anthony, and Dan Goldman
Shooting War. 2007. Grand Central Publishing, ISBN 9780446581202, 192p. ☿
>The year is 2011. While uploading footage about eminent domain for his Burn Baby Burn video-blog, cocky hipster Jimmy Burns happens to capture a suicide bombing of a Brooklyn Starbucks. As the next new media sensation, he is sent as a journalist by a corporate media giant to Iraq, where he is used by jihadist terrorists and scorned by fanatical U.S. Marines. Ironic humor and a riveting mix of photographs and digital painting raise provocative questions about the impact of corporate media, American imperialism, and the war in Iraq.

Modan, Rutu
Exit Wounds. 2007. Drawn & Quarterly, ISBN 9781897299067, 172p. ☿ Ⓨ Ⓐ
>Koby, a Tel-Aviv taxi driver, gets a mysterious call from Numi, an Israeli soldier. She suspects that his estranged father, who is her lover, is an unidentified victim of a suicide bombing in Hadera. As they search for answers, Kobi discovers surprising elements of both his father's and his own life, and Numi begins to wonder about her idealized beliefs. Mudan, one of Israel's best-known cartoonists, portrays the dual nature of a modern life in a country in ongoing war: the unruffled manner of those hardened by violence and the emotional scars that trickle down through generations.

Novgorodoff, Danica
Refresh, Refresh. 2009. First Second, ISBN 9781596435223, 144p. ☿
>Josh, Cody, and Gordon have just finished high school when their Marine reservist fathers leave their Pacific Northwest town for extended tours in Iraq. They are forced to grow up quickly to cope with poverty, absent moms working double shifts, and the unnerving tension of refreshing their e-mail again and again to check for word from their fathers. This stress changes the way they spend their time together, moving from daily fights in a backyard boxing ring to more brutal games with homemade weapons, mimicking soldiers' lives. Novgorodoff reveals emotion in an understated fashion, engaging the reader in the toll war takes on those who remain at home.

Sacco, Joe
Palestine. 1996, 2002. Fantagraphics Books, ISBN 9781560974321, 288p. Nonfiction, ☿ Ⓨ Ⓐ
>From Ramallah to Nablus to the refugee camps on the Gaza strip, Sacco meets with a wide variety of Palestinians, recording their faces and their stories. Older people recount tales of being driven from their homes in 1948, while children share their stories of stone throwing that leads them to join up

with one of the various political factions of the Palestine Liberation Organization. Sacco interviews mothers who have lost children in random shootings, men who have been interrogated and done time in prisons, and people whose houses have been bulldozed. This American Book Award winner is a grueling piece of graphic journalism; the detailed, anguished images bring the reader right into the never-ending stories of hopelessness and despair.

Spiegelman, Art
  In the Shadow of No Towers. 2004. Pantheon, ISBN 0375423079, 42p. Nonfiction. ⅋
    The morning of 9/11/01, Spiegelman and his wife, residents of Lower Manhattan, were running to get their kids from their schools near ground zero when they witnessed the collapse of the North Tower, an image that was seared into the author's mind. These powerful vignettes portray Spiegelman's process of struggling with his neurotic sense that the sky is falling while portraying the impact of the communal trauma and pain. Borrowing heavily from the weekly strips of more innocent times gone by, the cartoonist tells of the double fear of terrorists and the U.S. government, which used the attacks to put in place "the new normal" inciting an "us versus them" vengeful mentality while bypassing a golden opportunity to initiate a global worldview.

Intersecting Lives: Small-Town Communities

Towns, suburbs, and villages support a wide community of people in these graphic novels. In small towns, people connect with their neighbors, creating a web of interactions that are bigger than the place itself.

Clowes, Daniel
  Ice Haven. 2001. Fantagraphics Books, ISBN 037542332X, 89p.
    Personal and public lives intertwine in Clowes's impressive creation of the town of Ice Haven, a typical gloomy American town. The kids include David Goldberg, a strange kid who gets kidnapped; Carmichael, a disturbed boy who is obsessed with Leopold and Loeb; and the anxious Charles, in love with his new stepsister. The adults: Random Wilder, a wanna-be poet, tortured by his elderly poet neighbor's local success; Harry Nabors, a comic book critic; and Mr. and Mrs. Ames, a detective team that visits Ice Haven to investigate the kidnapping. Ice Haven becomes a real place through Clowes's detailed illustrations, his character's probing monologues and dialogue, and the interface between the characters.

Hernandez, Gilbert
  ▶*Heartbreak Soup*, **Love and Rockets.** 2007. Fantagraphics Books, ISBN 1560977833, 288p.
    Palomar is a fully realized Central American town that Hernandez created over a span of 20 years. Chelo, the midwife, introduces all the characters,

remembering their births, their complex family histories, and how they grew up and evolved. When the busty Luba arrives, competing with Chelo as the town's bath giver, the gossip travels like wild fire. These stories have all the richness of real small-town living, as the ups and downs of the inhabitants' interconnected lives are portrayed with heart and humor. Award-winning cartoonist Hernandez brings this place to life with his wonderful dialogue, complex storylines, and crisp, realistic line.

Katsumate, Susumu
Red Snow. 2009. Drawn & Quarterly, ISBN 9781897299869, 246p.

Katsumate exposes the hardships and the monotony of coexistence in a rural village just on the cusp of modernization. Isolated in a hilly and forested region, the villagers are bound by traditional roles and rituals. Farmers, old women, prostitutes, and monks are all caught up in daily existence, which includes marital abuse, betrayal, rape, and childish flirtations. These vignettes are both unsentimental and poetic, resulting in a genuine look at this particular place and time.

Lat
Kampung Boy. 2006. First Second, ISBN 1596431210, 142p. ☃

Life in a Malaysian *kampong* (village) is richly portrayed through the eyes of Lat, who tells his story from birth through life as a young teen, when he leaves his village. The common theme of growing up, from the freedom of childhood to taking on of progressive responsibilities, takes on greater significance in the rural, idyllic, preindustrial rubber plantation village in which it is set. Lat lovingly depicts the *kampong*, the closeness of the residents, the life-cycle rituals, and the fun of growing up there: diving naked from trees, catching fish by hand, and panning for tin, leading readers to feel an intimacy with this unfamiliar corner of the world.

Mezzo and Pirus
King of the Flies: Hallorave. 2010. Fantagraphics Books, ISBN 9781606993200, 64p.

Eric lives an empty life in a French suburb, sponging off his doting mom, popping pills, seeking sex, and running around town in his disconcerting oversized fly mask. Half of the intersecting stories in this first volume of a trilogy are told from Eric's point of view, while the others are told from the perspective of an aggressive alcoholic businessman, a young woman who is having sex with her old boss, Ringo, a crazed bowler, and other residents, all stuck in their addictive, perverse, violent lives. Mezzo's art, with its dark palette, rife with telling details and strange points of view, engrosses the reader while lifting the veil on the ugliness that lurks beneath the disquieting surface of this sad town.

Simmonds, Posy
Tamara Drewe. 2008. Mariner Books, ISBN 0547154127, 136p. Y A

When Drewe, a saucy London journalist, returns home to her inherited country house and brings her rock-star boyfriend, the balance of the small town is upset. From the yuppie guests at a literary retreat to the town girls, everyone in the village reacts the presence of these Londoners, beginning a chain of romantic and melodramatic events fueled by envy, gossip, and mischief. The inhabitants of this dull and idyllic rural English village are varied; the story comments on the changing nature of working-class villages that have been overrun by rich weekenders seeking peace in the country. Simmond's muted palette creates lovely images of the landscapes, farms, and homes and of the telling expressions in this novel of manners, inspired by Harding's *Far from the Madding Crowd*.

Urrea, Luis Alberto, and Christopher Cardinale
Mr. Mendoza's Paintbrush. 2010. Cinco Puntos Press, ISBN 0791933693231, 64p. ♨

This beautiful graphic novel reads like a love letter to its fictional setting, the rural Mexican town of Rosario. With chunks of the town periodically disappearing into the multilayered silver mines below and mummified bodies of monks, built into the walls of their 17th-century church, popping out every year, the inhabitants run the gamut from gossiping old ladies to young boys, awakening to the delights of girls. Watching all the goings-on is Mr. Mendoza, the self-acclaimed moral conscience of the village, brandishing his paintbrush to reveal all the residents' secrets. Cardinale's vibrant drawings resemble detailed block prints, depicting the physical lushness and the magic of life in this rich village.

Places That Go Bump in the Night: Horrifying Haunts

Haunted houses are a popular horror setting that twist the warm connotations of "home" and capitalize on readers' belief in the supernatural. Cobwebs, flickering lights, gloomy staircases, moving shadows, creaks, thuds, and moans all come with the dark forces that make familiar places ominous and threatening.

Corben, Richard, and Simon Revelstroke
William Hope Hodgeson's The House on the Borderland. 2000. DC Comics, ISBN 1563895455, 85p.

Two boys hiking in Ireland's countryside are chased from a pub by the townsfolk. Hidden in the ruins of a castle that teeters on an abyss, the boys find a 19th-century manuscript, a journal of the past resident's lifelong fight against the "swine-beasts," hair-raising primordial creatures that lived in the foggy abyss, creeping into the house, possessing his sister and his dog. As the boys read of his terror, they themselves begin to hear eerie sounds, calls of the swine-things longing to find another human portal into the real world once again. In this excellent adaptation of Hodgeson's 1908 novel, Corben captures the dread of deep, lurking dark forces erupting into our daily lives in both his text and his eerie drawings.

Hill, Joe, and Gabriel Rodriguez

▶ *Welcome to Lovecraft,* <u>Locke and Key</u>. 2008. IDW Publishing, ISBN 9781600702370, 152p. ☿ Ⓨ Ⓐ

After their father is brutally murdered, the three Locke kids move with their mom to live in their father's childhood home, Keyhouse, a huge Victorian in Lovecraft, Massachusetts. They are all traumatized and trying to deal with their grief, but the house that was meant to shelter them becomes a nightmare when the youngest boy discovers that he turns into a ghost when he goes through a certain door and that there is a deadly spirit living in the well. Bram Stoker Award-winning cartoonist Hill builds tension and terror that are beautifully illustrated by Chilean artist Rodriguez in this compelling, creepy haunted-house series.

Rankin, Ian, and Werther Dell'Edera

Dark Entries. 2009. Vertigo Comics, ISBN 9781401213862, 214p.

John Constantine is convinced to put aside his loathing of television and to bring his occult detective skills to a haunted-house reality show that seems to be serving its contestants with more than manufactured scares. Best-selling Scottish crime novelist Ian Rankin's comics debut revives beloved antihero Constantine, who attempts to save the girl once again in a contemporary haunted-house story that plays with the idea of hell in a media-saturated society. Artist Dell'Edera adds a black-and-white noir feel, bringing to life the personal demons that plague each of the house's contestants.

Seagle, Steven T. and Teddy H. Kirstiansen

House of Secrets. 1997. Vertigo Books, ISBN 1563893622, 128p. ☿

Abrasive teenager Rain hooks up with a younger innocent runaway and a no-talent grunge band in Seattle, where they squat in an old, furnished house that seems too good to be true. Rain's premonitions about the house come to fruition when she is summoned through the pantry door to another dimension to stand witness in a series of spirit trials, meting out severe justice to people who have kept harmful secrets. The first volume introduces the interesting premise, that "there ain't a person alive who isn't a walking, talking house of secrets." Spooky indie art portrays the Victorian haunted house as a character that will draw readers to eagerly read on in the series to find out how this courtroom and the spirits took up residence in this creepy house.

Simmons, Josh

House. 2007. Fantagraphics Books, ISBN 1560978554, 1v. (unpaged). ☿

A teenager walks into a forest and finds a massive, boarded-up Victorian building. He meets up with two girls, and they move a huge stone to enter and explore the secret passages and hidden underwater town within. They go through a trap door, and their fun adventure changes dramatically into an ever-darkening nightmare. Simmons expresses the emotions experienced by the threesome and the mood without words in his detailed drawings, which move the reader from the wonder of exploring old buildings to a world that grows smaller and darker until they find themselves in a place of utter terror.

Sturgis, Matthew, Bill Willingham, and Luca Rossi
Room and Boredom, House of Mystery, Vol. 1. 2008. DC Comics, ISBN 9781401220792, 128p. ♀

Architecture student Fig is chased from her burning home by two scary apparitions; she takes with her only a bundle of blueprints for a sprawling Victorian, B-movie type house she obsessively dreams about. When she passes through a mystery door, she is in a bar in the house she has designed, which sits on a cosmic crossroad where a cast of characters from all times and dimensions travel. Fig discovers that she is trapped there indefinitely and begins to try to unravel the mystery of why the house owns her and how she can escape the mysterious house.

Dreamscapes: Panoramas of the Author's Psyche

Graphic novels are an ideal medium for rendering the topsy-turvy world of dreams, where scenes are nonlinear, gaps in time abound, and much is left to the reader's imagination. The following titles illustrate the depths of the psyche, an internal landscape where anything goes.

B., David
Nocturnal Conspiracies. 2008. NBM/Comics Lit, ISBN 1561635413, 124p.

In beautiful inking of black, grays, and blues, David B. has created elegant and eerie representations of 19 dreams, which he had from his 20s to his mid-30s. Suspense is prevalent as the content of the dreams is filled with chases by Nazis, Bosch-like monsters, child-killing terrorists, cops, and assassins. These danger-filled dreams have their own unique mystifying logic and threatening narrative, and the gorgeous art brings the reader into the author's Kafkaesque unconscious realm.

Doucet, Julie
My Most Secret Desire. 2006. Drawn & Quarterly, ISBN 1896597955, 1v. (un-paged).

Doucet's pulsating dream journal is full of repeating images exploring gender, sexuality, and body image. She dreams she is a man who rapes some-one; her apartment is full of guillotines; she eats a friend's penis and gives birth to cats; and her teeth fall out. The dreams are full of disturbing details and a sense of self denigration. Award-winning Canadian artist Doucet is blatantly honest, with no apparent hang-ups, although many of her dreams end with her awakening in her bed, slyly relieved that it was just a dream. Densely inked and heavily detailed, Doucet's chaotic panels seem to be at the edge of bursting with her neurotic sleepy-time tales.

Mashiba, Shin
Yumekui Kenbun: Nightmare Inspector. 2008. Viz Media, ISBN 1421517582, 184p. ☸

Hiruko's nourishment is nightmares, which he consumes by accompanying people into their dream worlds and helping them achieve a desired outcome. A young man who feels unloved has a yearly nightmare that Hiruko explores, finding clues that bring the dreamer a longed-for peace with his father. Every night, a young woman dreams that she writes "tomorrow will be a repeat of today." She seeks out Hiruko and accepts the monotonous nature of life. This interesting manga premise offers the reader many sojourns into the world of nightmares and the potential power of dreams to change waking life.

Max
▶ *The Extended Dream of Mr. D.* 2000. Drawn & Quarterly, ISBN 1896597262, 75p. ⓎⒶ

Mr. D, a 40-year-old, profoundly discontented, married working man, can no longer bear the emptiness he experiences. One night, he falls asleep and then wakes up in a psychiatric ward 40 days later, motivated to recount the intense dreams and dreams within dreams that healed him. Mr. D reaches deeply into his own psyche and connects with and runs from characters that represent parts of his self that he cauterized earlier in response to a formative childhood experience. Max's expressive drawings and the suspense of the mystery encourage the reader to root for Mr. D and to engage in analyzing his prolonged curative dream.

McKay, Windsor
Little Nemo in Slumberland. 2007. Checker Book Publishing Group, ISBN 1933160217, 288p.

Nemo (Latin for no one) is searching on earth, through space, and in mythic lands for Slumberland, where he has been summoned by King Morpheus to be his daughter's playmate. These self-contained Sunday strips always end at a significant moment, with the last panel reserved for Nemo waking in his elegant bed. Nemo is portrayed without emotional expression or narrative context; he is merely the dreamer, allowing the reader to project interpretations of these sophisticated dreams. McKay renders the architectural and exotic dreamscapes in elegant lines, from strange perspectives, with unconventional scaling. This pioneering strip (1905–1914) has influenced generations of cartoonists artistically and is the granddaddy of dream comics.

Reklaw, Jesse
Dreamtoons. 2000. Shambhala Publications, ISBN 1570625735, 126p. ☿

This collection of dreams comes from Reklaw's online weekly dream strip, Slow Wave, in which he illustrates the dreams of contributors. He has a talent for showing off the absurd, humorous, and bizarre nature of dreams in four-panel comic strips. There are about 100 dreamtoons, including tales about a god that leaves a message on an answering machine about the approaching millennium; a pet rabbit that gives an unauthorized interview; and a guru who resides in the bottom shelf of a refrigerator. Reklaw illustrates a world we all share in this wonderful collection that readers may find both strange and familiar at the same time.

Veitch, Rick
Crypto Zoo (Collected Rare Bit Fiends), <u>The Dream Art of Rick Veitch</u>. 2004. King Hell Press, ISBN 9780962486469, 152p.

Suffering from depression and exhaustion, Veitch recorded his dreams as a part of his therapeutic treatment. These trips into his unconscious life were analyzed to increase his understanding of himself. This is the most complex of the three Rare Bit Fiends dream collections (titled in homage to Windsor McKay's post-Nemo dream comic); the stunning images illustrate wild surrealistic dreams, and there is an essay by Veitch about his perspective on the meaning of dreams.

Chapter Four

Language

Language in graphic encompasses words, images, or the marriage or juxtaposition of the two. The comics medium has its own vocabulary that informs the narrative in pacing, dialogue, and style. The lettering, word balloons, panel layout, coloring, inking, and gutters (the space between the panels) are some of the elements of the language that go beyond the text.

Beyond the writing, the style of the art is another key factor of the language. The appeal of style is particularly dependent on the readers' personal taste, making a neutral appraisal difficult; one person's poetic is another person's prosaic.

The visual language of comics has been widely explored in theoretical texts including Scott McCloud's *Understanding Comics* and Will Eisner's *Comics and Sequential Art*. General reviews have only recently started to grapple with the language of graphic novels. The lists in this chapter identify some of the aspects of graphic-novel language, offering readers a place to find titles that they will enjoy.

Putting the Novel Back in Graphic Novels: Literary Comics

One of the basic arguments against the term "graphic novel" is that it encompasses many types of books, many of which are not even fictions, let alone novels. The titles on this list reflect a common definition of novels: complex fictional narratives that deal with human experience. These works combine image and words magnificently and create stories whose weight leaves readers thinking about the stories long after the closing page.

Blain, Christophe
Isaac the Pirate. 2003. ComicsLit, ISBN 1561633666, 96p. ⓎⒶ

Isaac Sofer, a poor 17th-century painter, is cheerfully content with Alice, his childhood love, odd painting jobs, and dreams of being a famous artist. A chance encounter with a sailor leads him to sign on as a portrait painter for a ship's captain on what turns out to be a pirate ship bound for Antarctica. French cartoonist Blain moves the narrative between Isaac's transformation from painter to pirate and Alice's attempt to be faithful during Isaac's unexpectedly long absence. Blain's communicative cartooning and delightful use of a warm color palette to create mood and emotion offer added pleasures in this insightful, romantic adventure tale.

Burns, Charles
Black Hole. 2005. Pantheon Books, ISBN 9780375714726, 368p. ⓎⒶ

Teenagers in a 1970s suburb are reeling from the spread of a sexually transmitted disease that leaves each victim disfigured in a unique manner, from boils to skin flaps, from second mouths to molting skin. Popular Chris falls for Ray and gets infected by him. Ostracized, they move to an encampment in the woods where other afflicted teens are living. Keith hasn't been infected, but his affection for Chris leads him to join forces with the outcasts. Burn's stunning, sharp inking is full of symbols and visual metaphors, deeply integrated with the text to produce a powerful, at times repulsive account of the dark side of suburbia and adolescent sexuality and alienation.

Cruse, Howard
Stuck Rubber Baby. 1995, 2010. Vertigo, ISBN 1401227139, 224p. ⚥ ⚥

White, working-class Toland Polk's progressive girlfriend introduces him to the black community in this fictional Southern town, where his budding friendships pull him into the civil rights movement. His first exposure to gays in the boisterous black bars he visits brings vague, conflicted feelings about his sexuality into focus. All the characters are fully realized, with stories of their own that build a portrayal of changing social mores, from the black Reverend and his gay son, to educated liberal activists, to Toland's racist brother-in-law. Polk's story of coming to terms with his homosexuality and finding his place in the whirlwind of racial tensions of the 1960s is captivating. Cruse's lovely detailed art enlarges on the stories humor and big heart.

Eisner, Will
Contract with God and Other Tenement Stories. 1978, 2006. W. W. Norton, ISBN 1563896745, 208p.

55 Dropsie Avenue, a 1930s Bronx tenement, is occupied by immigrants and other poor souls struggling with the hard realities of life and dreaming of better days. Frimme Hirsch returns home in a relentless downpour from his only child's funeral, enraged at a God that would punish a man of good deeds An aging has-been opera singer lures a young married street singer into

her apartment and they share dreams of fame and fortune. The power-hungry building supervisor is duped by the child he takes advantage of. Residents go up to the mountains in search of a rich spouse or a break from unhappy matrimony. Eisner's lovely, realistic art illuminates the human condition, the heartbreak, passion, sadness, and disappointments, with great compassion in this landmark work that introduced the graphic novel format in the United States.

Larcenet, Manu
Ordinary Victories. 2004, 2005. NBM/ComicsLit, ISBN 1561634239, 128p.
  Marco is a burnt-out photojournalist who quits therapy and leaves Paris for a house in the country. Plagued by severe panic attacks and pessimism, he tries to make sense out of the difficulties of life, while learning to take pleasure in the small things. Marco begins a long-term relationship, photographs the industrial shipyard where his father worked, and struggles with accepting his father's Alzheimer's. The cartoony characters, wonderful dialogue, and expressive use of color make these realistic life stories into a literary piece that evokes strong emotions and thoughts on love, loss, responsibility, and class. Marco's maturation and discovery of how to live in his skin continue in the second volume, *Ordinary Victories: What Is Precious.*

Moore, Alan, and Dave Gibbons
Watchmen. 1987. DC Comics, ISBN 1435242793, 413p. ♉ Ⓨ Ⓐ
  It's the 1980s, and the ominous threat of nuclear war is hanging over cold-war America. The Crimebusters, a group of superheroes, are awakened from their apathetic retirement to investigate the murder of one of their own. Each of these superheroes is a multifaceted character coping with his own personal history, neuroses, and disappointments. As they recreate a new generation of masked vigilantes, the government decides to shut them down, leading to an unforeseen ending. Moore and Gibbons create a dense, morally profound world that challenges contemporary ideas on the use and abuse of power, secret identities, and the meaning of and trust placed in "heroes." The art is amazingly detailed, seamlessly moving the complex storylines through time and space. This benchmark graphic novel remains a stunning, provocative literary read.

Shaw, Dash
▶ *Bottomless Belly Button.* 2005. Fantagraphics, ISBN 9781560979159, 702p.
  The Looney family has gathered at its beach house to process the shocking announcement that, after 40 years of marriage, the parents are getting divorced. Peter, now married and with a young son, takes it hardest, searching for answers and raging against their decision. Claire, going through a divorce herself, distances herself from everyone except her teenage daughter. The youngest and most alienated, Peter, who is portrayed as a frog, hides in his room until he meets a young woman and shares the remainder of the time with her. Shaw's emotional iconography includes varying patterns of water, sand, and the sun, which echo deeply with the undercurrent of one family's life as it passes through change and time.

Ware, Chris
Jimmy Corrigan: The Smartest Kid on Earth. 1999, 2003. Pantheon Books, ISBN 0375714545, 380p. ⓎⒶ

   Jimmy Corrigan, an emotionally stunted and socially inept 30-something, receives an invitation from the father he has never met to visit for Thanksgiving. In meeting his father, he struggles with his conflicted responses and his inability to engage in conversation, let alone build relationships and tolerate multifaceted emotions. A second narrative about Jimmy's grandfather's 1860s relationship with his abusive father enriches the current narrative with a historical perspective of inherited depression and dysfunction between fathers and sons. Dream and fantasy sequences and timelines add layers of complexity to this multigenerational novel. This masterpiece is difficult to read, both visually and because of the hopelessness and deeply sad content, but it is dense with visual symbolic meaning and compassion that lead to a rewarding experience.

Walking Down Memory Lane: Retro Stylin'

   The word "retro" derives from the Latin prefix *retro*, meaning "backwards" or "in past times." It refers to obsolete trends, mode, or fashions that come to enjoy a renewed popularity at a later time. Nostalgia for "simpler times" and the modern "cool factor" often drive the widespread use of "retro" iconography and imagery in art, advertising, and industrial design. The art in the following titles is in a retro style, generally that popular between the 1940s and the 1970s.

Blanchet, Pascal
White Rapids. 2006. Drawn & Quarterly, ISBN 9781897299241, 1v. (unpaged). �

   This fine-looking account of the rise and fall of the town of White Rapids (Rapide Blanc) begins in the early 1920s in the Montreal boardroom of Shawinagan Water & Power when the decision is made to build a hydroelectric dam and a village in the uninhabited "wild north" of Three Rivers. Blanchet illustrates the life of this happy village from its opening in 1934 through its 1969 nationalization and automation, which lead to the demise of the village. Elegant muted drawings reflect the changing aesthetic from art deco through the 1960s, and lovers of design will appreciate the clever blending of word and image in this lovely blend of fact and fiction.

Cooke, Darwyn, and Dave Stewart
DC: The New Frontier. 2004. DC Comics, ISBN 1401203507, 1v. (unpaged). � ⓎⒶ

   This fantastic superhero alternate history places the DC Universe in the real-world cultural context of the tumultuous 1950s. Superman and Wonder Woman are working for the government and with vigilantism outlawed; Batman is even more of a loner. The war is over, and the simplistic dichotomy between good and evil has vanished with it. The cold war, the start of the civil rights movement, and the dawn of the nuclear ear are the new challenges. It's the obscure human heroes such as the Challengers of the Unknown and the Losers who must do battle in these thorny conflicts. Cooke's art has an audacious line and uses upbeat colors that reflect the aesthetic of the times with its brash optimism and midcentury modern space-age design.

Hensley, Tim
Wally Gropius. 2010. Fantagraphics Books, ISBN 9781606993552, 64p.

Wally Gropius's father, a gas magnate, has given him an ultimatum: marry the saddest girl in the world on his 18th birthday or lose his vast inheritance. Wally's interested only in playing with his pitiful band "The Dropouts" and in peppy Jillian, with her expertise in national anthems. The veneer of silly 1960s teen life is unexpectedly cracked open with satirical puns and jarring 21st-century incidents, such as the Abu Ghraib torture. Sometimes this parody of contemporary issues works; sometimes it falls flat. The retro design is the winner in this graphic novel. With vibrant panel compositions rendered in bright colors, Hensley's fantastic cartooning is an affectionate and off-beat homage to the aesthetic of Archie and Richie Rich.

Maruca, Brian, and Jim Rugg
Afrodisiac. 2010. Adhouse Books, ISBN 9781935233060, 96p.

No one can defeat Afrodisiac, the world's greatest, baddest antihero pimp. He rules his Wilkesborough with his powers of love and kung-fu fighting, aided by "foxy" buxom white women. Each story provides a new origin for Afrodisiac and a new villain over whom to prevail, including Death, Dracula, and Tricky Dick Nixon (in love with an intergalactic princess!). This hilarious pastiche of 1970s "blaxploitation" films, oddball Marvel characters, and pop culture is packed with jiving dialogue, zany premises, and lots of weird chaos. Plenty of retro action here in both content and art; Rugg often mimics the old grainy printing-process pointillism, the faded palette, and the yellowing pages of 1970s comic books.

Rabagliati, Michel
▶*Paul Has a Summer Job.* 2003. Drawn & Quarterly, ISBN 1896597548, 1v. (unpaged). ☃

After Paul drops out of high school, he is saved from the drudgery of his printing job by an offer to be a counselor at a camp for disadvantaged children. He is scared of being alone in the Northern Canadian forest and doesn't like kids. After achieving a difficult rock climb, Paul gains confidence and learns to open his heart, have fun with the campers, and take responsibility for others. He also experiences the sweetness of first love with his co-counselor, Annie. Award-winning Canadian cartoonist Rabagliati's retro ink drawings express a lot in this beautiful story of a teenager taking his first step into adulthood.

Regnaud, Jean, and Emile Bravo

My Mommy. . . . 2007. Ponent Mon, ISBN 9788496427853, 118p. ☺ Ⓨ Ⓐ

Jean is filled with apprehension when he has to say his name and what his parents "do for a living" on his first day of "big kid's school." He knows what his daddy does, but he doesn't even know *where* his mommy is. Jean's new, older next-door neighbor starts reading secret postcards that are supposedly from his mother, filled with her traveling adventures. French cartoonist Regnaud captures the things little kids do—fighting with a little brother, sneaking TV time, playing marbles—yet there is an undertone of sadness and confusion for Jean as he tries to understand his mother's absence. The innocence and discovery of the hard truths of childhood are beautifully illustrated by Bravo's full, warm palette and simple, evocative drawings.

Seth

It's a Good Life if You Don't Weaken. 1999, 2007. Jonathon Cape, ISBN 0224079182, 196p. Ⓨ Ⓐ

The protagonist, a chain-smoking, old-fashioned malcontent, has difficulty finding satisfaction in the present while he longs for a sentimental fantasy of the good old days. An obsessive collector, he spends years uncovering the story of Kalo, an anonymous 1940s cartoonist, who had a single cartoon published in the revered *New Yorker* magazine. Award-winning Canadian cartoonist Seth's fluid line work and his retro duotone palette are reminiscent of children's-book illustrations and cartoons of the 1940s, completing the romantic, nostalgic feel.

Talk, Talk, Talk: Dishing up the Dialogue

Dialogue is traditionally presented in comics in speech balloons. The size and font can vary for each character or to suggest loudness or tone. If you love witty repartee, dizzying debate, or just plain everyday talk, the graphic novels on this list may satisfy.

Baker, Kyle

Why I Hate Saturn. 1990, 2008. Vertigo Books, ISBN 0930289722, 208p. Ⓨ Ⓐ

Ann, a laidback freelancer for a fashionable New York style magazine, hangs out in bars, drinking scotch and trading sarcastic observations with her chauvinist friend, Ricky. Ann's wacky sister Laura, the alleged "Queen of the Leather Astro-Girls of Saturn," is in danger and comes to live with Ann, creating an odd-couple situation until Laura suddenly disappears. Baker's witty dialogue, all written under the panels rather than in word balloons, offers amusing and sardonic viewpoints on relationship issues, insecurities, and everyday life in the trendy lane.

Bendis, Brian Michael

▶ *Fortune and Glory.* 2000, 2010. Marvel, ISBN 9780785143093, 160p.

Award-winning cartoonist Bendis attempts to break into Hollywood with a screenplay of *Goldfish*, his early, well-received independent graphic novel.

Flabbergasted by the big screen machine, he cycles between joy when things seem to be looking good and despair when plans fall through. Bendis is a master of dialogue, and his copious word balloons careen across the page, perfect for the lively and exasperating interchanges in the series of meetings he has with Hollywood players. Bendis portrays his internal thoughts and his willingness to play the game with great honesty and turns his disappointment into a hilarious account of Tinsel Town talk.

Briggs, Raymond
Ethel & Ernest. 1998. Alfred A. Knopf, ISBN 0375407588, 103p. Ⓨ Ⓐ

Working-class Tory Ethel meets steadfast Labor supporter Ernst, and they fall in love over the course of a week in 1928. They marry, buy a house, and bring up their only child. Ernst has a long career as a milkman, and they live through World War II and grow old, dying within a year of each other in 1971. Briggs's care and detailing shine in both the warm illustrations and the flawless dialogue; the lovers' compliments, the small quarrels, and Ethel's comments on four decades of Ernst reading her the newspaper headlines. This 40-year conversation instills familiarity and affection for British illustrator Briggs's poignant biographical tale of his parents' romance and marriage and of an era of British working-class lives.

Kurtzman, Harvey
The Grasshopper and the Ant. 1960, 2001. Denis Kitchen Publishing, ISBN 09710080, 80p.

Pleasure-loving Grasshopper grooves with Butterfly, beats on his bongos, and waxes eloquent on his carpe-diem philosophy. Hardworking Ant replies with concise reports about how many grains he has gathered while Grasshopper lazes about. This jazzy, vibrant dialogue continues through the changing seasons, each with a different monochromatic color scheme, until the barren winter is upon them. Kurtzman, founder of *Mad* magazine, spins some satire into his beatnik variation on the simple Aesop's fable, where Grasshopper learns the hard way that hard work pays off—that is, if fate is with you. Beautiful brushwork and hopping dialogue, packed with jokes and existential exclamations, offers readers a lot to reflect on in this fun little gem.

Robinson, Alex
Tricked. 2005. Top Shelf Productions, ISBN 1891830732, 349p. ♒ Ⓨ Ⓐ

Ray Beam, a jaded rock star whose career has taken a downturn, finds a muse in cute temp Lily. Caprice replays negative behaviors when she gets involved with a deceitful, married forger. Belligerent IT technician Steve goes off his meds and becomes obsessed with Beam. A teenager runs away to New York in hopes of finding the father she never met. Robinson builds up each character's story separately until they all link in an unexpected confluence of events. This hefty book is text heavy, with natural dialogue moving across the page in harmony with the cartoony images. Robinson's talent dazzles as he visually represents Steve's fall into insanity through word balloons. Dialogue fans will enjoy this fun, conversation-filled read.

Vance, James, and Dan Burr

Kings in Disguise. 1990. W. W. Norton, ISBN 9780393328486, 184p. YA

Freddie Bloch's mother dies, his unemployed alcoholic father disappears, and his older brother goes to jail. Twelve-year-old Freddie is left to fend for himself during the Great Depression. He meets up with kindly Sam, "King of Spain," who teaches him as they hop trains, looking for their next meal. Freddie's eyes are opened by his encounters with the dispossessed and the labor politics of the times; he learns priceless lessons about humanity as he is forced to grow up quickly. This powerful historical read is enhanced by crisp illustrations and realistic, heartfelt dialogue that capture the times and the characters' development with great skill and impact.

Kinetic Cartooning: Animated Artistry

Early animated cartoons are closely tied to comics in shared imagery and storylines. In fact, many of the early silent cartoons were animated comic strips. The influence and love of animation of the first half of the 20th century is apparent in a number of contemporary graphic novels. The following titles follow in the tradition of these classic animated cartoons and comic strips, sharing their visual vocabulary and dynamic nature.

Annable, Graham

Book of Grickle. 2010. Dark Horse Comics, ISBN 9781595824301, 200p.

From commentary on consumerism with dialogue that consists solely of brand names, to a driver so distracted that he doesn't register a body flying off his windshield, to a couple of kids throwing rocks at a frog, Annable's stories present horrible moments that become funny or poignant in his talented hands. The content is as simple as the drawings; nearly indistinguishable characters fly across the pages, their string limbs coming out of their t-shirt torsos and their goggle eyes moving with frenetic energy. Annable creates emotional expressions that give his stick figures weight and charm. His animation skills are apparent, his timing, expressions, and wonderful sense of movement drawing the reader into his darkly humorous world.

Chieffet, George, and Stephen DeStefano

Lucky in Love: A Poor Man's History. 2010. Fantagraphics Books, ISBN 9781606993545, 120p.

Lucky Testatuda is 15 in 1942, gifted at fabricating stories that bolster his self-esteem as he darts around Hoboken stealing rationed gas, chasing girls, and watching Westerns. War is looming, and Lucky's dreams of being in the Air Corps fight for space with his rich sexual fantasies. He serves as a mechanic in Hawaii and comes home disillusioned and aimless. The gritty dialogue and Lucky's realistic escapades add to a period piece's frank look at immigrant and wartime experience. DeStefano's classic cartooning is incredible; he captures the feel of 1940s Little Italy and renders the fairly unlikable protagonist with sympathy and humor. Every panel is an absolute delight and brims with homages to Golden-Age cartoonists and beyond.

Deitch, Kim, and Simon Deitch

▶ *Boulevard of Broken Dreams*. 2002. Pantheon Books, ISBN 0375421912, 160p. ⓨⒶ

Early animator Ted Mishkin is hounded by his own devilish creation, Waldo the Cat, to drink and insanity. Ted made a name for himself at the 1930s Fontaine Studios with his dark Waldo character. As Disney's sentimental animation gains popularity, the studio needs to reinvent the free-wheeling Waldo into a cute sidekick for a flying rat. Love affairs, tragedies, and the interaction between Ted and his manager brother, Al, add to this portrayal of the brilliance and madness of creativity. Deitch's style is dark, and shadows and dark lines portray the debauchery and lost dreams of his characters and their industry. Yet their fantasies and animated creations burst out of the pages with energy, breaking through panels, bringing inanimate objects to life, and taking the reader on a dizzying ride through this fictionalized animation history.

Holcombe, Walt

Things Just Get Away from You. 2007. Fantagraphics Books, ISBN 1560978430, 209p.

A cigar-smoking, wise-cracking King of Persia falls in love with a commoner when he overhears her talking with the birds at the town well. When she falls ill, he and his faithful friend and camel, Jamila, leave on a quest for a mythical emerald that will cure her. But love is not what it seems to be in this Eisner Award–winning novella, a theme that Halcolme returns to in many of the stories collected in this wonderful book. Halcolme's skilled black-and-white art is complex and fluid, and the activity of the characters and the settings nearly burst out of the panels, creating a cartoon dynamism that packs a punch. The humorous and whimsical liveliness of Halcolme's cartooning is an effective balance for the emotional content of thwarted love, fears, and sadness.

Millionaire, Tony

Billy Hazelnuts. 2005. Fantagraphics Books, ISBN 1560977019, 109p. ⓨⒶ

The mice on Rumperton Farm decide to fight the old lady and her cat with a golem crafted from garbage pickings and a skull full of flies. This feisty creature attacks the cat with a meat grinder but is wounded. Child astronomer Becky comes to his rescue, naming him Billy, applying sweet salves, and giving him hazelnuts eyes. When Billy runs off to find the moon as it slips over the horizon, Becky follows. Fantastical adventures commence, including a battle with a flying pirate ship captained by an alligator robot and a celestial excursion through a planetary graveyard. Millionaire's dynamic, old-fashioned illustrations animate both the characters and the landscapes with a bursting energy in this strange fusion of gruesome and endearing escapades.

Neely, Tom
> *The Blot.* 2007. I Will Destroy You, ISBN 9780974271583, 180p. ☑Ⓐ
>> The protagonist of this story, an unnamed Everyman, wakes up one Tuesday to his normal daily routine. Carefree and whistling, he opens his daily paper to find an ink blot spreading on the page. His confusion increases and turns into downright fear as this amorphous blot spreads into parts of the neighborhood, occasionally eclipsing him in total darkness or bubbling out of his mouth. Each segment of this story represents his grappling with the existence of the blot, from his attempts to hide from it to his learning to embrace it through a woman he falls in love with. Neely's lyrical, lively style, reminiscent of the Popeye stories, has a jaunty bounce that contrasts beautifully with the uncontrollable dark elements of the pervasive ink blot in this existential allegory.

Stearn, Ted
> *Fuzz & Pluck: Splitsville.* 2008. Fantagraphics Books, ISBN 9781560979760, 240p.
>> Fuzz, a downtrodden, insecure teddy bear, and his friend, Pluck, a defeathered, hot-tempered chicken, work as busboys at a fast-food diner. Pluck gets fired after fighting customers and becomes a gladiator, fighting talking animals and a sour, mutant half of a grapefruit. Fuzz gets chewed up by a dog while delivering a sandwich and is added to a little girl's collection of squabbling toys until he escapes. Scenes of furious fighting come off as silly humor, just as in the old funny-animal cartoons that they recall. Stearn enlivens his totally dissimilar characters through expression, movement, and sassy dialogue as they stumble through their nutty exploits with their guardian angels watching over them until they are reunited again.

Page-Turning Panels: Suspenseful Reads

Pacing in graphic novels is established through compelling plot and in establishing time visually. Readers who relish the anticipation that comes with building suspense may enjoy these graphic novels.

Brubaker, Ed, and Sean Phillips
> ▶ *Sleeper: Season One.* 2009. Wildstorm, ISBN 9781401223601, 286p.
>> Superhero/spy Holden Craver is working undercover in a terrorist organization. When his handler is shot, no one is left to vouch for him, leaving him in limbo. Carver needs to rationalize the murders he commits while trying to stay alive in a world of colorful evil-doers. This dilemma offers Brubaker great material for both a considered character study and a highly suspenseful cat-and-mouse thriller.

Delano, Jamie, and Jock
> *Hellblazer: Pandemonium.* 2010. Vertigo Comics, ISBN 9781401220358, 126p.
>> John Constantine is back! The hard-smoking, cussing occult detective is framed for planting a bomb in the British Museum by an alluring Muslim

woman. The Secret Service lets him off to investigate an Iraqi POW with supernatural powers who is torturing U.S. soldiers. The famed supernatural enforcer heads to warring Iraq with the woman to ferret out and find the demonic god that controls this spirit, dodging war zones and using his wit to overcome the spirits. Delano rips a suspenseful thriller, and Jock's atmospheric art blends the human and spirit world to great effect.

Ellis, Warren, Bryan Hitch, Paul Nearry, and Laura Depuy
Relentless, The Authority, Vol. 1. 2000. Wildstorm, ISBN 1563896613, 192p. ☷
Terrorist Kaizen Gamorra believes that superhero team Stormwatch has been obliterated, leaving him free to use his troops of superhuman killers to take over the world. After destroying Moscow, he finds his plans thwarted in New York when superhero leader Jenny Sparks, the Spirit of the 20th Century, brings Stormwatch out of hiding to save the world. Award-winning cartoonist Ellis creates a three-dimensional community of characters whose powers and actions explode off the page. The art is amazing, zooming in for character close-ups and moving out for spectacular, action-packed battles and explosions, providing the reader with the satisfaction of watching a heart-pumping action flick that takes the moral high road.

Johnson, Mat, and Warren Pleece
Incognegro. 2008. Vertigo, ISBN 140121097X, 136p. ☷
Harlem journalist Zane Pinchback is so light skinned he can pass as white. Pinchback makes use of this to travel undercover in the South to report on lynchings and racially motivated incidents under the pen name Incognegro. When his dark-skinned brother is accused of killing his white girlfriend, Pinchback goes deep into Mississippi to investigate and to uncover the real killer before his brother is violently murdered. Award-winning cartoonist Johnson's well-plotted twists are in themselves gripping enough for the mystery to stand on its own. On top of this, the reader vicariously experiences the tension of Pinchback's racial exposure and the ongoing state of fear that blacks in the 1930s South lived in, resulting in an absorbing, provocative read.

Kieth, Sam
Four Women. 2002. Homage Comics, ISBN 1563899108,1v. (unpaged).
Four friends of varying ages are on a car trip to a wedding. Their car breaks down in the middle of the night on an remote country road. Two men stop and try to get into the locked car, banging on it and smashing it by driving their truck over it. One of the women gets pulled halfway out, and another takes control of the power locks and sacrifices herself to save her friends. The reader experiences the assault from within the car, leaving a sense of horror and questions about what he or she would do in the same situation. In this chilling page-turner about cruelty, vulnerability, survival, and forgiveness, Kieth has crafted a compelling version of every woman's worst nightmare.

Lapham, David
Innocence of Nihilism, <u>Stray Bullets</u>. 2005. El Capitan, ISBN 0972714561, 232p. Ⓨ Ⓐ

Two low-level thugs are stopped by the police while disposing of a corpse, starting a senseless killing spree. A girl is traumatized when she witnesses a brutal double murder, setting her up for a life of troubles. A naïve, college-bound boy and an older woman who lives with criminals are thrown together. Lapham's interweaving stories introduce characters that intersect in unexpected ways as they muddle through dysfunctional family life, child abuse, thefts, and murders. The psychological truths of the characters, experienced through their dialogue, thoughts, and expressions, make them easy to identify with and create a unique high-tension read.

Rucka, Greg
Whiteout. 2007. Oni Press, ISBN 9781932664706, 126p. ☻

U.S. Marshall Carrie Stetko longs for the isolation that her post in Antarctica has granted her. Things get complicated when a body turns up, and then two more, followed by more in various camps around the continent. After an attempt on her life, Stetko unravels a plot to smuggle gold out of the continent, and, in doing so, she experiences an internal transformation of her own. The rhythm of the drawings support this tightly paced and well-written mystery with a mood all its own.

Straczynski, J. Michael, and Gary Frank
Midnight Nation. 2004. Top Cow Productions/Image Comics, ISBN 1582404607, 304p. ☻

LAPD Lieutenant David Grey, lonely and cynical after his wife leaves him, has his soul stolen by the "The Walkers," psychedelic zombie-like creatures of the night. He is suspended in "the in-between," a parallel world where all the invisible people—the lost and lonely who have fallen through the cracks—exist. A beautiful, enigmatic spirit, Laurel, takes him on a year-long walk across the country to New York in an attempt to either retrieve his soul or become one of the zombies. The reader is drawn into the thought-provoking, compassionate intrigue, eager to find out who wins the age-old battle between good and evil, between hope and despair.

Tezuka, Osamu
MW. 1976, 2007. Vertical, ISBN 1932234837, 582p.

Under Michio Yuki's good-looking, charming, successful mask lives a sociopathic torturer and murderer. After committing his brutal crimes, he confesses to a friend and sometime lover, Father Garai. They are bonded for life as the sole survivors of a military poison gas leak, MW, which Yuki breathed in, destroying his conscience. Tezuka's exploration of the complexities of good and evil embraces many topics, including societal fears of chemical/nuclear weapons, crooked politics, and the Church. Yuki's horrifying, amoral crimes are steps in his attempts to uncover the governmental cover-up of the gas leak and to locate the deadly MW. The story builds a tension that keeps readers turning the pages of this dark, compelling manga.

Urasawa, Naoki
Monster. 2006. Viz Media, ISBN 9781591166412, 216p. ☿ Ⓨ Ⓐ
　　A brilliant brain surgeon, Dr. Kenzo Tenma, leaves Japan to work in a German hospital. While trying to find a balance between being a "player" in the hospital business and saving lives, he decides to operate on a young boy whose parents have been killed rather than on the city's illustrious mayor. Despite a demotion, Dr. Tenma is pleased with his choice, but, years, later he is shocked to find out that he has created a murderous monster. This 18-volume series is a dark and compelling thriller whose many plot twists deal with moral quandaries that create a strong undertow of suspense.

Moving on from Classics Illustrated: Graphic Adaptations for Grown-Ups

Classics Illustrated comic book series (1941–1971) published adaptations of literary classics with the goal of making challenging stories, from *Moby Dick* to the *Iliad*, accessible to young people. Now that graphic novels have achieved a level of artistry and sophistication that was unimaginable at that time, cartoonists have been adapting books that go beyond the dumbed-down visual mediocrity of their predecessors. In fact, many best-selling fiction authors, including Dean Koontz and Janet Evanovich, have written stories for graphic-novel treatment in an attempt at cross-pollination, exposing their fans to graphic novels. This list collects outstanding graphic adaptations that complement or enlarge on their source material.

Aguirre-Sacasa, Roberto, and Mike Perkins
Captain Trips, Stephen King's The Stand, **Vol. 1.** 2009. Marvel, ISBN 9780785142720, 160p.
　　A security guard starts the spread of a highly contagious virus across the country when he runs from the deaths of his co-workers at a special government lab. The deadly mutation of the common flu virus was developed as a top-secret weapon, and the military is doing everything it can to keep the public from finding out, killing reporters, quarantining towns, and dumping truckloads of corpses in the ocean. Based on Stephen King's best-selling novel, this adaptation is true to the original, a considered visual retelling that captures the warning about humanity's vulnerability to biological warfare pathogens.

Auster, Paul, Paul Karasik, and David Mazzucchelli
City of Glass. 1994, 2004. Picador, ISBN 0312423608, 138p. ☿
　　Isolated, grieving mystery writer Daniel Quinn feels his identity slipping when he gets late-night calls looking for a detective named Paul Auster. He

pretends to be Auster and is hired to protect Peter Stillman from his abusive father, who is getting released from jail. Quinn becomes obsessed with the elder Stillman's eccentric wanderings through the streets of New York, leading him down a dark path. Karasik and Mazzucchelli adapt Auster's metafictional and verbal games into a visual format, capturing the fluctuating rhythms and dense prose through clever and iconographic images. *City of Glass* is a stellar example of how a graphic adaptation can, as Art Spiegelman comments in his introduction, "create a strange doppelganger of the original book."

Cooke, Darwyn
Richard Stark's Parker: The Hunter. 2009. IDW Publishing, ISBN 1600104932, 140p. Y A

Cooke's adaptation of Richard Stark's (Donald Westlake) tale of a cold-hearted antihero begins with a 20-page wordless sequence showing Parker slashing through Manhattan traffic to seek vengeance on his former double-crossing partners and the wife who left him for dead. His face is not shown in this sequence, making it all the more revealing when we see the rage and cruelty that have been hinted at in his angry body language, his rude interactions, and the rugged, steely-blue inking. Cooke's stellar visual storytelling and his ability to build mood perfectly complement Stark's hard-edged prose. Parker is fully realized here as the immoral predator who will do whatever it takes to get what he sees as his, keeping the reader both repelled and enthralled, just as the prose original did.

Crumb, Robert
Book of Genesis. 2009. W.W. Norton, ISBN 9780393060124, 1v. (unpaged). ☉ Y A

From Adam and Eve's playful romp in the Garden of Eden to Joseph's fear when thrown into a pit by his brothers, the biblical stories offer Crumb myriad opportunities to portray emotions that he excels in: lust, wrath, and desperation. Crumb's masculine, glowering God, with flowing robes nearly concealed by his rolling mane and beard, follows in the footsteps of classical depictions of the punitive Old Testament patriarch. Based primarily on Robert Alter's accomplished translation and the King James version of the Bible, this retelling of Genesis includes the violence and the carnality in a faithful, mature illustration of Genesis sans Crumb's signature shock-and-mock style.

Hamilton, Jim
Ray Bradbury's Fahrenheit 451. 2009. Hill and Wang, ISBN 9780809051014, 149p. ☉

Guy Montag is an enthusiastic career fireman in an oppressive world where firemen start fires to burn books. The knowledge and thought that books represent are outlawed, replaced by numbing pills and entertainment walls playing dumbed-down programs whose actors become the viewer's "family." Montag begins questioning his happiness when his wife overdoses, and he strikes up a friendship with a teenager who is fully alive and questioning. In this well-crafted adaptation, Hamilton's visual interpretations of the raging fires consuming books and their readers, the deadened, fun-seeking characters, and the (frighteningly familiar) huge, omnipresent screens reinforce Bradbury's 1953 message, instilling dread in the hearts of book-loving readers.

Keller, Michael, and Nicolle Rager Fuller
Charles Darwin's On the Origin of the Species. 2009. Rodale Books, ISBN 9781605299488, 192p. Nonfiction. ☿

Illuminated by Rager Fuller's sumptuous and informative illustrations, Keller clearly presents Darwin's theories on the laws of variation and natural selection. This adaptation is enriched with biographical information relayed through conversations between Darwin and his circle upon his return from the Galapagos Islands. Related discoveries, including Mendel's genetics, continental drift theories, and the discovery of DNA, and the human genome are discussed, as is the fiery debate about creationism and evolution. At the end, Darwin wonders at the beauty and elegance of life on this planet, a sentiment that the authors clearly communicate in this stunning and accessible adaptation.

Panter, Gary
Jimbo in Purgatory. 2004. Fantagraphics Books, ISBN 1560975725, 33p. ⓨⒶ

In this "mis-recounting" of the second book of Dante's *Divine Comedy*, Panter's punk character, Jimbo, wanders through a high-tech afterlife, encountering pop-culture icons including John Lennon, Yul Brynner, and Bruce Lee. Each person, robot, or creature that Jimbo meets stands in for a part of Dante's journey. The narrative is driven by quotations from a dazzling array of sources in a nod to Dante's referencing of the classics and his literary and social peers. Panter grows the chain of influence with quotations taken from writers from Boccaccio to Raymond Chandler and from sources from limericks to rock lyrics. An exceptional visual achievement, each complete page is a cohesive whole reminiscent of an illuminated manuscript and represents a canto from *Purgatorio*. This adaptation is dense and dazzling in the diverse ways it illuminates, echoes, builds on and renews Dante's epic poem.

Big Bang for Your Buck: Memorable Novellas

Longer than a short story but shorter than a novel, great novellas require special skill. The following short graphic novellas make an impact with their ability to evoke emotion and to build meaningful themes in a minimum of pages.

Baru and Jean-Marc Thevenet
Road to America. 1990, 2002. Drawn & Quarterly, ISBN 1896597521, 45p. ⓨⒶ

When Said Boudiaf is discovered by boxing promoters, he is committed to avoiding the politics of Algeria's lengthy and bloody mid-20th-century uprising against French colonial rule. He leaves his small, lower-class Algerian village and his revolutionary brother to fight in France. There he is the butt of racism, even when he becomes a European champion. Said just wants to box, but both the French and the Algerians want his allegiance and use him as a propaganda tool. The interesting blend of a historical and a sports story and the beautiful illustrations in rich colors, with their detailed sense of time and place, make this novella an absorbing quick read.

Breutzman, Nicholas, Shaun Feltz, and Raighne Hogan
Yearbooks. 2009. 2D CLOUD, ISBN 9780578019833. 44p. ⚥

Awakening from a nightmare in which a teacher turns into a bat to avoid the honesty in her students' drawings of what a sad day looks like, Ryan readies himself for another day of being bullied at high school. His only friends are Michelle and his mentor, Mr. Feltz. Mr. Feltz boasts of his drawings of junkies and abortion clinics, but, when he finally sees them, Ryan is disturbed by the unemotional, coarse drawings. His respect is further destroyed when Ryan witnesses something he wishes he hadn't seen. The merging of the haunting storyline, the off-kilter artwork, and the fluorescent coloring evokes the messy feelings of high school and innocence lost.

Briggs, Raymond
▶ *When the Wind Blows.* 1982. Penguin Books, ISBN 9780140094199, 48p. ⚥

Jim and Hilda, a retired blue-collar couple, cheerily prepare their emergency supplies for a reported nuclear attack on England by the Soviet Union. Trusting in the "powers that be" to look after them, they try to make sense of the cold war, able to see it only through the lens of World War II. The sweetness in their relationship, the simple, straightforward illustrations, and the humor alleviate some of the sinking feeling that the reader begins to have after the shock of the blinding flash of the falling bomb.

Crane, Jordan
The Last Lonely Saturday. 2000. Fantagraphics Books, ISBN 1560977434, 1v. (unpaged). ⚥

This perfect, wordless "picto-novella" tells the sweet story of an elderly widower preparing for his regular Saturday trip to the cemetery. He writes his daily letter to his wife, which he adds to his weekly pile, and picks out flowers to bring to the graveside of his beloved Elenore. Crane's amazing design-bold colors and minimalist line drawings express so much about love, loss, and death that it's hard to imagine a reader putting this award-nominated novella down with dry eyes.

Santoro, Frank
Storeyville. 1995, 2007. PictureBox, Inc., ISBN 0978972279, 38p.

Will, an out of work drifter in the rough world of 19th-century Pittsburgh, hears that his long-lost friend Rudy, "The Reverend," has been spotted in Montreal. Will heads north on the roofs of train cars in search of Rudy, whom he last saw when they broke out of jail together. Will perseveres through months of bumming around Montreal and finds an unexpected answer to his search when he finds "The Reverend." This experimental comic about true friendship contains 15 three-toned panels on each oversized page in which Santoro sketches people, towns, and landscapes in a wonderful, free-wheeling style that reflects the content of the tale.

Sturm, James
Market Day. 2010. Drawn & Quarterly, ISBN 9781897299975, 96p. Ⓨ Ⓐ

Mendelman, a moody artisan, leaves his pregnant wife and travels all night from his 19th- century Eastern European shtetl to sell his handmade rugs at the market. Mendelman's foreboding is realized when he finds that his craftsmanship is not valued at the new Emporium (a 19th-century Wal-Mart) and that he must sell the rugs for a fraction of what he earned previously. Sturm skillfully contrasts the hubbub of the market with the slow pace of Mendelman's life and captures the anxieties of an individual at the mercy of historical shifts.

Tomine, Adrian
Scenes from an Impending Marriage. 2011. Drawn & Quarterly, ISBN 1770460349, 56p.

Originally written as a guest favor for Tomine's wedding, this little gem is a keenly observed prenuptial slice of life. Incidents such as an embarrassing meeting with a fired DJ, unpleasant exchanges with employees at possible reception venues, and anxious disagreements between the bride and the groom over who to invite (or not to invite, as the case may be) add up to a charming and familiar portrayal of the shenanigans and pressures of planning a wedding.

Idiosyncratic Idiom: A World of Their Own

The comics medium lends itself to the expression of unique visions. The works on this list transcend stylistic diversity to create singular worlds crafted out of their creator's idiosyncrasies. This personal vocabulary and iconography, while perhaps mined from the creator's unconscious, presents a consistent internal logic that results in self-contained worlds.

Bell, Marc
Shrimpy and Paul and Friends. 2003. Highwater Books, ISBN 0966536371, 1v. (unpaged).

Mischievous Shrimpy loves to provoke his roommate, Paul. Shrimpy's antics include giving birth from his knees to 12 tiny Shrimpys, stealing Paul's brother's nipples and performing a ritual rendition of "Soapin' up the Hawg," and inspiring the insect-like Ib-Ubs to turn Paul's home into a kingdom of

Towers. When things go awry, Paul assembles friends, including octopus Taco, Chi-Man, and Sue the Tooth to help him set things right and to restore peace between the roommates. Bell's art is both lush and cute at the same time, jam-packed with wonderful detail. While the stories are superficially nonsensical, Bell weaves strands of mystical illumination into the silliness and creates tight, engaging narrative in his distinctive, playful world.

Dame Darcy

Dame Darcy's Meatcake. 2010. Fantagraphics Books, ISBN 9781606993460, 200p.

Dame Darcy's beautiful, macabre world is peopled with eccentric characters, including rasping Richard Dirt (a woman), seductress Effluvis (a land-loving mermaid), bickering Hindrance and Perfidia (a two-headed girl), depressed Strega Pez (a witch who communicates through a bloody throat gash), and the token male, Max Wolf (an upright wolf in a tuxedo) These characters, dressed in gorgeous, flowing clothing, exist in a highly detailed Victorian gothic world filled with the sinister and the decadent: bloodshed, obsessions, erotica, dismemberment, ghostly possessions, and death. Bawdiness and whimsy lighten these baroque, gruesome stories, which read like bizarre dreams, steeped in Darcy's own unique aesthetic of gothic romantic horror.

Deitch, Kim

The Search for Smilin' Ed. 2010. Fantagraphics Books, ISBN 9781606993248, 161p.

Deitch begins a frenzied search for Smilin' Ed, a 1950s kids' TV show host, who has allegedly died, although his body has never been found. Every lead turns into a dead end, until his famous creation, Waldo the Cat, the incarnation of devilish id, takes over the quest. Waldo finds a subterranean archive of human pop culture where bearded pygmies use aliens to gather materials. Smilin' Ed is there, doing his wacky show for demons. Dietch's lifelong cast of bizarre characters comes together with his surreal storylines and jam-packed crosshatched illustrations that skew the reader's perspective. Readers may find themselves suspending disbelief as they are swept into this hallucinatory ride where metafiction meets madness.

Marder, Larry

▶*Beanworld: Wahoolazuma!* 2009. Dark Horse Books, ISBN 9781595822406, 272p. ☘

Beanworld revolves around Gran'Ma'Pa, the divine tree of life that provides the single food source that only the gambling Hoi-Polloi can process into Chow. Mr. Spook, the hero of Beanworld, leads the Chow Sol'jer Army on raids underground to the gambling Hoi-Polloi Ring Herd to steal the Chow. On goof-off days, they enjoy frenzied dances to the Boom'r Band's funky music and puzzle over sculptures in the Look-See Show. Marder creates a zany domain based on a complete interdependent food chain, where everybody's survival is contingent on playing out a role. This wonderful, cartoony world is filled with emotion and creativity that draws the reader into its fantasy logic, perhaps prompting a heartfelt shout of wonder with the Boom'r Band's slang exclamation: Wahoolazuma!

Rege Jr., Ron
Skipper Bee-Bye. 2000, 2006. Drawn & Quarterly, ISBN 1896597963, 256p.

An elephant in a classy hat inherits big money but yearns for the love of a cute mouse-girl. She and her brother reside in a treehouse, where they run the family printing business and go to the Lik-Lik club for fun. Strange insect creatures swarm around these characters, bringing them together and separating them through interwoven stories. Rege's simple line drawings create an utterly unique vocabulary that builds a mystifying world where meaning seems apparent on one page and then elusive on the next. Most stories are wordless except for sound effects, with Rege's peculiar, abstracted cartooning shorthand building emotional and visual impact.

Woodring, Frank
Weathercraft. 2010. Fantagraphics Book, ISBN 9781606993408, 100p.

Woodring has been telling hallucinatory, wordless tales of Frank, a clueless anthropomorphic cartoon creature, for more than 20 years. In *Weathercraft*, Frank takes a backseat to the wretched Manhog, part man, part pig, who responds to ongoing torture by the shape-shifting demon Whim. Frank and his crudely shaped pets, Pupshaw and Pushpaw, wander through a bizarre, danger-laden landscape, shooting at everything that moves and helping Manhog in his demeaning travails with a lift or something to eat. Eventually, Manhog is redeemed, but not for long! Wooding's mesmerizing cartoon domain depicts a series of unfathomable events strewn with mystical symbols that have a dark karmic logic all their own.

Tintin Take-Offs: It's All in the Line

The clear-line style was established by Hergé, the Belgian creator of Tintin, in 1930. Dutch cartoonist Joost Swarte coined the French term *ligne claire* in 1977. In Hergé's art, the uniform, strong lines denote movement and emotion. There is no sense of depth; flat expanses of strong color with contrasting tones provide emphasis, rather than shading. Cartoony characters stand out against detailed, realistic backgrounds. Many of the stories are adventures of one sort or another, playing on Tintin's genre. The titles on this list are examples of the work of cartoonists who pay tribute to Hergé and make this elegant style their own.

Burns, Charles
X'd Out. 2010. Pantheon Books, ISBN 9780307379139, 1v. (unpaged).

Doug, an injured high school boy, is addled by painkillers and walking a very thin line between dreams and reality. When awake, he attempts to piece together what happened to his masochistic love interest and to connect with his depressed father. While asleep, he ventures into a surreal, creepy place where alien-like creatures eat maggots from rotting meat and fetuses are found in his eggs. Burns employs a clear-line style in these exploits, endowing Doug's dream counterpart, Nitnit, with a tuft of hair on his bald, bandaged head that is reminiscent of Tintin's cowlick. The length, size, and coloring of this first in a series of Doug's adventures are based on Franco-Belgian-style comics formatting. This one's the most disturbing, inverted homage to Hergé yet.

Giardino, Vittorio
▶ *No Pasaran!* 2000. NBM Publishing, ISBN 978–1561632619, 64p.

In 1938, Max Friedman leaves the comfort of his home in Geneva to return to Civil War–wracked Spain in search of his friend Major Treves, a Republican Loyalist. Treves disappeared when he stopped the murder of a soldier who had abandoned his ammunition-depleted post. Friedman journeys to the front as Franco and his Nazi allies advance and arouses the suspicion of Franco's secret police, Stalinists, Trotskyists, and antifascist forces. Amid the intrigue, Friedman avoids politics in pursuit of finding his friend. Giardino's clear-line style realistically depicts Barcelona's burnt-out streets lined with bullet-pocked art nouveau buildings. His detailed settings and flat colors complement the fully formed characters and historical plot in this excellent adventure.

Little, Jason
Shutterbug Follies. 2002. Doubleday Graphic Novels, ISBN 9780385503464, 153p. ☿ ⓨⒶ

Bee, a budding photographer, enjoys making copies of the racy photos she develops at a one-hour photo processing lab. When a famous crime photographer drops off film containing what appear to be posed photos of murders, Bee becomes suspicious. She starts following him, uncovering his sordid life, oblivious to the potential dangers. Little's clear-line style is graceful. The backgrounds are detailed, the characters cartoony, and the flat, saturated, pop colors are a delight to the eye.

Lutes, Jason
Berlin. 2001. Drawn & Quarterly, ISBN 1896597297, 209p. ⓨⒶ

Art-student Marthe Muller meets socialist journalist Kurt Severing on a train ride to Berlin, which eventually leads to a love affair. Their story is interspersed with the story of a woman who leaves her brutal husband and becomes a communist, a policeman of the Weimer Republic, and followers of the rising Adolf Hitler. These absorbing stories provide a realistic glimpse into life in the short-lived liberal democracy of the Weimar Republic as the Nazis rose to power. Lutes's beautiful art is in the clear-line tradition, and his extremely detailed illustrations of Berlin and his ability to convey mood and emotion with line result in a moving historical novel.

Modan, Rutu
Jamalti and Other Stories. 2008. Drawn & Quarterly, 9781897299548, 174p.

This collection of stories illustrate Modan's understanding of the peculiarity of everyday life and its tragedies. A serial killer puts underwear on the heads of his victims; a nurse who attends to a dying romantic suicide-bomber has doubts about marrying her chauvinist Israeli boyfriend. A father believes an unidentified plane circling his kibbutz is his long-missing soldier son. Modan experiments with her own takes on clear-line, ending with a beautiful example of the style. The characters appear as cartoony cutouts against the softly colored, detailed backgrounds, void of shading. Their emotions and reactions are clearly portrayed in the simple, crisp lines of their expressions, resulting in a mature clear-line style.

Swarte, Joost
Is That All There Is? 2011. Fantagraphics Books, ISBN 9781606995105, 120p.

This retrospective volume collects Swartes's beautifully designed, satirical stories from 1972 to the present. The oddly coiffed Jopo de Pojo, Swarte's alter ego, has adventures tinted by naiveté, as he makes his way through the art and music world. Also included is the robust professor Anton Makassar, waxing eloquent on passing fashion or on how to use Zip-a-Tone screens. Swarte's training as an industrial designer and his love of the clear-line style are evident in his detailed settings, full of elegant objects, architecture, and cars. His magnificent flat coloring, concise line, and caricatured characters work well for his social commentary and ironic humor.

Tardi, Jacques
The Extraordinary Adventures . . . of Adele Blanc-Sec. 2010. Fantagraphics Books, ISBN 9781606993828, 96p.

Adele Blanc-Sec is a daring writer, traveling in 1911 to Paris with a kidnapped woman stashed in a trunk. Her goal is to get hold of a newfangled invention that will help spring an innocent from jail, but she is distracted by intrigue surrounding a live pterodactyl that is menacing the inhabitants of the city. Bumbling policemen, scheming politicians, and maniacal scientists all complicate events that get stranger as the adventures progress. The influence of the clear-line style is evident in Tardi's muted palette and detailed portrayals of a realistic Belle Époque Paris. The odd, cartoony characters, prehistoric monsters, and madcap antics come together to create a fun intriguing take on Tintin's early-20th-century French serial adventures.

Pantomime Comics: Pictures Speak Louder . . .

The earliest known wordless novel, *The Passion of Man* (1918), was produced by artist Frans Masereel in response to the horrors he witnessed in World War

I Europe. Wordless novels are a medium of protest against social injustice and political strife because they tackle issues that leave people at a loss for words. Pictures communicate powerful ideas across language and literacy barriers. Wordless novels can demand extra effort from readers who are accustomed to depending on text, and some of these stories have words in pictures to provide context. The list is organized by date to track the wordless graphic novel's evolution over time. Start with the first, and you're bound to develop your visual competency and fire up your social conscience as you "read" on.

Masereel, Frans
Passionate Journey. 1919, 2007. Dover Publications, ISBN 9780486460185, 176p.

Unfolding like the silent black-and-white films that inspired Masereel, 165 expressive woodcuts tell the story of a man who steps off a train into a world of urban wonders and decay. Over time, this "Everyman" experiences love, difficult working conditions, and the loss of a child. Spiritual undertones swell as the man is transformed by life, reaching a crescendo in a martyred death scene, followed by the suggestion of resurrection. Humanist Frans Masereel, a friend of German expressionists George Grosz and Kathe Kollwitz, is considered a grandfather of the modern graphic novel. While *Passionate Journey* is bound to the cultural times in which it was created, this story of transcendence in an ordinary life will speak (silently) to contemporary readers.

Ward, Lynd
God's Man: A Novel in Woodcuts. 1929, 2004. Dover Publications, ISBN 0486435008, 160p.

Ward's protagonist, a young man in the midst of a crisis of faith, makes a pact with an evil force to sell his God-given artistic talents for fame and fortune. After experiencing the dark side of life, the man repudiates earthly pleasures. Sweeping woodcuts with dramatic perspectives create a sense that the protagonist's dilemmas are larger than life. Moralistic sentiments and stereotypes in this pictorial narrative should be viewed in the context of pre-Depression era America. (*God's Man* was released the same week the stock market crashed.) Ward's view of the woodcut technique as a process of bringing to light what is already there parallels his strength in bringing aspects of humanity that are lurking within the shadows into sharp focus.

Gross, Milt
He Done Her Wrong: The Great American Novel. 1930, 2006. Fantagraphics Books, ISBN 9781560976943, 256p.

If the first titles in this section are starting to sound similar to you, you might enjoy some lighter wordless fare in Milt Gross's 1930 parody of these popular wordless novels. Country boy falls in love with city girl, who is taken away by a dastardly villain. A series of misadventures in a mix of surprising locales ends with boy getting girl back again. While Gross's reference to this as a great American novel is tongue in cheek, his strong period cartooning results in a funny graphic novel that still amuses readers in our day. Gross, a newspaper cartoonist, was famous for his development of a Yiddish-English dialect in comics.

Drooker, Eric

▶ *Flood! A Novel in Pictures.* 1992, 2007. Dark Horse Books, ISBN 1593076762, 1v. (unpaged). ♉ Ⓨ🅐

This striking book contains three thematically connected stories about the consequences of loss and poverty in an uncaring, decaying city. In the title story, a man, slowly losing his identity, walks in a relentless rain storm that takes on biblical proportions. Drooker uses the medium fully to depict his characters' internal disintegration. As the numbers of panels per page multiples progressively, the reader experiences the man's sense of claustrophobia as he fades into anonymity. Despite the dismal ending, the lyricism in Drooker's expressionistic scratchboard art undercuts the pessimism and presents the impression of hope.

Kuper, Peter

The System. 1997. Vertigo, ISBN 1563893223, 103p.

Political cartoonist Peter Kuper thematically follows in the footsteps of his humanist forbear, but diverges enough in treatment to make this a landmark wordless graphic novel. Kuper takes the standard story of urban decay and inequality and adds multiple complicated plotlines played by a cast of characters. Kuper creates a cubist world out of stencils and spray paint that conveys the "system," spewing out corrupt politicians, criminals, and cons, all the while groaning with the sounds of class warfare. If you like a bit of a visual challenge, you may find satisfaction in this unique graphic novel.

Lanier, Chris

Combustion: A Story without Words. 1999. Fantagraphic Books, ISBN 1560973145, 56p.

The protagonist in the book, a soldier, begins to explore the rationale behind the war he is fighting when he witnesses a protester setting himself on fire. *Combustion* depicts one man's moral and spiritual crisis on the battlefield, which eventually leads him to defy his (unknown) country and end up lost behind enemy lines. Lanier's amazing scratchboard art is full of symbols and layered meaning. This is a powerful antiwar story that will resonate with the reader long after the last image.

Ott, Thomas

Cinema Panopticum. 2005. Fantagraphic Books, ISBN 1560976497, 104p.

This wordless novel presents a series of bizarre psychological horror tales within an interesting metafictional silent-film frame. Alone at a carnival, with no money to go on the rides, a gloomy young girl discovers an old-fashioned "Cinema Panopticum" where she can watch silent horror shorts on machines. Reminiscent of EC horror comics, each film is more grotesque than the last, as the protagonists in each fall into Ott's clever and twisted plot traps. The reference to silent movies is echoed in the realistic scratchboard art, which looks like a black-and-white film with all its atmospheric grays. If you like this one, check out other wordless titles by this Swiss master of psychological horror.

Winchluss
  Pinocchio. 2011. Last Gasp, ISBN 9780867197518, 192p. 🆈🅐
      This dark, sumptuous interpretation of Carlo Colodi's children's classic by French cartoonist Winchluss is wildly inventive narratively and artistically. Created by a scientist, Pinocchio is a robotic soldier who, like his wooden puppet predecessor, wanders away from his creator, landing himself in a series of dangerous situations in a warped fantasy fairyland. A depressed Jiminy Cockroach accompanies him on his adventures, Monstro the whale is a contaminated mutated fish, and there is a pulp noir mystery woven throughout. Winchluss seamlessly moves between multiple cartooning styles, using each wordless panel to drive the dramatic tale of a mind-boggling, modern-day Pinocchio.

Visual Variety Shows: Stylistic Smorgasbords

The following graphic novels each contain numerous different visual styles between their covers. If you thrive on variety or admire versatility, these visual tours de force will be feasts for your eyes!

Kupperman, Michael
  Tales Designed to Thrizzle. 2009. Fantagraphics Books, ISBN 9781606991640, 144p.
      Time-traveling investigative team Snake 'n' Bacon go to the past on a bacon-smuggling case in all their animated cartoon glory. Old-timey, optimistic "Cousin Grandpa" solves his daily nonsensical conundrums in beautifully hatched line work. A violent Einstein and Twain duo is straight out of the four-color adventure comics of the 1950s. Two nonfiction pieces show off Kupperman's 1930s woodcut style and his realistic illustration skill. From spoofy comic book covers and mock advertisements to eye-popping endpapers, Kupperman creates a fitting style for each. This colorful campy collection is also funny in diverse ways, containing visual gags, scatological humor, silliness, and the darkly absurd.

Madden, Matt
99 Ways to Tell a Story. 2005. Penguin Books, ISBN 1596090782, 205p. ☋

Playing on Raymond Queneau's "Exercises de Style," which took a basic text and expressed it in 99 different styles, Madden does the same for the sequential art. A man is working at his computer, gets up, and walks out. Another person calls down, asking him what time it is (1:15). He opens the refrigerator and wonders, "What the hell was I looking for, anyway?" This simple narrative is told from various points of view and panel layouts and in varying verbal and textual versions. Madden depicts the scene in superhero, horror, funny animal, and Western genres and various cartooning styles, including those of George Herriman and of underground and current independent comics. This is a fascinating and fun look at the diversity that exists in the comics medium.

McKean, Dave
▶ *Cages.* 1998, 2010. Dark Horse, ISBN 9781595823168, 496p. ⓎⒶ

Artist Leo Sabarsky moves into a new apartment and interacts with other residents of his building, including a philosophical author, a spiritual jazz musician, and a botanist who has a forest growing in her apartment. Mysterious forces are at play as they all struggle with creativity, relationships, and being trapped in their own lives. McKean intertwines the characters' stories with fantasies, metafictions, myths, monologues, divine dialogue, and wordless riffs. The main storyline is expressionistic, using duotone pen-and-ink drawing that veer off into minimalist line drawing, haunting digitally enhanced photography, bright abstract acrylics, avant-garde multimedia collage, and more. British artist McKean's ambitious work is an example of mastery in a remarkable array of styles and techniques and a beautiful union of word and image.

Seagle, Steven T. and Teddy Kristiansen
It's a Bird. . . . 2004. DC Comics, ISBN 1401201091, 124p. ☋ ⓎⒶ

Comics writer Steven responds with angry resistance when his editor offers him the prime assignment of writing Superman comics. Memories surface of his first time reading *Superman* in a hospital waiting room, listening to the adults talk about his grandmother's death from a shameful genetic disease. As this childhood story unravels, Steven goes into an emotional whirlwind as he analyzes a character and a concept he doesn't understand, from Superman's costume to traits such as invulnerability, power, and a secret identity. Steven works through his emotions while deconstructing this beloved icon. Adding another layer of complexity, each of the 21 aspects he explores is beautifully rendered in a different visual style.

Sikoryak, R.
Masterpiece Comics. 2009. Drawn & Quarterly, ISBN 9781897299845, 65p. ⓎⒶ

This wonderful parody on the 1960s *Classics Illustrated Comics* presents Adam and Eve as Dagwood and Blondie, Ziggy as Candide, and Charlie Brown as Kafka's man-turned-cockroach, Gregor. *Wuthering Heights* is rendered in the pulpy 1950s style of EC horror comic books, *Crime and Punishment* offers up Silver Age Superman as Raskolnikov and *The Scarlet Letter* features Little LuLu as the young Pearl. The pairing of cartooning style and classic literature is clever, as is the spoof of old comic books, complete with ads for contests and reader's queries about the stories. Sikoryak is a master at mimicking the styles of cartoonists ranging from the early 20th century's Windsor McKay (Little Nemo) to the late 20th century's Jim Davis (Garfield).

Spiegelman, Art

Breakdowns: Portrait of the Artist as a Young %@&*! 2008. Pantheon Books, ISBN 9780375423956, 87p.

Spiegelman begins this book with a 30-page cartoon memoir of his influences and theories about comic art. The middle of the book is a reprint of the 1977 *Breakdowns*, a large-format anthology of his work from 1972 to 1977. These pieces are highly experimental; Spiegelman is breaking through the panels, playing with time, content, and humor or the lack thereof. He moves with ease between styles, including expressionist woodcuts, gag-cartoon style, avant-garde cubist, pop, psychedelic underground, and early cartoon-strip styles. In the afterword, Spiegelman presents his history working in the medium he so loves, along with the history of the publication of *Breakdowns*.

Talbot, Bryan

Alice in Sunderland. 2007. Dark Horse Books, ISBN 1593076738, 319p.

Award-winning British cartoonist Talbot plays actor, tour guide, and lecturer as he guides the reader on an astounding journey through Sunderland, England's local history and folklore, Lewis Carroll's life, and the history of comics. From these interwoven narratives, Talbot touches on a multiplicity of themes, including myth, art, politics, imagination, interconnectedness, war, and theater. Using multimedia line work, engraving, watercolors, and photography, Talbot creates a baroque collage of styles from Victorian to underground to indie, scattered with homages to Hergé, Hogarth, and McCloud. A true tour de force, this inventive work takes the reader on an entertaining historical and metafictional expedition through the rabbit hole and back again.

Ware, Chris

The Acme Novelty Library. 2005. Pantheon, ISBN 9780375422959, 120p. ⓨⒶ

This gorgeous book is a treasure chest of design delights, including oversized, page-long comic strips, glow-in-the-dark constellations, an Acme photo history, self-assemble dioramas, and pages of faux vintage ads. Many of Ware's characters are represented, including dimwitted Big Tex, lost space robot Rocket Sam, insecure Quimby the Mouse, and middle-aged incarnations of Rusty Brown and Jimmy Corrigan. Ware's art is masterful; he moves from heavily hatched to flat cartooning, from minimalist, iconic shapes to fully detailed panels that use a range of color palettes, including black and white, muted, extremely bright, and duotone. The mood ranges from dark humor, to warm sympathy, to sad alienation, complementing the visual variety and resulting in an astounding work that engages the senses, mind, and emotions over long periods of time.

Mining the Minutiae: Graphic Diarists

Taking a long, honest look at the little things in life and their responses to them, the authors of these graphic memoirs illustrate the minutiae of daily existence. Daily writing provides some diarists with artistic structure, while for others it is a way to capture time as the days flow by. The titles on this list tend to be light fare, numerous slices of life that don't probe too far inside. Readers who enjoy the language of everyday life will find fitting reading material here.

Beaty, Nate
BFF: Brainfag Forever. 2008. Microcosm Publishing, ISBN 9781934620007, 224p. ☿
 Beaty guides the reader through this collection of his mini-comics, *Brain Fag* (which means mentally fatigued). *BFF* distinguishes itself from the legions of indie or DIY (do it yourself) biographical comics by the honest insight that Beaty offers as he journals about romantic relationships, money, and societal pressures. His primary subject matter is the process of finding and believing in his artistic voice. As he develops over time, his minimalist drawings fluctuate from scratchy line to beautiful detailed line work.

Bell, Gabrielle
Lucky. 2006. Drawn & Quarterly, ISBN 189729901X, 111p. Nonfiction. ☿
 Bell chronicles her daily life with honesty and warmth, covering about three months across 2003 and 2004. She covers a lot of ground, relaying her experiences as an artist working minimum-wage jobs and modeling for art classes and her ongoing hunt for a reasonable studio apartment in New York. Dialogue and characterizations of her friends and roommates are delightful, building a strong sense of her interpersonal relationships, while the narration provides insight into her inner struggles. Award-winning Bell's simple line illustrations initially appear to be utilitarian but develop and enrich the text as her stories goes on.

Brown, Jeffrey
Undeleted Scenes. 2010. Top Shelf Productions, ISBN 9781603090582, 350p. Nonfiction.
 This chronological collection of stories is a good place to launch into Jeffrey Brown's poignant and witty world of autobiographical comics. He starts with one-pagers that capture moments of his childhood (fights, superhero fantasies), moving on to his 20s, when his life is defined by his infatuations with various women, and finally coming to an account of becoming a father.

It includes humorous stories such as *Every Girl Is the End of the World for Me*, about a reconnection with an ex-girlfriend. Brown portrays himself as a passive slacker through scratchy, awkward line drawings, a somewhat simple characterization that allows readers to identify with his emotional experiences.

Chiappetta, Joe
Silly Daddy. 2004. Reed Graphica Book, ISBN 1594290199, 256p. Nonfiction. ☝ Ⓨ Ⓐ

Chiappetta began his comics journal at the age of 22, when his daughter, Maria, was born. He writes about being an artist and striving to be a good dad and reveals his shame about a few parental wrongdoings, creating a slice of life that readers can sympathize with from the start. His bohemian, anarchist ways lead to a divorce and feelings of grief over being separated from his daughter on a daily basis. Chiappetta's visits with Maria, his second marriage, the birth of his son, and his conversion to Christianity are explored with both straight and imaginary storytelling as he provides an engaging look at his daily life.

Kochalka, James
American Elf. 2004. Top Shelf Productions, ISBN 189183049. 518p. Nonfiction. ☝ Ⓨ Ⓐ

Kochalka began writing about one incident from each day in 1998 and decided to continue this practice for five years. He portrays himself as an awkward elf, coming to grips with the mysteries of life. This collection transmits the cadence of his daily life: going pee, eating, drawing, rocking out with his band, playing with his cat, and generally observing small details every day. It also takes on bigger pieces: his love for his wife, his sense of isolation, and the experience of having a newborn baby are all portrayed in odd and moving comics.

Pekar, Harvey
American Splendor and More American Splendor: The Life and Times of Harvey Pekar. 1986, 2003. Ballantine Books, ISBN 9780345468307, 320p. Nonfiction. Ⓨ Ⓐ

This collection includes pieces from 1976, when Pekar began writing autobiographical comics, through 1984. Known for writing about his daily life and work as a filing clerk in Cleveland, Ohio, Pekar in this collection mainly focuses on his struggles with getting published, his addiction to collecting jazz records, and his women and money troubles. A variety of cartoonists illustrated this American Book Award winner, which portrays the life of the common man with great honesty and touching detail.

Porcellino, John
▶ *King Cat Classix.* 2007. Drawn & Quarterly, ISBN 9781894937917, 382p. Nonfiction. ☝

This hefty collection of Porcellino's award-winning mini-comics covers daily events in his life from 1989 through1996 focuses on the meaningfulness of small events. From encounters with animals, girlfriends, his family, and friends, to joy in nature and music, Porcellino stands in as an everyman, eliciting the reader's identification with his moving or humorous experiences. This book also tracks the changes in his minimalist line drawings over time: very scratchy and full of emotion in his younger years, moving to a more contemplative line as he matures.

Cutting through Conventions: Experimental Exercises

The following titles are chosen because they give the reader a glimpse into the cartoonists' creative process, from panel layout to coloring. The reader can see the artist pushing some aspect of the format beyond its traditional limits. Pick up one of these titles if you enjoy watching artists playing with their work.

Fawkes, Ray
One Soul. 2011. Oni Press, ISBN 1934964662, 176p.
    Eighteen life stories are told in parallel in this innovative graphic novel. Covering characters spanning human history, from a prehistoric hunter to a punk British drug addict, Fawkes creates a stirring and sympathetic story for each one. Each two-page layout consists of 18 panels, 9 on each page, each dedicated to one of the narratives. This infrastructure allows Fawkes to break through linear time. The reader can read all 18 narratives simultaneously as a multilinear whole or follow each individual story separately by going through the book 18 times. *One Soul* offers a fascinating experimental paradox where, depending on the reader, the parts may be greater than the whole or the whole greater than its parts. Visually, Fawkes masterfully crafts cohesive compositions on each two-page spread, and thematically he creates a sense of a collective universal experience of life.

Mazzucchelli, David
▶*Asterios Polyp.* 2009. Pantheon Books, ISBN 9780307377326, 384p. ♀ ⓎⒶ
    Asterios Polyp is down on his luck, wallowing in videos of life with his ex-wife in an apartment cluttered with unpaid bills and garbage. On his 50th birthday, lightning strikes and his apartment burns down, forcing him to find a new life and confront his past. Flashbacks reveal his past as an eloquent architecture professor, more enamored of his own academic dualistic theories than of his soft, quiet wife, Hana. While Mazzucchelli's palette is limited to the printer's primary colors, these colors represent characters, time periods, emotional states, and even philosophical ideas. For instance, the present-day narrative is colored primarily in yellow, while, in flashbacks, Asterios is portrayed in cyan, which represents intellect, and Hana in magenta, representing emotion. The balance between these colors varies according to the power dy-

namics, character interactions, and the setting. As Asterios evolves into a more three-dimensional character, the two-tone color dichotomies diminish. Maz-zucchelli also uses style, lettering, and panel size symbolically, adding depth and dimension to this clever and inventive graphic novel.

Shaw, Dash
Body World. 2010. Pantheon Books, ISBN 9780307378422, 1v. (unpaged).

Professor Paulie Panther, a shady drug encyclopedia editor and addict, arrives in Boney Borough in 2060 to test a bizarre new plant that is growing near the high school. The mysterious drug has no effect when the user smokes it alone, but when the smoker is in the presence of another person, the two people become one, sharing each other's consciousness, memories, thoughts, and impulses. Teacher Jem Jewel, student Pearl Peach, and her heartbroken ex, Bill-Bob Borg, all smoke the plant with Panther. When depicting the people's altered states, text, bodies, and facial features overlap, colors are layered, and stark black-and-white ink splashes combine, creating a psychedelic brew. Using computer-generated art and his angular cartoony style, Shaw is inventive with color, layout, and format in this quirky, high-concept sci-fi drama.

Trondheim, Lewis
Mister O. 2002, 2004. NBM, ISBN 1561633828, 32p. ☹

Mister O, a circle with stick limbs, dot eyes, and a line mouth, is determined to get over the chasm that is in his path. He tries a new strategy on each of the 30 pages in this book, using bridges, springs, wings, and a catapult and even consuming gassy food for self-propulsion. Each attempt is a spectacular failure as he plunges into the unseen depths below. Award-winning French cartoonist Trondheim breaks each page into 60 postage-stamp panels where the continual drama plays out, each line necessary to depict a large range of actions, ideas, and emotions. Stripped down to the bare essentials, Mister O is minimalist in concept, plot, and execution, eliciting curiosity and laughs from readers of all ages.

Veitch, Rick
Can't Get No. 2006. Vertigo, ISBN 1401210597, 352p.

Manhattan executive Chad Roe's veneer of success crumbles when his company is hit with a lawsuit over the ubiquitous indelible graffiti made by his company's popular "ultra-permanent marker." Chad spirals into a substance-induced bender, during which his entire body is tattooed with his own marker. He wakes up to witness the planes hitting the Twin Towers, a shared catastrophe that connects him to other outcasts as he embarks on a strange road trip. Award-winning cartoonist Veitch sets the pace of this wordless narrative, with a baroque, stream-of-consciousness poem about God, nature, and humanity running below the panels. The parallel visual and prose narratives cycle between dissonance and harmony, resulting in an intriguing experiment in the relationship between text and image.

Yokoyama, Yuichi
Travel. 2008. PictureBox, ISBN 9780981562209, 202p.

Three men board a train together and travel through the city, countryside, and suburbs to arrive at the lakefront. There is no plot beyond this, and no words. Yokoyama masterfully captures the motion as this journey shifts through various perspectives—from looking out of the train to looking in and through the eyes of the three men, their fellow passengers, and the people the train passes. Abstract and heavily patterned artwork and flowing panels break time down into fleeting moments. The reader can speed through Yokoyama's distinct, innovative train trip or linger over mundane moments, such as when raindrops slip down the window or shadows dapple a passenger's face.

Sensory Semantics: Reading beyond the Eyes

Whether you're reading the words or "reading" the pictures, graphic novels are usually a visual experience. The following titles may stimulate reader's sense of touch, taste, sound, or smell, in addition to sight.

Carre, Lille
The Lagoon. 2008. Fantagraphics Books, ISBN 9781560979548, 80p.

Young Zoey hears her grandfather reminiscing about the haunting song of an amphibious creature in the lagoon by her home. After a late-night visit, the creature serenades Zoey's mother, drawing her into the depths of the lagoon, to be followed by her bewildered husband. Zoey seems immune to the creature's power, resulting in an act of revenge that leads the story into darkness. Carre's fluid drawing brings to life the sounds of the woodsy lagoon, winding its way around the characters, intertwined with the rhythms of Zoey's house—a metronome, tapping fingers and whistling. The undertones of sexuality and horror in this peculiar story are lyrically aural, lulling the reader into Carre's strange poetic reality.

Evens, Brecht
▶*The Wrong Place.* 2009, 2010. Drawn & Quarterly, ISBN 9781770460010, 184p. [Y][A]

Robbie has a fun-loving charisma that nobody can resist. When his drab childhood friend Gary has a party, all the energy and conversation revolve around Robbie's hoped-for arrival. Naomi throws her caution to the wind at the Disco Harem, where she falls for noncommittal regular Robbie, only to find her loneliness increased after an evening of passion. Swirling color, densely layered or applied with transparency, and loose, expressive lines draw the reader into a vicarious experience of dancing, having sex, and being packed into crowded city spaces. The pounding disco music and excited crescendos and the awkward quiet of social chatter are "heard" through the magic of Even's gestural rendering and a mixed cocktail of sumptuous, expressive watercolors.

Larson, Hope
Gray Horses. 2006. Oni Press, ISBN 193266436X, 112p. ♀ ⓎⒶ

Noemie travels from France to go to art school in Chicago, where she befriends a local student, Anna, and is silently pursued by a photography student. Larson's graceful black inking creates swirling images, text, and word balloons and contrasts beautifully with the white and peach tones of the organically shaped panels. The reader is swept into the sensory poetry of Noemie's internal perspective as her imagination reveals a series of vivid dreams about a girl's frantic escape on a powerful horse. Larson excels at depicting Noemie's new sensual pleasures, the smell emanating from the bakery across the street, the ringing bell of the ice-cream man, and the feel of the sun and wind on her skin.

Sakabashira, Imiri
The Box Man. 2009. Drawn & Quarterly, ISBN 9781897299, 124p.

A secretive man rides his scooter through a Japanese city with his cat-like companion and a mysterious box. A lizard monster breathes fire on him, primitive masks speak to him in pictographs, and every room he passes is occupied by bizarre creatures torturing school girls for a creepy voyeur. While sound effects are prevalent in manga, this alternative wordless manga brings them to center stage; the sound of the scooter sets the pace, the creaking as the top of the mystery box opens, the rowdy blows of the torturers, and their victims' cries of pain bring an eerie mood to the journey. Sakabashira skillfully overlaps and varies the size of the letters to modulate volume and creates stillness in segments where sound effects are absent.

Tanaka, Veronique (Bryan Talbot)
Metronome. 2008. NBM Comics/Lit, ISBN 156163526X, 68p.

A pianist sits smoking and watching his clock as he looks around the room at reminders of his failed love affair. These objects move the narrative back in time, revealing the story of the lovers' meeting, their moving in together, and their eventual breakup. Each page is divided into 16 panels. On the first page, all panels are of a ticking metronome. The following page displays rows of the metronome interspersed with the ticking of the second hand on a watch, setting the tick-tock pace, which persists throughout the book. The soundtrack brings the reader into the emptiness of the room with the protagonist and creates a sense of the inevitability of change through time.

Wagner, Matt, Amy Reeder, and Marley Zarcone
Extra Sensory, <u>Madame Xanadu</u>. 2011. Vertigo, ISBN 1401231594, 144p.

Immortal Madame Xanadu, a minor DC character, originated in King Arthur's Camelot and, in the 1960s, has set up shop on New York's Lower

East Side, where she advises on all things supernatural. In this volume of this award-winning series, Madame Xanadu encounters characters with unsettling gifts of the senses. An eight-year-old boy's olfactory powers can solve a mystery. A young woman's taste buds tell her where the food has been before it gets to her mouth. An advertising executive hears voices that lure him to violence and carnal temptations. Additional stories about sight, touch, and the sixth sense are each illustrated by a different female artist in a lush array of styles that reflect these unusual sensory experiences.

Imaginings Envisioned: Calvin and Hobbes for Grown-Ups

The brilliance of cartoonist Bill Watterson's portrayal of Calvin's wise cohort, Hobbes, is the result of the visual device of bringing the lion to life only when he and Calvin are alone. When other characters come on the scene, Calvin's internal reality evaporates and Hobbes becomes only a beloved a stuffed animal. The graphic novelists on this list are likewise able to give form to their characters' world of make-believe, visually representing the fantasies that facilitate their comprehension of the distressing circumstances of their lives and the world around them.

B., David
▶ *Epileptic.* 2002, 2005. Pantheon Books, ISBN 0375714685, 368p. Nonfiction.
♻ YA A

French cartoonist David B.'s older brother's severe epilepsy defines his childhood family life. David and his sister are overlooked, while his parents search for a cure, moving from one alternative practitioner to the next: macrobiotic communes, mediums, and magnetic therapists. David copes by depicting his worries and frustration in his artwork and by drawing surreal family histories, complete with fantasy monsters that break through into David's real-life experience. This emotionally honest story is told in beautiful bold black-and-white ink, creating a study of how fantasy can carry a child through demanding times.

Cotter, Joshua W.
Skyscrapers of the Midwest. 2008. Adhouse Books, ISBN 0977030474, 282p.
Y A

The protagonist, a fifth grader, blurs the lines between fantasy and reality as a survival mechanism to cope with bullying at school, harsh punishment at home, and the death of his kind grandmother. A giant version of his favorite robot action figure, Stealth Nova, always arrives with a beacon of light (a lantern) to save him. He is continuously bothered by his younger brother, El Jefe, who has his own imaginary protector, his stuffed animal T-Rex come to life. All the humans have cat-like faces and sometimes become robots, adding another dimension of fantasy to Cotter's potent depiction of the power of imagination in helping children to survive cruel childhood ordeals.

Hornschemeier, Paul

Mother, Come Home. 2009. Fantagraphics, ISBN 1560979739, 128p. ⚉

When young Thomas's mother dies, his father, a Logician, escapes into a world where he is floating, looking for his "hidden" wife. The father's dissociation from reality leads him to neglect Thomas, who has to become the "groundskeeper" of the house, his mother's garden, the forest, and the mother's grave ("hiding place"). Thomas starts losing control, and his only sense of power comes from pretending he is a noble, caped lion while wearing a mask that his mother had given him. Hornschemeier's spare, solemn drawings exquisitely depict the father's and the son's attempt to defy their overwhelming grief and guilt, each in his own make-believe world.

Kelly, Joe, and J. M. Ken Niimura

I Kill Giants. 2009. Image Comics, ISBN (9781607060925), 184p. ⚉

Barbara is falling deeper and deeper into an imaginary world where she is a maiden-knight who has special powers and weapons to kill the monsters who are constantly drawing closer. Her visible rage and strange ways result in her being bullied and feeling totally alienated from her peers. When a Titan appears in the guise of a tornado, Barbara confronts him with great bravery and subsequently exposes her feelings of terror. The swirling illustrations strikingly illustrate the inner world that she has created, where monsters represent the fears caused by a family tragedy.

Matsumoto, Taiyo

Gogo Monster. 2009. Viz Signature, ISBN9781421532097, 455p. ⚉

Yoki is shunned by his classmates because of his fantastical drawing and strange visions. Alone, he slips deeper and deeper into "the other side," where spirits contact him in raindrops and the powerful Super Star rules all. When a new boy befriends Yoki, he finds that his ability to see "the other side" is slipping from him. Set exclusively in his Japanese elementary school, this poignant story spans two years in which Yoki slowly leaves behind the imaginary world that has kept him safe from alienation and his feelings of loneliness.

Small, David

Stitches. 2009. W.W. Norton, ISBN 978039306857, 329p. ⚉

National Book Award Finalist *Stitches* is an infuriating but ultimately redemptive story of a child's endeavor to survive his detached family life, ruled by repression and anger. David's father, a radiologist, gives him numerous X-ray treatments for sinus problems. For three years, David's parents disregard a lump on his neck, which leads to the removal of his thyroid and a vocal cord. Left without a voice, David bears the physical manifestation of the family curse—silence. Caldecott Award–winning children's author Small depicts the fantasy play that helped him find his voice, both literally and symbolically.

Chapter Five

Mood

Mood is one of the hardest appeal elements to define. First, there is the mood of the work itself, which can be a highly subjective variable, depending on the reader's response. In graphic novels, the art, the shading, and the coloring can help determine the mood of the story. Finally, there are also lists that cater to a particular mood of the reader, suggesting, for instance, titles to read when you are in the mood for a laugh or a cry or want to learn something new.

What? Looking for a Laugh from Your Comics?? Funny Funnies

Despite the name, it's difficult to be genuinely funny in the comics medium. With cartoonists who explore the socially unacceptable and terrible truths of modern life, dark humor is more common in graphic novels. Other kinds of humor require a level of craftsmanship that is hard to find, since much humor is dependent on timing, which is uncontrollable when the reader sets the pace. The titles on this list are all funny, although each is humorous in its own way.

Crumb, Robert
The Book of Mr. Natural. 1995. Fantagraphics Books, ISBN 1560971940, 126p.
Is bearded, balding, robed Mr. Natural a wise guru or a charlatan selling sham enlightenment to the hippie "booshwah" San Francisco crowd? Probably both. This collection of stories from 1967 through 1995 about one of Crumb's most beloved characters shows the diminutive holy man as down to earth,

expounding madcap advice such as "the whole universe is completely insane" in return for money or other degenerate favors. Flakey Fount, the stand-in for Everyman and Mr. Natural's most faithful disciple, is continuously frustrated by his guru's putdowns and non sequiturs, but "Natch" pulls him back with the promise of self-honesty and the lure of lustful women. Crumb's raunchy wit and expert, grotesque cartooning satirize New Age spirituality and middle-class suburban life.

Daly, Jim

Red Monkey Double Happiness Book. 2009. Fantagraphics Books, ISBN 9781606991633, 112p. ☷

These oddball Cape Town crime adventures star laid-back Dave, a cartoonist with monkey feet, and his clueless slacker friend, Paul. Dave and Paul are smoking weed and talking about life when they hear strange glunking noises in the apartment above, producing visions of a thousand Russian dwarves assembling for a boot dance on Dave's ceiling. A capybara escapes from a wetlands animal sanctuary. When Dave and Paul go to find him, they are freaked out by glowing green eyes in dried-out patches of the wetlands. South African cartoonist Daly's beautiful, detailed art and stoner dialogue mix transcendental musings, conspiracy theories, and deadpan humor in these hilarious, absurd mysteries.

Fingerman, Bob

▶ *From the Ashes: A Speculative Memoir.* 2010. IDW Publishing, ISBN 9781600106002, 175p.

When Bob and his beloved wife, Michelle, appear to be the sole survivors of a nuclear bomb, they initially revel in the opportunity to spend time together and their new freedom from the electronics that plagued the lives of these overworked New Yorkers. The foodie cannibals, mutants, and zombies ("Reanimated Americans") who cross their paths are tame compared to the right-wing zealots who are using a corporate underground bunker as a baby breeding farm. Fingerman's laugh-out-loud, genre-mixing satire is a wonderful example of how to find humor in an alarming situation while poking fun at the folly of humankind.

Koslowski, Rich

Three Fingers. 2002. Top Shelf Productions, ISBN 1891830317, 134p. Ⓨ🄰

Struggling filmmaker Dizzy Walters sees potential in the charismatic Ricky the Rat. The success of their first animated cartoon catapults Ricky to stardom, allowing him to escape from Toonsville, an oppressed, segregated slum. Other Toons can't equal his success, and rumors fly about "the ritual," a mutilation that mimics one of Ricky's unique features. Ashamed, Ricky turns to boozing, his life crumbling. Told in mockumentary style, this book contains interviews of players done in a cartoony style and "archival" materials on animation history presented in a photorealistic style. An absurd premise, wonderfully executed, Koslowski's story is engaging and laugh-out-loud funny.

Mignola, Mike
Amazing Screw-on Head and Other Curious Objects. 2010. Dark Horse Comics, ISBN 9781595825018,1v. (unpaged). ☻ [Y][A]

In the title story of this collection of droll, odd stories, Abraham Lincoln calls on his secret agent, "Screw-on Head," to investigate the theft of an ancient document on world destruction. Mister Groin helps screw this wacky protagonist onto an appropriate body to foil villainous Emperor Zombie's plans. The five remaining stories are indeed curious, chock full of stodgy old men, hot-air balloons, strange magical objects, snakes, devils, ghosts, Martians, and more. Award-winning cartoonist Mignola's unabashed silliness and amusing quips, combined with his distinctive steampunk-meets-horror style, will keep fan's coming back to reread over and over again.

Nilsen, Anders
Monologues for the Coming Plague. 2006. Fantagraphics Books, ISBN 1560977183, 1v. (unpaged).

A bird and the woman who feeds him converse, two men (one whose head is a scribble) wander around discussing semiotics, and a man talks about his job search with his dog. Nilsen interweaves these existential exchanges with monologues by the characters. His scratchy, minimalist drawing allows his absurdist humor to take front stage, the scribbly head man informing the reader during a monologue how easy it is to make God laugh (he finds everything funny) or wondering whether, if Jesus were to come back and succumb to a life of crime, he would join the Aryan Brotherhood or the Nation of Islam in prison.

Powell, Eric
Nothin' but Misery, <u>The Goon</u>. 2003. Dark Horse Comics, ISBN 1569719985, 160p. ☻ [Y][A]

The Goon, an indestructible brute of a man, is the strong-arm for the missing mob boss, Labrazio, in a shady Depression-era city. Along with his sidekick, Franky, and the Buzzard, an ex-sheriff who feeds off the undead, the Goon fights off a takeover by zombie hordes. He is a shady antihero, a thug who is respected for his enthusiastic protection of the common folk from weird monsters, including talking squids, a hillbilly werewolf, and Santa's child-hungry elves. These zany stories mix slapstick, supernatural horror, and 1930s pulp adventure with offbeat faux advertisements for items such as the Billy Lobotomy Kit ("All heads taken from convicts and soulless heathens!"). With ghoulish humor throughout, *The Goon* is pure laugh-out-loud fun.

Trondheim, Lewis
Harum Scarum, <u>The Spiffy Adventures of McConey</u>. 1997. Fantagraphics Books, ISBN 1560972882, 48p.

A naïve rabbit med student in 1930s Paris is drawn into hilarious, precarious situations after he witnesses a mad scientist turning lizards into monsters. Along for the ride are friends: the canine bumbling Inspector Ruffhaus and a feline gonzo journalist on the lookout for his first big scoop. Government agents, foreign spies, and nasty villains of all varieties are also in pursuit. The wisecracking dialogue is sharp, the situations are wacky, and the pace is thrilling. Award-winning French cartoonist Trondheim communicates humor both verbally and through his atmospheric cartoony drawing in this comical all-ages romp.

Meditative Moments: Contemplative Comics

Some of the titles on this list present pensive protagonists, reflecting on aspects of life. Other titles are meditative in their mood. All share the quality of leaving the reader thoughtful, musing on the profound observations on living they contain.

Dakin, Glenn

Abe: Wrong for All the Right Reasons. 2001. Top Shelf Productions, ISBN 1891830228, 174p.

Dakin's alter ego, Abraham Rat, a bespectacled and big-nosed loafer, continuously finds enjoyment to be the secret to life. Superheroes, fairies, and historical figures make appearances, but these flights of fancy feel grounded in the real world in British cartoonist Dakin's capable hands. The sketchy, energetic line drawings convey Abe's compassion and humor as he contemplates the details, listens to the silence, and digs deep to find the truths in the often absurd situations in which he finds himself. This collection shows Abe maturing through the years, his sense of wonder and the meditative tone leaving the reader with a smile and a desire to look for the wonder in the world.

Estes, Max

Hello, Again. 2005. Top Shelf Productions, ISBN 1891830635, 156p.

William, a young man with heavy bags under his eyes, ruminates on the heavy guilt he carries. He saw his father in flagrante delicto with his babysitter, which led to his parents' divorce. As a prank, he unmoored a boat from the dock, and the drunken sailor aboard was never again seen. Currently he's sleeping with his best friend's fiancée! When his conscience comes to visit in the form of the sailor's ghost, he is forced to reflect on his actions and learns some critical lessons about taking responsibility and letting go of his old baggage.

Kelso, Megan

▶ *Squirrel Mother.* 2006. Fantagraphics Books, ISBN 1560977469, 147p. ∀

Many of the stories in this thought-provoking collection describe coming-of-age moments. As her mother prepares to leave her, a young girl cuts into the dress her mother sewed for her. Another young girl finds magic in dancing the waltz, while her mother takes her own dreamy time-out. A troubled aunt locks her niece out of her house while babysitting for her. Under the simple veneer of Kelso's soft, beautiful drawings, all the stories are teeming with complex subtext: implications, questions, and shifting perspectives. The narrative build slowly, and the revelations in last panels create the desire to immediately re-read the story to reflect on its hidden meanings.

Orff, Joel

Thunderhead Underground Falls. 2007. Alternative Comics, ISBN 1891867881, 1v. (unpaged). ☷

This touching book opens with Ken and Lara, two college kids, on an exhilarating car ride through an open plain on a snowy night. Orff weaves flashbacks to develop the intimacy of their relationship into the story of their parting weekend before Ken leaves for military basic training. Each moment is full, whether it's taking a walk, hanging out with friends, or buying groceries, and the sense of each event's significance is intensified in the face of Ken's departure for war. The contemplative mood results from Ken's knowing that, when he comes back, he will never again experience all life's routine activities and moments in the way that he does now.

Porcellino, John

Thoreau at Walden. 2008. Hyperion, ISBN 1423100386, 99p. Nonfiction. ☷

Porcellino combines quotations from Henry David Thoreau's *Walden* and *Journals* and his essays *Walking* and *Civil Disobedience* to tell the story of Thoreau's two years of subsistence living in a cabin on the uninhabited shore of Walden Pond. Thoreau hoes the earth to grow beans, enjoys the sun on a summer day, and interacts with an owl on a walk. These acts are imbued with simple bliss. Thoreau's observations and ideas are still potent to readers today. Porcellino's minimalist line, the earthy coloring, and the many wordless panels enhance the reader's ability to experience the quiet, slow changes of the seasons and the sounds of nature.

Sacks, Adam

Salmon Doubts. 2004. Alternative Comics, ISBN 1891867717, 1v. (unpaged). ☷

The life cycle of a school of salmon is used to whimsical effect as a meditation on basic questions of identity. Henry is a shy fish whose desire to connect with others leads to contentment with his fate: swimming upstream, spawning, and dying. His best friend, Geoff, is mulling over existential issues. Geoff decides to disregard his innate drives and ventures out alone into the wider world of the ocean beyond. Simple images, full of motion, show the vast size of the school, each fish looking like the next, but the dialogue highlights the individual differences.

Weing, Drew

Set To Sea. 2010. Fantagraphics Books, ISBN 9781606993682, 1v. (unpaged). ☷

A colossal loafer dreams of becoming a famous nautical poet, but his attempts at writing are vapid. One night, he falls asleep on a pier and wakes up a deck hand on a ship. This kidnapping is a blessing in disguise, as he matures through hard work and experience. Readers will treasure each page of We-ing's gorgeously rendered drawings and the deep satisfaction provided by this thoughtful tale.

In the Deep, Dark Shadows: Bleak Noir

Noir, a French term for 1940s crime films, describes both a mood and a type of crime story. Well suited to the comics medium, the graphic-novel noir crime story has seen a resurgence in popularity the. The art is shadowy and the characters are cynical in their bleak urban settings. These noir crime stories are laced with pessimism and an undercurrent of sexuality, and they are heavy on the hard-boiled dialogue and violent plot twists.

Azzarello, Brian, and Victor Santos
Filthy Rich. 2009. Vertigo, ISBN 1401211844, 200p.

Richard "Junk" Junkin is a down-on-his-luck car salesman and former football star whose career was ended by injury and a gambling addiction. His disappointment breeds hostility and repressed rage, boiling under his ladies'-man exterior. When his boss suggests he may be better suited to keeping an eye on his rebellious, socialite daughter, Junk finds himself lusting after her. Her exploits at the ritzy nightclubs she patronizes often get into the tabloids, but, one dark night, one escapade leads to murder, and life gets even shoddier for Junk. Set in 1950s New York, this story is pure noir. The dialogue is pulpy, the plot is convoluted and full of greed, sex, and violence, and the art is murky with shadows.

Benson, Mike, Adam Glass, and Shawn Martinbrough
Luke Cage: Noir. 2010. Marvel Comics, ISBN 9780785139423, 1v. (unpaged). ☪

Urban legend Luke Cage (aka "The Power Man") is back on the streets of 1920s Harlem after 10 years in prison. He is suspicious when Stryker, an old friend who is now a Prohibition mob boss, tells him that his lover is dead. He searches for her while unraveling the back-alley choking of a white, upper-class woman. Cage lives up to his legend as he kills his way to surprising answers related to double-crossing friends, viciousness, and pas-sion. The hard-boiled clichés in the dialogue are balanced by the incredible dark art, depicting Harlem, the violence, and the characters in perfect noir fashion.

Berry, Hannah
Britten and Brulightly. 2009. Metropolitan Books, ISBN 9780805089271, 112 p. ☪

Depressed private-eye Fernandez Britten and his peculiar "partner"/alter ego, Brulightly, a wry, talking teabag (huh?), accept one final case as they try to uncover the foul play behind a supposed suicide. The plot has all the twists and turns of a double-cross mystery with a good dose of hard-boiled talk à la Raymond Chandler. Berry's attractive watercolors of greyish shades of blue and green cloak the story in a moody fog. The perpetual rain, the black-circled eyes in Britten's sculptural face, and the interesting use of perspective all add to the crafting of the heavy noir atmosphere.

Fialkov, Joshua Hale, and Noel Tuazon
▶ *Tumor*. 2010. Archaia, ISBN 9781932386820, 200p.

Has-been L.A. private investigator Frank Armstrong is drinking his sad life away when a mobster offers to pay him dearly to find his daughter. The same day, he is diagnosed with a terminal brain tumor. Armstrong plows ahead, determined to do something good before he dies. His symptoms increase hourly. As he becomes increasingly incoherent, he confuses the past, his wife's murder, and his current case. Fialkov's excellent story, brimming with plot twists, deception, and darkness, plays with themes of memory and of history repeating itself. The stark black inking, with greys indicating flashbacks, captures the increasingly muddled state of Frank's mind as he maneuvers through this complex noir crime story.

Matz and Luc Jacamon
The Killer. 1998, 2003. Archaia Studios Press, ISBN 9781932386448, 128p.

The unnamed protagonist, an educated assassin, is waiting longer than expected on his current stake-out. As he waits, he starts to lose his cool and begins to ruminate, revealing his history, the stress and loneliness of his profession, and his belief in the hostile, predatory nature of humanity. The story takes a turn when he discovers he has been framed, and his first concern becomes to extricate himself from this situation and then to retire. Parisian writer Matz's intriguing look at the breakdown of a hit man is spare and psychological in the vein of classic French noir films and Jacamon's cartoony realism creates fantastic moods with varying color palettes and interesting panel layouts.

Tatsumi, Yoshihiro
Black Blizzard. 1956, 2010. Drawn & Quarterly, ISBN 9781770460126, 128p.

Susumu Yamaji, a down-and-out pianist, believes he killed a man in a drunken stupor. He is bound for jail by train and handcuffed to hardened killer Shinpei Knota, with whom he shares an unknown common past. When an avalanche derails the train, Yamaji is forced to flee with Knota into a furious blizzard in the mountains. The police are in hard pursuit through the freezing wilderness, and the dilemma hangs heavy: which of the prisoners will lose their hand and life in order to truly escape. This noir thriller was revolutionary when published in 1956, the face-paced, cinematic artwork and dynamic perspectives resulting in an electrifying visual experience.

Heartbreakers: When You Need a Good Cry

These stories share a common theme: protagonists who have lost loved ones and their attempts to move on, or not, as the case may be. Emotionally rich and moving, these are titles that will leave few readers with dry eyes.

Girard, Pascal

▶ *Nicolas.* 2008. Drawn & Quarterly, ISBN 9781897299715, 69p. Nonfiction. ☿
    Pascal and his brother are goofing around together, recording a Ghostbuster cassette tape in the "before" scene that opens this tender graphic novel. "After" Nicolas dies, Pascal is initially in denial, later trying to make sense of the death and struggling with his loss. Nicolas's presence is with him (he always carries his picture with him) as he grows up, attends high school, and moves away. Girard's award-nominated vignettes of moments in the long process of accepting a brother's death, craft a story that is much greater and deeper than its parts.

Harkham, Sammy

Poor Sailor. 2003. Gingko Press, ISBN 158423184X, 1v. (unpaged). ☿
    Thomas and Rachel, a devoted couple, are building a house for themselves, alone in the quiet and privacy of the country. Their love feels profound as they go through their daily activities. Thomas's brother visits, bringing enticing tales of his seafaring adventures in hopes of luring him from his contented life out to sea with him. One misfortune after the next visits Thomas, and the imprudence of his decision grows increasingly apparent, ultimately culminating in a heartbreaking tragedy.

Jason

Hey, Wait. . . . 1999, 2001. Fantagraphics Books, ISBN 9781560974635, 1v. (unpaged). ☿ ⓨⒶ
    Bjorn and Jon are best buddies, playing pranks, discovering girls, and dreaming about being comic-book authors when they grow up. When they decide to start a Batman fan club, they choose a secret test to join that proves lethal for Bjorn. Time passes, and Jon lives the life of a guilty survivor, unable to make a meaningful life for himself as his grief and regret eat away at him. Award-winning Norwegian cartoonist Jason's distinctive anthropomorphic dog-headed humans tell a sorrowful tale of a life wasted by guilt and grief.

Pedrosa, Cyril

Three Shadows. 2007. First Second, ISBN 159643239X, 268p. ☿
    "Back then . . . everything was simple and sweet. . . ." Louis and Lise live in the sheltered forest and dote on their dear son, Joachim. The family's freedom and contentment are shattered with the ominous appearance of three shadowy horsemen who linger on the hill above their vale but fade into the mist when approached. When Lise discovers that they have come for Joachim, Louis flees with his son on a dangerous journey across a river to a place where he hopes he can protect Joachim. Pedrosa's beautiful book is a luminous and heartrending expression of the complexities of fear, rage, and grief that a parent feels when confronted with his or her deepest fear.

Torres, Alissa, and Sungyoon Choi

American Widow. 2008. Villard Books, ISBN 9780345500694, 209p. Nonfiction. ☿
    On September 11, 2001, Eddie Torres kissed his pregnant wife and left home for his second day of work in the North Tower of the World Trade Cen-

ter. This story explores a victim's grief, anger, and disorientation when her personal life abruptly intersects with world politics. Torres reveals her pain and the chaos of getting through the maze of aid bureaucracies, coping with single parenthood, and dealing with posttraumatic stress and depression. *American Widow* is a moving love story, a tale of heartbreaking loss, and a deep tribute to one of the lives lost in the tragedies of 9/11.

Winick, Judd
Pedro and Me. 2000. Henry Holt, ISBN 0805089640, 192p. Nonfiction. ⚇

In 1993, Winick joined MTV's show *Real World-San Francisco*, rooming with HIV-positive Pedro Zamora, a sweet and charismatic AIDS educator. Winick overcame his misconceptions and lack of knowledge about the disease, and he and Pedro became fast friends. Pedro accepted that he was compromising his health by participating in the show in order to reach a huge audience in his mission to break down stereotypes and to prevent AIDS. Shortly after appearing on the reality show, at the age of 22, Pedro died, with his many loving friends and family around him. This beautiful graphic novel pays tribute to Zamora's remarkable life and expresses Winick's ongoing gratitude and love for his dear friend.

Family Fun: All-Ages Graphic Novels

Comics are for kids! This is a common refrain of the high-brow in response to adult graphic novels. These titles are geared for the enjoyment of both kids and adults. So curl up with your favorite kids and enjoy an excellent comic book!

Deutsch, Barry
Hereville. 2010. Amulet Books, ISBN 9780810984226, 139p. ⚇ [Y][A]

Mirka Herschberg, "yet another troll-fighting 11-year-old Orthodox Jewish girl," dreams of slaying dragons. Her opportunities to fulfill this dream may seem limited in the contemporary Orthodox community of Hereville. Mirka has to use her smarts and talents when she crosses paths with a witch's talking pig, which sends her on an adventure to find a special sword. Deutsch's art is delightful, his characters are well developed, and he seamlessly combines fantasy and religious life. Readers age 10 and up will be charmed and find a solid role model in Mirka as she follows her hero's quest.

Hergé
▶*Rackham's Treasure,* <u>Adventures of Tintin</u>. 1945, 2002. Mammoth, ISBN 1405206233, 62p.

Children eight and up will love following young traveling reporter Tintin and his cherished dog, Snowy, in search of Captain Haddock's treasure, hidden by pirates long ago. Hard-of-hearing, bumbling Professor Calculus offers Tintin his shark-proof submarine to travel to a Caribbean island and into the bowels of the captain's ancestral home. Blistering barnicles! Thundering typhoons!

Belgian cartoonist Hergé's beautiful clear-line art creates priceless verbal and physical interplay among Tintin, Snowy, the captain, and the professor. The laughter, mysteries, scientific discoveries, and international sites will transport readers young and old into Tintin's high adventures.

Holm, Jennifer, and Matthew Holm

Babymouse: Queen of the World! 2005. Random House, ISBN 0375932231, 92p.

Babymouse, a smart and playful mouse, dreams of being the Queen of her class. To do so, she must ingratiate herself with the most popular girl, Felicia Furrypaws. She finagles an invitation to Felicia's sleepover, only to realize that the popular crowd's idea of a good time doesn't compare to the fun she has eating cupcakes and watching monster movies with her best friend, Wilson the Weasel. The Holmses (a brother-sister team) charmingly portray Babymouse's search for glamour and imaginary adventure, from conquering a squid in her locker to traveling through space in search of the much-desired party invitation. A fun read with a message encouraging pride in one's individuality, this will be enjoyed by kids age five and up.

Hosler, Jay

Clan Apis. 2000. Active Synapse, ISBN 096772550X, 158p. ☃

A goofy honeybee, Melissa, is under the wing of Dvorah, a spinner of wonderful tales about a bee's life cycle. The reader learns about the biology, community life, and ecology of honeybees, as Dvorah teaches Melissa about undergoing her metamorphosis from larva to bee, swarming to create a new hive, pollinating flowers, and making honey. Hosler has a gift for presenting a lot of information embedded in an engaging, sweet story. His simple cartooning creates various characters with distinct personalities in this winner for nature lovers young and old.

Renier, Aaron

Spiral-Bound (Top Secret Summer). 2005. Top Shelf Productions, ISBN 1891830503, 178p. ☃ [Y][A]

Shy elephant Turnip is encouraged to explore her artistic side in a summer sculpture class. Sassy rabbit Ana longs to be an investigative journalist. She hooks up with photographer Emily, a bird, to write for the underground paper about the planned sculpture show at the city pond, where a feared monster has been sighted. Renier creates a world where believable animal characters co-exist and learn lessons through daily life interactions. Drawn in a fun and endearing style, *Spiral-Bound* is an enchanting read for adults and kids age eight and up. If you enjoy this one, be sure to read his current all-ages adventure book, *The Unsinkable Walker Bean.*

Runton, Andy

Owly: The Way Home & The Bittersweet Summer. 2004. Top Shelf Productions, ISBN 1891830627, 157p. [Y][A]

No need for birds and insects to be scared of Owly, a lonely little owl who is a friend to all creatures. In *The Way Home*, he rescues and nurses Wormy back to health after he was swept away from his parents by a thunderstorm. Owly distracts a few nectar-loving hummingbirds who are tempted by Wormy by buying them flowers. They happily live together until summer is over, hoping their new friends will return the next year. These simple, wordless stories will charm kids age six and up and will engage parents also with the sweet warmth of friendship and the need to accept goodbyes and overcome differences.

Sakai, Stan
Yokai, <u>Usagi Yojimbo</u>. 2009. Dark Horse Books, ISBN 9781595823625, 62p.

On a hazy night when the Yokai (monster spirits) are roaming the forests, noble samurai rabbit Usagi slays a few of them to save a girl. Usagi meets an ancient "demon queller," who informs him that it is the Night Parade of a Hundred Demons, where the Yokai rise up and capture a living soul to lead them to world domination. Usagi struggles to overcome his internal fear and battles the mighty Yokai. Brilliantly painted with shimmering watercolors and fully realized characters, Sakai's story will delight readers age nine and up and encourage them to jump into the fun, award-winning series *Usagi Yojimbo* (Bunny Bodyguard).

Smith, Jeff
Bone. 2004. Cartoon Books, ISBN 188896314, 1332p. ᕼ ⓎⒶ

For kids 11 and up, this mammoth volume collects 13 years of Smith's epic, humorous fantasy cartoon. The saga starts when three cousins, bright Fone Bone, trickster Phoney Bone, and comical Smiley Bone, are chased out of Boneville for attempting a con dreamed up by Phoney. The cartoony cousins are scattered in a vast desert, to meet up again for adventures in the Valley, a magical land filled with Rat Creatures, Dragons, Giant Bees, a peasant turned princess, and an old crone, among others. Smith succeeds in his attempt to make his own distinctive cross between *Lord of the Rings* and Donald Duck that transcends conventional fantasy with its humor and appeal to readers from pre-teen through adult.

Spiegelman, Art, and Francoise Mouly (editors)
It was a Dark and Silly Night . . . , <u>Little Lit</u>. 2003. Harper Collins Publishers, ISBN 0060286288, 48p.

Each delightful and humorous short tale begins with "It was a dark and silly night." and then goes off in 13 imaginative directions. Lemony Snicket and Richard Sala depict children's encounters with a mysterious Yeti (whose "silly" stands for "Somewhat Intelligent, Largely Laconic Yeti") who entices them from the warmth of their homes. Neil Gaiman's tale portrays a jello-fight bash in a cemetery that wakes up the hard-partying dead. Kaz presents a child who is convinced he must be adopted because his family is so abnormal. An outgrowth of the avant-garde *Raw* magazine, this collection exposes readers to a variety of comic styles. Children and parents alike will be eager to read and reread their favorites.

Educational Interludes: Visual Learners, Take Notice!

Nonfiction graphic novels provide wonderful reading material for the visual learners among us. One of the wonderful things about comics is the medium's excellence in combining education and entertainment. The following titles provide information on a great variety of subjects and are significant additions to the growing field of graphic nonfiction.

Aoki, Keith, James Boyle, and Jennifer Jenkins
Bound by Law? (Tales from the Public Domain). 2006. Center for the Study of the Public Domain, ISBN 0974155314, 76p. Nonfiction.

> Akiko, a spirited documentarian, is filming a day in the life of New York City when her cell phone's Rocky-themed ringtone chimes. The copyright holders state that it will cost her $10,000 for the right to have the song in her documentary, providing a perfect opening into the complexities of intellectual property law. The reader, together with Akiko, learns concepts and practical applications of "fair use," copyrights, and public domain, with examples of court decisions and works that have been adapted from copyrighted material. This smart example of using comics for a thought-provoking treatment of a messy nonfiction subject offers a fun alternative to hitting the law books.

Barry, Lynda
What It Is. 2008. Drawn & Quarterly, ISBN 9781897299357, 210p. Nonfiction.
☼ ⓎⒶ

> What is an image? What is imagination, experience, memory? Barry asks many questions surrounding creativity and responds with deeply resonating collages that include everything from excerpts of children's schoolwork to wonderful watercolor animals, monsters, and plants. Interspersed with these musings are moving autobiographical comics about her artistic development from childhood to her 30s. The last third of the book is a workbook with exercises and tips to help readers release their creativity from the traps of thinking too much and self-judgment. This wonderful meditation on creativity doubles as a how-to book akin to a visual *Writing Down the Bones: Freeing the Writer Within.*

Beuhl, Paul (editor)
Wobblies!: A Graphic History of the Industrial Workers of the World. 2005. Verso, ISBN 1844675254, 305p. Nonfiction.

> This centennial commemoration of the founding of the Industrial Workers of World brings to life famous figures in the Wobblies labor movement, such as Mother Jones, Joe Hill, and Emma Goldman, along with significant events, strikes, legends, and songs. Cartoonists including Peter Kuper, Spain Rodriguez, and Trina Robbins contribute striking pieces in styles reminiscent of socialist art. An excellent bibliography rounds out this important work. This

is a timely reminder of the conditions that this radical, grass-roots movement was born of and the power of solidarity in fighting rich corporate interests. If you appreciate this, check out editor Beuhl's amazing graphic adaptation of Howard Zinn's *A People's History of the American Empire.*

Fujitaki, Kazuhiro
Manga Guide to Electricity. 2009. No Starch Press, ISBN 9781593271978, 206p. Nonfiction. ⍾

Rereko is failing electricity studies in her advanced home planet, Electopia, and is sent to Earth to learn the fundamentals from an electrical engineer researcher, Hikaru. Starting with the basic theory of how electricity is created, each subsequent section of the book introduces concepts in a clear manner and builds on previous information. Voltage, amperage, current, Ohm's Law, batteries, magnetism, and motors are covered in great detail, with diagrams and text segments to reinforce the material. Examples of how we use electricity daily include flashlights, sensors in MP3 players, and televisions. Check out other manga guides that offer accessible information on topics such as statistics, databases, physics, calculus, and molecular biology.

Gladstone, Brooke, and Josh Neufeld
The Influencing Machine. 2011. W. W. Norton, ISBN 0393077799, 192p. Nonfiction. ⍾

Gladstone, co-host of NPR's *On the Media*, is the cartoon host of this compelling history of the media from ancient Rome's public daily notices, the Acta Diurna, to the press's role in feeding the nation's paranoia during the McCarthy era, to the active role of reporters in creating news during the Watergate scandal. Controversial issues, including self-censorship, political coverage, and war journalism, are explored in full detail, including a meaty analysis of institutional biases. Award-winning graphic journalist Neufeld's smart, detailed images are a perfect visual complement to Gladstone's keen and entertaining deconstruction of the media influencing machine, which suggests how we can be responsible consumers and partners in shaping contemporary media.

Gonick, Larry
Cartoon History of the Universe. 1997. Three Rivers Press, ISBN 0385265204, 368p. Nonfiction. ⍾

Award-winning cartoonist Gonick covers the three billion years from the Big Bang to Alexander the Great in this funny, well-researched history. Silly humor and a swift pace move the reader through the Big Bang, the emergence of cellular life, the dinosaurs, human evolution, and early civilizations, including Israelites, Assyrians, and Egyptians. Gonick is knowledgeable and provides perspectives different from those in conventional textbooks, with a focus on the accomplishments of women and blacks and the viewpoints of commoners and rulers alike. Two volumes follow this one with more informative and fun bits that lead the reader through the Renaissance.

Lay, Carol

The Big Skinny. 2008. Villard Books, ISBN 9780345504043, 195p. Nonfiction.

After a lifelong fight with fat that included yo-yo dieting, diet pills, hypnosis, and comfort eating, cartoonist Carol Lay decided to change her "fattitude" and become a "big loser." She developed commonsense habits such as daily weighing, making fresh-food choices, and exercising daily to maintain her weight loss. The book includes dieter's challenges, advice for getting past stumbling blocks, gymless workouts, calorie charts, and menu plans The graphic-novel treatment of dieting is refreshing and fun, with charming illustrations of mouth-watering, low-calorie foods to inspire the reader. Lay's weight-loss approach is nonjudgmental and is based on making a decision to change and shifting your focus from what you can't have to what you want to have.

McCloud, Scott

Understanding Comics: The Invisible Art. 1994. HarperPerennial, ISBN 006097625X, 216p. Nonfiction. � Ⓨ Ⓐ

McCloud's landmark exploration of comics theory is itself an intellectually provocative and entertaining example of the comics medium. McCloud is an affable visual guide through the history and definition of the medium and its vocabulary and techniques. This wonderful graphic theory of comics supports the vitality of the medium as art and literature. Abstract concepts including icon recognition, "closure" between panels, and perception of time become clear and visible in McCloud's witty and astute panels.

Ottaviani, Jim

▶ *Fallout.* 2001. G.T. Labs, ISBN 0966010639, 239p. Nonfiction. ♝

This well-researched graphic novel looks deeply into the "political science" around the creation of the atomic bomb. The first part covers scientist Leo Szilard's discovery of nuclear chain reaction and the subsequent development of the Manhattan Project. To resolve the conflicting objectives of the military and the government, head physicist Robert Oppenheimer acted as a diplomat. The second part presents the aftermath: Szilard's attempts to curb development of the bomb and the government interrogation of Oppenheimer after he questioned the production of the hydrogen bomb. Award-winning cartoonist Ottaviani explores the dangerous juncture between science and politics in this brilliant cautionary tale that is well illustrated by a group of artists, resulting in an engaging, fascinating read.

Stavans, Ilan, and Lalo Alcaraz

Latino, U.S.A.: A Cartoon History. 2000. Basic Books, ISBN 0465082211, 173p. Nonfiction. ♝

Presented as a theater production with narrators including a skull, a toucan, a maestro (teacher), and the author himself, this graphic novel covers Latino history from Columbus's arrival in 1492 through NAFTA and beloved pop singer Selena's 1990s murder. With an emphasis on Mexicans, Cubans, and Puerto Ricans, the narrators present definitions, famous people, historical periods, and Latino social issues such as racism, bilingualism, and immigration law. Stavans provides a historical perspective different from that presented in standard textbooks on events such as the Battle of the Alamo and the Rough Riders. Alcaraz's fun cartooning integrates well with the content, and an in-depth index helps readers locate a wealth of information.

Violent Rides: Gory Graphics

In the 1950s, EC comics upped the ante for horror with its well-written, lurid, and wildly popular comics. Readers were enthralled with the content, from all varieties of grisly deaths to themes of sexual transgression. Congressional hearings prohibited the comics' bloodbath and all scenes of "depravity, lust, sadism and masochism." Horror comics went out of fashion for a time, but for those readers with a thirst for blood, these titles show that the bloodbath is back with a vengeance. Be warned: graphic horror is, well, graphic. Not for the faint of heart.

Ellis, Warren, and Ben Templesmith
Fell, <u>Feral City</u>. 2007. Image Comics, ISBN 9781582406930, 1v. (unpaged).
> Detective Richard Fell has just been transferred across the bridge to Snowtown, an industrial underbelly plagued with heinous crime and savage attacks by feral dogs. The police department is a joke, ignoring the violence that Fell aims to address. Fell is not above hands-on battle with the criminals, adding to the ongoing gore. Templesmith's moody art exposes the perverse essence of Snowtown in these brutal and sad vignettes.

Ennis, Garth, and Steve Dillon
Gone to Texas, <u>Preacher</u>. 1996, 2009. DC Comics, ISBN 9781410222796, 336p.
Ⓨ Ⓐ
> Preacher Jesse Custer is a dedicated small-town preacher until he is inhabited by Genesis, the offspring of an angel and a demon escaped from the heavens. The angels send a vicious cousin of Death, the Saint of Killers, to capture the preacher, and The Grail, a secret sect that protects Jesus' bloodline, gets in on the action. The Preacher teams up with his ex-lover and a vampire to cross the country in search of God, who has relinquished his job and gone missing. This over-the-top mix of the supernatural, horror, religion, and blood sends the reader on a wild and violent ride.

Gray, Justin, and Jimmy Palmiotti
Face Full of Violence, <u>Jonah Hex</u>. 2006. DC Comics, ISBN 1401210953, 144p.
> Heavily scarred bounty hunter Jonah Hex is back in town, and he's ready to draw the first blood. This coldhearted, tough-as-nails former Confederate soldier rescues a kidnapped boy from fighting rabid dogs, avenges

a brutal rape, punishes the attackers who scalped the members of a wagon train, and faces a town filled with trigger-happy nuns. Rendered in a realistic, dynamic style that keeps the gore flying off the pages and the body count climbing, Hex is resurrected once more in these classic tales of Western vigilante justice.

Mignola, Mike
Seeds of Destruction, **Hellboy**. 1993, 2003. Dark Horse Comics, ISBN 1593070942, 128p. ☢ ⓨⒶ

In 1944, soldiers and psychics have gathered in isolated church ruins where the Nazis are channeling a mysterious occult force in a last-ditch effort to win the war. When the dust fades, there is a hornless red demon boy with a tail and a stone arm. Fifty years later, Hellboy is a sympathetic, strong hulk that works as head agent for the Bureau of Paranormal Research. The malevolent sorcerer that conjured him sends a bizarre monster to kill his adoptive father in order to draw Hellboy into his realm. Other stories in this series have more gore than this origin story, but the violence is always tempered by engaging narrative, Mignola's distinctive dark, rough art, and humor, making it the only series appropriate for teens on this list.

Ōtsuka, Eiji, and Sho-u Tajima
MPD-Psycho, **Vol. 1.** 1997, 2007. Dark Horse Manga, ISBN 159307770X, 181p.

Yousuke Kobayashi, a police detective with a gift for profiling perpetrators, is investigating a serial-murder case in which the female victims are mutilated and their dismembered heads hung from trees over their naked bodies. Kobayashi gets a horrifying package from a psychopath killer who recognizes the detective as one of his own, forcing him into a whirlwind of emotions that end with him killing this man. Kobayashi's multiple-personality disorder is exposed, and he goes to jail but is still used by the crimes unit for his gift for profiling criminals such as a cannibal killer and an architect who grows human flowerpots for landscaping. These grisly plotlines and the stark illustrations of tortured victims are for those who can stomach pure horror.

Ryan, Johnny
Prison Pit. 2010. Fantagraphics Books, ISBN 1606993836), 116p.

A masked alien brute is abruptly dumped from a spaceship into the titular prison pit and left to survive among inmates who are even more repulsive than he is. He moves from one battle to the next, each one upping the ante in the blood-spurting severed-limb department. Ryan's ability to create every more gruesome permutations on the basic sick-brute-fights-sick-brute scene is astonishing. Add on primitive art, juvenile jokes, and furious energy to produce a total gross-out read. For those who like their gore straight, with no plotline, no character development, and no meaning, *Prison Pit* will hit the spot.

Templesmith, Ben
Gentleman Corpse, <u>Wormwood</u>. 2008. IDW Publishing, ISBN 9781600100475, 123p. ౹

> Wormwood is a sentient worm that lives in the eye socket of a demon-hunting corpse with a crazed grin and a pentagram etched into his rotting forehead. Friend of otherworldly deities, Wormwood is in charge of protecting Earth from creatures from other dimensions. With his robot sidekick, a lap dancer, and the ghost of Trotsky, he unravels a series of gory deaths involving people torn open from the inside by tentacled monsters from the dark side. Templesmith's great art takes advantage of color schemes to reflect the action and mood, and his dry humor cuts through the creature killing and machine-gun gore.

Vasquez, Jhonen
Johnny the Homicidal Maniac: Director's Cut. 2009. Slave Labor Graphics, ISBN 0943151163, 168p.

> Johnny gleefully kills those who slight him or just irk him and, sometimes, just "randoms" on the street. Two sentient Pillsbury Doughboys who encourage his sadism and suicidal thoughts live with him in a small house that has decomposing carcasses nailed to the wall, beings in various states of torture, and a monster living behind a wall. In order to keep the monster at bay, Johnny must keep the wall painted with fresh coats of his victim's blood. Johnny also creates a comic book called *Happy Noodle Boy,* frightens Squee, his timid neglected neighbor, questions his bloodthirsty existence, and discovers he is controlled by supernatural forces. Vasquez's energetic Goth art work really shows off the unrestrained bloodbath in this crazy cult revenge fantasy.

An Assortment of Riches: Outstanding Anthologies

Comics anthologies, which collect work that is too short for bound publication or excerpts from larger works, have had a surge in popularity in recent years, with many being edited by well-known cartoonists. Included are pieces by rising cartoonists and short stories or excerpts by established artists. Not included on this list are fabulous one-shot comics anthologies such as *McSweeney's 13* and Yale University Press's *An Anthology of Graphic Fiction, Cartoons and True Stories.* The collections on this list are perfect for when time constraints require a quick read and are also a great way to discover newcomers and rising cartoonists.

Abel, Jessica, Mat Madden, and Neil Gaiman (editors)
▶ *The Best American Comics.* 2010. Houghton Mifflin Harcourt, ISBN 9780547241777, 329p.

> Publisher Houghton Mifflin added comics to The Best American Series in 2005, each year collecting excerpts from graphic novels, comic books,

mini-comics, and comic strips. Series editors Abel and Madden gather possible entries, and their guest editor for the year picks the final entries. Established comic artists are well represented, including Peter Kuper, Ben Katchor, Hernandez Brothers, Bryan Lee O'Malley, and Peter Bagge. Emerging talent includes John Pham, Theo Ellsworth, Lauren Weinstein, and Michael Cho. Selections reflect the guest editor's taste but stay within the independent mainstream's range of styles and storytelling. This series provides meaty forewords by the editors and lists of notable comics that weren't included, resulting in an all-around great anthology that reflects current independent comics.

Buford, Brendan (editor)

Syncopated: An Anthology of Nonfiction Picto-Essays. 2009. Villard Books, ISBN 9780345505293, 151p.

Buford collects 16 nonfiction comic essays, including memoirs, biographical profiles, historical essays, and journalistic pieces. Excellent essays include Nate Powell's portrait of Tulsa's 1921 riots, in which thousands of black residents were killed; Rina Piccolo's piece on the evolution of postcards; and Greg Cook's powerful treatment of direct quotes from FBI interrogations of prisoners at Guantanamo. Biographical highlights include Sarah Glidden's travelogue of a family trip to China to pick up her adopted sister and profiles of psychologist Erik Ericson by Paul Karasik and of jazz musician Boris Rose by editor Buford. Buford self-published issues of Syncopated in "zine" format beginning in 2002. Given the general high quality of this bound publication of new material and the current popularity of graphic nonfiction, readers will hope for a regular publication of these "picto-essays."

Harkham, Sammy (editor)

Kramer's Ergot, Vol. 6. 2006. Buenaventura Press, ISBN 097668487X, 336p.

Kramer's Ergot offers a visual knock-out featuring multipaged short stories and one-pagers. It includes works created by 24 international contributors, from established masters including Gary Panter, John Porcellino, and Ron Rege Jr. to the best in the new generation of comic artists, including Vanessa Davis, Marc Bell, C. F., and Souther Salazar. This volume also contains historical reprintings of comics by Suiho Tagawa and Marc Smeets that fit right in with the contemporary imagery. *Kramer's Ergot*, published periodically, is the cream of the avant-garde in present-day comics anthologies, focusing on comic art specifically. Each volume is beautifully packaged and bursting with aesthetic delights.

Kibuishi, Kazu (editor)

Flight, Vol. 5. 2008. Villard Books, ISBN 9780345505897, 363p.

Volume 5 of this Eisner Award–nominated anthology includes 21 stories by American cartoonists, many of whom are producing web-comics. Highlights include Richard Pose's excellent piece about a passionate sports fan's disillusionment in his sports hero, Sarah Mensinga's understated challenge to religious dogma, and Svetlana Chmakova's take on elementary school bullying. *Flight* is a yearly anthology of indie short stories that has a unique premise: all the comics relate in some way, whether literally or figuratively, to flying, resulting in many thoughtful pieces, with elements of science fiction and fantasy that reflect on the human experience. *Flight* tends to be uneven in quality, but, overall, the beautiful art is its strength, the vivid coloring and diverse styles exposing readers to a new generation of comic artists.

Reynolds, Eric (editor)

Mome, **Vol. 19.** 2010. Fantagraphics Books, ISBN 9781606993491, 1v. (unpaged).

This volume opens with a psychedelic piece, the first in a series by Josh Simmons that focuses on race issues, and includes a story about *Love & Rockets* character Roy by Gilbert Hernandez and a horror tale by Tim Lane. Other highlights are a pornographic Steve Ditko homage by D. J. Bryant and Oliver Schrauwen's gorgeously executed story about a wheelchair-bound man's imaginary life. Published quarterly since 2005, this alternative-comics anthology offers established and emerging artists the chance to reach a wide audience and a platform to hone their crafts in ongoing serialized stories and standalones. Readers who enjoy literary comics where storytelling is a priority will find much to enjoy in this tremendous anthology.

Wilson, Sean Michael (editor)

Ax: Alternative Manga. 2010. Top Shelf Productions, ISBN 9781603090421, 399p.

This excellent collection of stories culled from Japanese *Ax* magazine dazzles with a huge range of subject matter and alternative manga styles. The art ranges from the lush mushroom landscape in "Mushroom City" to the simple line drawings of "Push-Pin Woman" to gothic grotesque in "Six Paths of Wealth" and the photo-realistic inking of "Rooftop Elegy." The subject matter is equally diverse, although it leans toward the subversive. It shuns the escapist manga conventions to show the darker side of life, including sordid sexuality, murder, existential angst, and scatological themes. Contributions on the lighter side include a history of a Japanese motorcycle in "Enrique Dobayashi's Eldorado" and a working man's answer to his midlife crisis in "The Story of Mr. H."

When the Spirit Moves You: Theology Lite

The recent entry of religion into the world of graphic novels present its messages in alternative formats. These are not stories based on religious texts; rather, these titles share a combination of standard narrative (science fiction, westerns, coming-of-age stories) with religious material or light discourses on faith.

Bashi, Parsua

Nylon Road. 2006. St. Martin's Press, ISBN9780312532864, 127p. Nonfiction. ☿

In her 40s, Bashi finally follows in the footsteps of the majority of her family and friends and leaves Iran's Muslim fundamentalism for Switzerland. Living in a capitalist free society, she converses with herself at different ages, sorting through her changing religious beliefs and coming to understand the effects of living under religious absolutism. One of the most difficult things to come to terms with is the daughter she left behind, of whom she lost custody when she filed for divorce from her abusive husband. Bashi's sense of humor and keen eye for details entertain while the story grapples with the intersection between politics and religious observance.

Morse, Scott

Visitations. 2003. Oni Press, ISBN 1929998341, 1v. (unpaged). ☿

A distressed woman seeking solitude in a church confesses to the pastor that she doesn't believe in god. The pastor challenges her when he picks three random newspaper stories covering tragic events and expresses how he sees the hand of God in each. She remains skeptical until the pastor recognizes her role in the final article, which is followed by a lifesaving divine intervention. The sketchy, sepia-toned art adds to the sense of mystery that Scott Morse conjures in his simple meditation on the connection between the divine and everyday life.

Ross, Steve

Marked. 2005. Seabury. ISBN 1596270020, 180p. ☿

In a contemporary occupied city where the rich literally blind themselves to the oppressed with eye masks and demons crawl into innocent people, infesting them with sickness, John the Baptist, a homeless man, is preaching on the radio. While working on a high-rise, a carpenter hears his call, shaves his head, and finds John, who sees that he is "the one" to save the people. This retelling of the *Gospel of Mark* provides a basic storyline of Jesus' teachings and his life, with some radical imagery that speaks to the power of this story.

Rushkoff, Douglas, and Liam Sharp

Akedah, Testament. 2006. Vertigo Comics, ISBN 9781401210632, 128p. ☿

A Big Brother government keeps tabs on all draft-age people through implanted identification tags. Jake doesn't have an implant because he grew up in France, but his father, the scientist who created the tags, is expected to implant a tag in his son. Jake becomes more involved with a revolutionary group, forcing his father to contend with the violent unintended consequences of his life's work. Rushkoff effectively interweaves scenes from the sacrifice of Isaac and the destruction Sodom and Gomorrah into this contemporary dystopian tale. Yahweh, along with the pagan gods Moloch and Astarte, are all vying for power as they watch the events unfold.

Sfar, Joanne
▶ *The Rabbi's Cat.* 2005. Pantheon Books, ISBN 0375422811, 142p. Ⓨ Ⓐ
    In 1930s Algeria, the rabbi's cat, peeved by its constant cawing, eats a parrot, and, lo and behold, he is able to speak! And talk he does, with great impertinence and theological knowledge. The rabbi decides the cat will be a bad influence on his young daughter, and the cat decides to outsmart the rabbi and become a bar mitzvah to win back the pleasures of the girls' petting. French cartoonist Sfar's vibrant line, glorious colors, and rich dialogue embed Jewish literature and lore into this moving family story. The reader gains a picture of a Sephardic Jewish community in transition and of Talmudic debate in a mature, sassy-talking-cat tale.

Sheinkin, Steve
The Adventures of Rabbi Harvey: A Graphic Novel of Jewish Wisdom and Wit.
2006. Jewish Lights Publishing, ISBN 1580233104, 123p. Ⓨ
    Rabbi Harvey is the biggest, wisest justice-wielding rabbi in the fictional frontier town of Elk Spring, Colorado. The townsfolk turn to him to settle disagreements, and he keeps them safe from frontier gangsters, using only his smarts and his wide-ranging knowledge of Talmudic knowledge and Hasidic folktales. The art adds to the absurd humor; the dusty palette and wood-patterned backgrounds evokes a rugged West populated by "old country" Jews—shtetl meets the Wild West. This hilarious, contemporary equivalent of the *Wise Men of Chelm* stories will appeal to both young and old alike.

Tezuka, Osamu
Buddha, Vol. 1. 2003. Vertical, ISBN 1932234438, 400p. Ⓨ Ⓐ
    This volume, the first of 14 in this biography of Buddha, begins with Master Sita sending out a Brahmin emissary to find the next God. The Brahmin finds Tatti, a boisterous boy who is at one with nature, able to possess animals through his sense of oneness with them. These characters become intertwined with the birth of Siddhartha, a child of great powers who will attain a level of enlightenment that will enable him to answer basic questions of faith such as "Why are we alive?" and "Why is there suffering in the world?" Tezuka uses historical fiction in a way that keeps it fun and profound at the same time, producing a thoughtful satisfying contemporary read.

World Views: Graphic Journalism

Graphic journalism has become an increasingly popular method of presenting world events. Some of these titles are first-person accounts, reminiscent of "gonzo journalism," in which everything is filtered through the perception of the cartoonist. Others are straight reportage using the comic-book format. All the titles on this list are excellent examples of how graphic journalism can inform and impact readers about local and world events.

Crowley, Michael, and Dan Goldman

08: A Graphic Diary of the Campaign Trail. 2009. Three Rivers Press, ISBN 9780307405111, 1v. (unpaged). Nonfiction. ♉

Starting with the Democratic takeover of senate in the 2006 midterm elections, this campaign diary follows early rumors of candidates, through caucuses and primaries to Election Day 2008. Crowley, the campaign reporter for *The New Republic*, covers all the candidates, providing background and campaign information, in addition to focusing on the Clinton/Obama battle and the resurgence of McCain's fight with Obama. Important issues of the campaign are covered, often by using a fictional reporter to give humorous commentary. Reportage is supported by the visuals: the text, mostly narration, is reminiscent of headlines, and the black-and-white, photo-referenced illustration lends a sense of the speed and drama of the news.

Kubert, Joe

Fax from Sarajevo. 1996. Dark Horse Comics, ISBN 1569713464, 207p. Nonfiction. ⓎⒶ

Comics publisher Ervin Rustemagic was trapped in his native Sarajevo with his wife and children when Serbian forces and the Yugoslav People's Army barricaded the city and began "ethnic cleansing" in 1992. Rustemagic's faxes to friends worldwide created a lifeline to the outside world in which he detailed his family's survival through 18 months of nightmarish war. Award-winning cartoonist Kubert records frequent bombings during which the family huddled in its basement bathroom, scrambling for food, witnessing children being killed by snipers, and hearing rumors of mass rapes. Kubert's remarkable reporting of one family's struggle tells the story of a once peacefully integrated city that saw tens of thousands of civilians killed as the world stood by.

Lefevre, Didier, and Emmanuel Guibert

The Photographer. 2009. First Second books. ISBN 9781596433755 267p. Nonfiction. ♉ ⓎⒶ

In 1986, photographer Didier Lefèvre was hired to document the experiences of a group of physicians from Doctors without Borders in Afghanistan. Following a cultural immersion course in Pakistan, they began a majestic and dangerous trek with a local arms caravan through Russian-occupied mountain regions to provide medical care in hard-hit remote areas. Lefèvre is pushed to his limits, both physically and mentally, as he learns that survival depends on respect for the rigid mores of the culture in which the doctors and he are travelers. The physicians are incredible, providing a range of medical care under makeshift conditions. This combination of photo documentary and comics is visually stunning. French cartoonist Guibert's raw drawings narrate Lefèvre's story, offering humane and deep insights into a region that is still at war today.

Neufeld, Josh

A.D.: New Orleans after the Deluge. 2009. Pantheon Books, 9780375714887, 193p. Nonfiction. ☻ ⓎⒶ

A.D. opens with a bird's-eye view of New Orleans as Hurricane Katrina sweeps through and the city is flooded. Neufeld masterfully zooms in on seven residents in the days prior to the hurricane and interweaves their day-by-day experiences of the storm, the flood, the diaspora from the devastated city, and the return to rebuild. Denise is packed into the filthy New Orleans Convention Center with other dehydrating "have-nots." Leo and Michelle evacuate and face the trauma of losing everything when they return. Abbas and Darnell ride out the storm in Abbas's family-run grocery store. High school senior Kwame evacuates, becoming a refugee, while his parents rebuild his father's church. Dr. Brobson weathers the storm with friends in his French Quarter home and is instrumental in post-Katrina rescue efforts. Neufeld's stunning bold colors, expressive drawing, and wonderful two-page spreads pull the reader into this multifaceted, award-nominated account of the storm and its aftermath.

Rall, Ted

To Afghanistan and Back. 2002. NBM, ISBN 1561633259, 109p Nonfiction.

Shortly after the 9/11 terrorist attacks, journalist Rall spent time in Afghanistan. This collection of *Village Voice* dispatches, editorial cartoons, a graphic novella, and photographs exposes the myth of precision bombings, the impossibility of defeating the Taliban, and the vested interest of major U.S. corporations in the continuation of the war in the Middle East. Rall also talks about the daily life of a war correspondent and his frustrations at being at the mercy of armed translators and drivers whose allegiances depend on the circumstances of the moment. Rall's simple, chunky drawings communicate the bleakness of Afghan existence, the poverty, and the dual reality of monotony and daily fear.

Sacco, Joe

▶ *Safe Area Gorazde.* 2000. Fantagraphics Books, ISBN 1560973927, 227p. ⓎⒶ

In 1995, shortly after a ceasefire was finally honored by the Serbians, Sacco arrived in Gorazde, a UN-designated safe area that had been surrounded by separatist Serbs and that had been under siege since 1992. Sacco's first of four visits to interview people celebrates their joy at the possibility of a peaceful future and in having their stories heard around the world. Through their personal accounts, along with stories of many others who died, Sacco builds the story of how Gorazde survived the starvation, bombings, mutilations, and mass graves.. The first-person accounts, his self-deprecating tone, and his realistic, detailed drawing portray the hardships and heroism of ordinary people caught in the horror of ethnic cleansing and desperate conditions.

Creeping over the Edge: When Only Disturbing Will Do

If you're seeking something lighthearted or that will make you feel good, you won't find it on this list. If, however, you're looking for a gripping view into a twisted world full of broken and demented souls wandering through lives steeped in disturbing circumstances, these titles are among the best.

Andersson, Max, and Lars Sjunnesson
▶ *Bosnian Flat Dog.* 2006. Fantagraphics Books, ISBN 156097740X, 112p.

While attending a Slovenian alternative-comic convention, Swedish cartoonist Sjunnesson receives a call from an old Slovene roommate who offers him his Kosovo war diary. When they go to pick it up, they are bombarded with ice-cream missiles in engraved shells from Sarajevo, one of which contains the diary. They embark on a frenzied, bizarre road trip, crossing paths with droves of kidnapping veiled widows, zombie ex-soldier prostitutes, the titular flat dogs (run-over but still living), and the refrigerated corpse of Tito. The manic, blocky art is like a hazy dream, fittingly expressing a dark reality loaded with brutality and absurdity, a comical and disturbing reflection of the "traumatized psyche" of the Balkans.

Cilla, Chris
The Heavy Hand. 2010. Sparkplug Comic Books, ISBN 9780979746581, 1v. (unpaged).

Big-time liar Alvin Crabshack leaves his disdaining girlfriends for a job with the eccentric Professor Berigan in Honeypot Caverns. He hitches a ride, during which he learns about the politics of the cavern, where rival research groups are studying bizarre cave creatures. Rejected by the professor, Crabshack continues on his journey, jam-packed with surreal elements and bizarre characters, including abused donkeys, hooded executives, killer pods, and a masked apocalyptic man. Big-nosed cartoony characters and druggy parties, cavern settings in bold black and white, and inky dream-like spreads of swirling story features all converge to form a demented shape-shifting brew where reality and fantasy blur.

Hanks, Fletcher
I Shall Destroy All the Civilized Planets. 2007. Fantagraphics Books, ISBN 9781560978398, 122p. ⊻Ⓐ

This collection of disturbing stories about a crazy superhero by overlooked Golden Age comic artist Fletcher Hanks presents Stardust, a crime-busting scientific marvel who metes out justice with great cruelty. When he thwarts the acquisitive Fifth Column's plans to overthrow the United States, Stardust turns the lesser leaders into icicles and the more powerful ones into rats, chased by a panther into the river. This penance supports his philosophy: "I don't kill, I just leave you somewhere to die in agony." Fletcher plays out all his weird fixations in these peculiar comics: grotesque punishments, plans for global destruction, and astonishing ray powers. The art complements the stories: primitive, with strange perspectives, in a flat, whirlwind of color.

Hine, David

Strange Embrace. 2003. Active Images, ISBN 0974056723, 204p.

Alex Steadman revels in using his clairvoyant powers to evil ends. He probes the mind of his landlord, an isolated, possessed old man, Anthony Corbeau. Corbeau's history is one of torture, sexual suppression, and madness. Anthony becomes obsessed with African art, collecting until it takes over his house, the powerful, subterranean images a pointed contrast to the repressed Victorian times. Alex, seeing the demonic madness that they share, is compelled to destroy the elderly Corbeau, resulting in a shocking ending to this unsettling tale of psychological horror.

Ligotti, Thomas, Stuart Moore, Joe Harris, Colleen Doran, and Ben Templesmith

The Nightmare Factory. 2007. Harper Paperbacks, ISBN 0061243531, 112p. ♻ ⓎⒶ

An anthropologist who goes to a small town to study an obscure midwinter festival is pulled into a dark Saturnalian cult with human sacrifice and men who devolve into worms. A psychologist knows there are higher forces involved when a woman consults him about her alarming dreams within dreams, all focusing on her becoming a mannequin. When the town's defunct sanatorium gets blasted, the souls of all who had been incarcerated there are freed to overtake the town. Writers Moore and Harris and a variety of horror artists craft chilling stories from Ligotti's psychologically twisted material.

Rickheit, Hans

Squirrel Machine. 2009. Fantagraphics Books, ISBN 9781606993019, 192p.

Edmund and William Torpor are entering adolescence in a 19th-century New England town. William plays bizarre instruments that his brother Edmond has created from scavenged animal carcasses. When they unveil their repulsive "Bovine Resonator" at a public concert, the people rise up in disgust at the brothers' aberrant invention. Outcast and badgered by their pornography-painting mother, the brothers discover a seemingly endless parallel world beneath their house where they are free to create their transgressive constructions and explore their relationship and their sexuality. Obscurantist artist Rickheit's meticulous drawings are beautiful, a juxtaposition that makes this enigmatic story even more viscerally disturbing.

Tatsumi, Yoshihiro

The Pushman and Other Stories. 1969, 2005. Drawn & Quarterly, ISBN 1896597858, 202p.

Tatsumi's stories take place in the blue-collar slums of Tokyo, where residents contend with rats, flimsy walls, sexual perversion, and crime. In

Piranha, a factory worker with a nagging lover gets his arm mangled in machinery for the insurance money, which will enable her to open her own brothel. *Sewer* tells of a worker in the sewers, where aborted babies are often found; who knows what to do with the remains when his girlfriend gets pregnant? Tatsumi has a talent for unflinching portrayals of both the realities and the despair of living in the seedy districts of the city.

What's It All About? Chewing on the Big Questions

Each of these titles attempts to answer questions about various aspects of living. Readers in the mood to stretch their minds and delve into aspects of what it means to be human and how we understand the world will find plenty of food for thought in the following stories.

Doxiadis, Apostolos, and Christos H. Papadimitriou
Logicomix: An Epic Search for Truth. 2009. Bloomsbury USA, ISBN 1596914521, 347p. ⓎⒶ
This amazing graphic novel uses three levels of narrative to tell the story of Bertrand Russell's life and the history of philosophical discourse. The book opens with Greek author Doxiadis speaking to the reader about the creative process of creating this book. The next level is Bertrand Russell lecturing about logic as it applies to the question of whether or not the United States should enter into World War II. While Russell is lecturing, his biography and the history of mathematics and logics through the mid-1900s are told through flashbacks. The authors manage to bring these topics to life for the reader through engaging images and by giving Russell's quest emotional context: his desire to manage the chaos of the world by searching for certainty in abstract ideas and the possibility of madness that looms over such an undertaking.

Ellsworth, Theo
Capacity. 2008. Secret Acres, ISBN 9780979960925, 336p.
Theo, the narrator of this charming book, invites the reader to literally join him using an "amazing viewing helmet" in his attempts to capture the stories of all the wooly and wild characters in his exceedingly imaginative mind. His goal is to tell these stories, but he soon becomes overwhelmed by the sheer volume and the mutability of his thoughts. He uses this investigative journey of consciousness as a frame for seven ("magical number") honest short stories that reflect the world within his head. The artwork is mind-blowing, with creatures and contraptions of all kinds in fantastical cities and forests, from dreams and waking life, all representing the age-old endeavor to understand and represent consciousness.

Hornschemeier, Paul
The Three Paradoxes. 2007. Fantagraphics Books, ISBN 9781560976530, 1v. (unpaged).

On a weekend visit to his parents' house, Paul is having trouble creating a cartoon about a boy with a magic pencil who is looking for answers and slaying monsters. On a walk with his father, he stops to take photos of spots where he has flashbacks of hurtful childhood events. Hornschemeier is reminded of Zeno's Paradoxes— the belief in change is misguided, motion is an illusion, and the destination always remains out of reach— which he presents in a comic book within the comic. Hornschemeier uses five different styles for various segments about moments that feel like the Paradoxes. Bound together, they create a thought-provoking reflection on the tricks of memory and the concept and experience of change.

Huizenga, Kevin
Curses. 2006. Drawn & Quarterly, ISBN 1894937864, 145p. Y A

Everyman protagonist Glenn Ganges shares mentally stimulating stories that read like essays. Thematically, they address various types of curses, from lost children to different notions of hell. During a zealous period of studying visions, Ganges himself sees an apparition the memory of which, years later, reverberates when he finds letters detailing a 19th-century case of a reverend's visions. Everyday events result in discourse about missing children, the Sudanese "Lost Boys," and Gange's supernatural quest to pluck an ogre's feather to overcome infertility. The meaning of hell is contemplated through a golf partner, a seminarian who is writing an Evangelist perspective on damnation. Award-winning cartoonist Huizenga's blend of fact and fiction and his wonderful, simple illustrations deliver layers of food for thought and emotional resonance.

Lane, Tim
Abandoned Cars. 2008. Fantagraphics Books, ISBN 9781606993415, 163p.

Lane explores what he calls "the great American mythological drama" in this interconnected collection of graphic stories. He presents the American dream "have-nots" at the intersection of loneliness, frustration, desire, and fear. They get into fights, run away from love, waste their nights in bars, all while looking for meaning in lives that have fallen short of their expectations. Lane tells their stories against the backdrop of American landscapes, pop culture references, including portraits of a young and old Marlon Brando, Elvis Presley, and Jack Kerouac, and the blues. The arresting black-and-white ink drawings, reminiscent of pulpy EC comics, and the literary bent of the text add to the melancholic existential questioning in these haunting tales.

Malkasian, Cathy
▶*Percy Gloom.* 2007. Fantagraphics Books, ISBN 9781560378459, 174p. Y A

Lazy-eyed Percy Gloom has reason to be cautious. The Gloom legacy includes committing suicide at an early age. With the encouragement of his inventor mom, Percy overcomes his fears to venture out for an interview for his dream job at "Safely Now": writing cautionary labels about the hazards of common household objects. When an angry woman sticks her infected toe into his mouth (woe is Percy!), it sends Percy through a strange landscape swirling with singing goats, funnel-wearing cultists, and chanting death-eaters. As Percy gains experience, he is able to let go of his perpetual fears and face loss and death. Malkasian's solid pencil drawings are a unique fusion of the charming and the grotesque that matches this playfully peculiar existential fable.

Putting the Graphic Back in Graphic Novels: "Adult" Comics

So you had to wade through all these lists of adult graphic novels to get to the sexy ones? Reading erotic prose is surely a different experience from seeing it. As with violence and other disturbing images, sex in graphic novels is right before your very eyes. Many cartoonists portray sex in their graphic novels, including Jaime and Gilbert Hernandez, Charles Burn, Garth Ennis, Howard Cruse, Julie Doucet, and Joe Matt. Beyond the mainstream, there is a thriving body of pornographic comics, from the erotic, to the raunchy, to pure smut. So, when you're in the mood, pick up a titillating title, slip into something comfortable, and feast your eyes on this small sampling of erotic graphic novels. Warning: one person's erotica is another's pornography. You may need to search beyond your public library for the titles on this list.

Cooper, Dave
Ripple: A Predilection for Tina. 2003. Fantagraphics Books, ISBN 1560975431, 136p.
Martin DeSerres, a 38-year-old who supports himself drawing mediocre kids' cartoons, gets a grant for a gallery show on "The Eroticism of Homeliness." He hands out cards to women he finds "wonderfully flawed." Tina, a young, fat girl, answers. She is shy at first, but, as she poses in leather and masks, she sees the power she exerts over Martin, encouraging an increasing boldness. Martin is obsessed with the rippling quality of her skin and falls in love with her. Their sex is perverse, not only in its kinkiness but also in the warped dynamic of power and longing that award-winning cartoonist Cooper expertly depicts. The unattractive surface may dull lustful responses, but some will appreciate this emotionally charged amorous story of erotic obsession.

Coovers, Colleen
Small Favors. 2002. Eros Comix, ISBN 1560975199, 128p.
Just looking at the cover of this graphic novel, with the subtitle "Girly Porno" and two retro-looking girls dancing and snuggling, projects a fun vibe. Adorable Annie is sucked into a subterranean world when she uses up her al-

lotment of masturbatory experiences and is presented with a five-inch fairy woman to keep her on the straight and narrow. But the fairy begins seducing Annie from the start, and the sex pretty much never stops. They invite the viewer to enjoy their affectionate and shameless experimentation, which is somewhat fantastical because of the height difference. Coovers enthusiastically crafts girl-on-girl porn that is playful, friendly, and sexy all at the same time.

Emerson, Hunt

Lady Chatterley's Lover! 1986, 2007. Knockabout Comics, ISBN 0861660498, 56p.

British cartoonist Emerson mixes humor into the sex in his graphic adaptation of the once shocking erotic novel by D. H. Lawrence. Constance marries Lord Chatterley shortly before he is wounded in World War I and left paralyzed and impotent. Frustrated by her sexual longings and his desire for an heir, she begins an affair with the lower-class game keeper. Lady Chatterley's sexual awakening is depicted through visual symbols such as waves, flames, and rippling effects. The illicit pair's carnal couplings around the grounds of the estate are heady with the power of flouting class and social mores, all lightened with Emerson's cartoony style, sense of fun, and humorous sight gags.

Giardino, Vittorio

Little Ego. 2006. Heavy Metal, ISBN 1932413626, 48p.

This lovely homage to Windsor McCay replaces Little Nemo, a prepubescent little boy, with Little Ego, a beautiful, somewhat shy young woman. Little Ego's dreams are full of adventures of the erotic variety, including lesbian encounters, stripteases in the Saharan desert, naked parties with sexy results, and an exploit with a mischievous umbrella. Little Ego wakes up from these dreams in a state of arousal and somewhat embarrassed, wondering what her analyst will make of her wild dreams. Italian comic artist Giardino offers a woman's sweet and sensual nighttime fantasies in lush, beautiful colored illustrations.

McKean, Dave

▶ *Celluloid.* 2011. Fantagraphics Book, ISBN 1606994405, 232p.

Disappointed that her lover won't be home on time after work, the protagonist prepares for a night alone. She is in for an unexpected surprise when she notices a film projector and watches the scratchy film of a couple making love. When the images fade, there is a magical door, and the naked woman opens it to discover a very sexy world beyond. Award-winning comics artist McKean has succeeded in his efforts to create an erotic graphic novel that is "beautiful, and mysterious, and engages the mind."

Moore, Alan, and Melinda Gibbe

Lost Girls, 2006, 2009. Top Shelf Productions, ISBN 1603090444, 320p.

Adult versions of Dorothy, of Oz, Alice, of Wonderland, and Wendy, of Neverland, come together in Hotel Hemmelgarten in 1913 Austria. Alice, now a decadent older woman, leads Wendy, a stressed English housewife, and fun-loving Dorothy into a world where sexuality is unleashed. All taboos are broken in pages and pages of carnal delight. Gibbe's gorgeous pastel drawings in an art-nouveau style reminiscent of fairy-tale illustrations present sex as sumptuous art. While some readers will be turned off by the sexualizing of iconic children's book characters and depictions of incest and pedophilia, others will experience this book as a significant work of sexually inventive comic erotica.

Waller, Reed, and Kate Worley
Complete Omaha the Cat Dancer, **Vol. 1.** 2005. Amerotica, ISBN 1561634514, 128p.

Omaha, an enthusiastic feline exotic dancer, is married to Chuck Katt and also enjoys dalliances with bisexual co-worker Shelly. Complications arise when Omaha gets involved with her boss, Charles Tabey, a crazy tycoon who turns out to be her husband's father. The story turns melodramatic but heartfelt as the characters talk and work through their issues around sex, morality, and love. This erotic series, which started in 1978, has staying power because it integrates sizzling sex into a soap opera storyline, starring three-dimensional characters with real relationships. All this and it's anthropomorphic, too. Omaha and the gang have animal heads on human bodies, respectfully bringing out the animal in these great human characters!

Dirty Stories, **Vol. 2.** 2001. Eros Comix, ISBN 1560974001, 132p.

True Porn. 2003. Alternative Comics, ISBN 189186758X, 224p.

Both of these anthologies are populated with sexy stories, by popular mainstream and alternative cartoonists, that span the erogenous spectrum from tender to nasty, comical to disturbing, sweet to bizarre. Starting with the orgiastic cover by Rick Altergott and the sexy frontispiece by Dan Clowes, *Dirty Stories* contains work by Renee French, Richard Sala, Dean Haspiel, Mack White, Mary Fleener, Dylan Horrocks, Bob Fingerman, and more. *True Porn* is less raunchy and more literary than *Dirty Stories*. It contains autobiographic sexual stories from the lives of Jeffrey Brown, Vanessa Davis, Aaron Renier, Ariel Schrag, and Josh Simmons. Sexually open but not always sexy, the erotica found here is honest in its exploration of the varied experiences of sexual desire, although both collections are lean on experiences outside the heterosexual realm.

Index

Underlined text represents series titles

About the Author

ABBY ALPERT is an experienced librarian, happily providing reader services to adults and children for more than 15 years. Abby produces and curates an online archive and daily nonprofit email that highlights the best of social cause media. Abby's enthusiasm for comic books dates back to the first grade, when she began reading. Her adolescence was spent devouring underground comics and, later, alternative art commix. She is grateful that she has been able to satisfy her hunger for comics well into adulthood, thanks to the continued evolution of the graphic novel. Abby lives in Illinois with her son and their dog.

CPSIA information can be obtained at www.ICGtesting.com
Printed in the USA
LVOW10s1931160714

394635LV00005B/208/P